KV-240-840

THE COMMITTEE ON LATIN AMERICA

Latin American economic & social serials

With a preface by Sir John Walker and a note on
periodical indexes by A J Walford and Peter Hoare

published on behalf of COLA by

CLIVE BINGLEY  LONDON

3

First Published 1969 by Clive Bingley Ltd
16 Pembridge Road London W11
Set in Univers and printed in Great Britain
by R E Gordon & Co Ltd London SW17
Copyright © The Committee on Latin America 1969
All rights reserved
85157 064 X

4

CONTENTS

PREFACE

by Sir John Walker KCMG OBE

Director General, Hispanic Council;
Luso Brazilian Council

When inaugurated almost twenty five years ago, the Hispanic and Luso Brazilian Councils decided that their main object should be the advancement of knowledge and understanding of the countries of Latin America and the Iberian Peninsula, with special reference to economic conditions, and their cultural and linguistic background. The councils set to work by means of their Education and Library Committees to implement these decisions at a national level and have been a spearhead in reviving interest in Latin America in the United Kingdom. This interest has gained impetus in the past few years but it must be nourished by more sources of information if it is to be maintained.

In their own fields, other agencies and institutions have also felt a need to keep themselves better informed and equipped with materials and programmes concerning this area. In order to achieve as much co-ordination as possible, and to stimulate action to meet the growing demand for information, especially on the economic front, a meeting took place on June 11 1963 at Canning House. There were present members of the ASLIB Economics Group; librarians and other representatives of government departments such as the Foreign Office, Board of Trade and Ministry of Defence; representatives of large firms, such as the Bank of London and South America Limited and Unilever Limited, of university libraries, including the British Library of Political and Economic Science, and of institutions such as CICRIS, the Library Association, the National Central Library and the Royal Institute of International Affairs.

I felt it a great privilege to take the chair at this meeting at which a project committee was established, under the name of the Committee on Latin America. It is now my pleasure to welcome the accompanying very practical outcome of its work in connection with one of its projects; a union list of Latin American economic and sociological serials in British libraries. The co-operation of the National Central Library (BUCOP) through the committee's chairman, Mr.K I Porter, has contributed much to this commendable result, which will bridge an important gap in our knowledge of Latin America. This project is the first of a number which the committee hopes will add greatly to the documentation of the area.

PERIODICAL INDEXES

a note by A J Walford and Peter Hoare

Two indexes to Latin American periodicals in economics and the social sciences that combine wide coverage and reasonable fluency of publication are both Pan American Union products — the PAU Columbus Memorial Library's **List of books accessioned and periodical articles indexed for the month** (1950–), and the **Index to Latin American periodicals: humanities and social sciences** issued jointly by the Columbus Memorial Library and the New York Public Library (1961 — quarterly). The first lists 6,000 items annually, of which about 1,000 concern periodical articles in econonomics and the social sciences. The second indexes about 130 journals, producing some 6,500 references annually; of these, possibly twenty five percent are relevant to economics and the social sciences in Latin America.

A third major source is the **Handbook of Latin American studies** (Washington DC, The Hispanic Foundation, Library of Congress, 1963– annual), which, as from volume 26, devotes alternate volumes to the social sciences and the humanities. Volume 26, the first to be devoted to the social sciences, carries more than 4,000 annotated entries for books and articles from about 600 periodicals (of which two thirds emanate from Latin America). About 1,000 of the entries are relevant to this survey. Admirably annotated and well indexed, this biennial coverage of the social sciences clearly meets the needs of the university student and research worker, rather than the business man.

There is a distinct falling off in coverage in the less specialised indexing and abstracting services. The United Nations (Geneva) Library's **Monthly list of selected articles** (now a bi-monthly) draws on thirty eight Latin American periodicals, but only very selectively, and it has perhaps 300 items annually on Latin American economics, including items in English language journals. The International Monetary Fund and International Bank for Research and Development Joint Library's monthly **List of recent periodical articles** offers, with considerably less timelag, about the same number of items. It draws on a very few Latin American periodicals only (for example, **Comercio exterior** (Mexico), **America Latina** (Rio de Janeiro), plus **Revista interamerica de ciencias sociales** (Washington), and **Social and economics studies** (Jamaica).

International bibliography for economics (1952-), an annual prepared by the International Committee for Social Sciences Documentation, has the advantage of drawing on about 2,000 periodicals, including a fair number that emanate from Latin America. A drawback is the timelag of between two and three years in appearance.

The weekly **Public affairs information service bulletin** (1915–) has much to recommend it as a current awareness service, but very few of the 1,500 journals it covers emanate from Latin America. However, articles on Latin American countries from other sources, especially North America, are quite

8

numerous. Thus the 1956 cumulated volume has fifty four references on Mexico and forty two on Cuba. The **Bulletin analytique de documentation politique economique et sociale contemporaine** (1946–), which appears ten times a year, has about 100 relevent articles annually, and **Economic abstracts** (The Hague, 1953– twice monthly rather fewer. In these less specialised abstracting and indexing services Latin American periodicals are not so prominent.

The Caribbean area is covered by three bibliographies, **Current Caribbean bibliography**, a valuable list published annually since 1951 by Caribbean Commission, last appeared in 1964 (cumulated volumes 9-11, 1959-61, part 1). Part 1 of this cumulation was never published, because the commision folded up in 1965. This bibliography covers political, economic and social affairs in the French, British, Dutch and US possessions in the Caribbean. It is arranged in classified UDC order, with alphabetical (author-subject-title) and chronological (author-title) indexes.

Caribbean studies (Puerto Rico, The University of Puerto Rico Institute of Caribbean Studies, 1961– quarterly) carries a welcome current bibliography, and covers an area defined as the Antilles, Yucatan, British Honduras, Central America, Panama, Columbia, Venezuela and Guyana. It is probably a selective (criteria questionable) list of books, pamphlets and articles. The **Selective list of recent publications catalogued** (Huerto Rey, Caribbean Economic Development Corporation, Caribbean Regional Library, March 1966– bi-monthly) is often useful for socio-economic publications, although it is highly selective.

INTRODUCTION

The subject scope of the serials in this list is indicated by the phrase 'economic and social' in its title; 'economic' is interpreted fairly broadly, to include, for example, serials concerning important products of the area, even if the main emphasis may be agricultural. The list concentrates on current and recent serials; titles known to have ceased before 1945 are generally excluded. Relevant serials are included in this list even if there are no known holdings for them in UK libraries. Users of this list will no doubt appreciate the difficulty of providing complete or even completely accurate bibliographical information in every case.

The main section of this work consists of title entries with the fullest possible information and known holdings grouped by area. These groups consist of two general categories, followed by specific area in alphabetical order. Serials published in each area are listed in alphabetical title order, together with serials published outside the Latin American region, but pertaining to it. The 'general' categories contain serials published by international organizations, or serials of a general nature published outside Latin America. 'Latin America' is itself interpreted broadly as the Americas south of the United States, together with the island territories normally associated with them, including Bermuda.

The form of entry, and various conventions employed, follow the general style of the **British union-catalogue of periodicals; new periodical titles.** Users of this list are invited to submit any additional information on holdings or relevant titles, or any comments they may wish to make, to the Editor, BUCOP, National Central Library, Store Street, London WC1.

The asterisk (*) against certain titles in the following lists indicates that they are indexed in the Index to Latin American periodicals: humanities and social sciences, mentioned in the foregoing article by Dr Walford and Mr Hoare.

A single asterisk (*) against the library symbol or its holding in the following lists indicates that there are issues missing from the holding indicated. A double asterisk (**) against the library symbol indicates that it holds issues of the title, but the extent of the holding has not been made known.

GENERAL AREA OF LATIN AMERICA

ALALC BOLETIN. Asociacion Latinoamericana de Libre Comercio. Cenci, Uruguay.
No. 1, Ap 1964—

BoLSA

ALALC SINTESIS MENSUAL. Asociacion Latinoamericana de Libre Comercio.
Montevideo. 1, J1 1965—

BoLSA

ALLIANCE FOR PROGRESS WEEKLY NEWSLETTER. Alliance for Progress
Information Team. Washington, D.C.

BoLSA **
HispLBC **

AMERICAN EN CIFRAS. Inter-American Statistical Institute. Pan American
Union; Department of Statistics. Washington, D.C. 1960—

BM 1963—
BoLSA **
HispLBC
RIIA **

AMERICA LATINA. Rassegna di Cultura e Lavoro delle Repubbliche dell'America
Latina. Milan. 1, Ap 1952—

AMERICAS. Pan American Union. Washington, D.C. 1, Mr 1949—
[Prev. part of: Bulletin of the Pan American Union. Also issued in Spanish
and Portuguese editions.]

BhmPL
BM 3 (1), Ja 1951—
BoLSA 1960—
EdinU 19, 1962/63—
HispLBC **
LivPL
NLS 17(2), 1965—
NottU 13, 1956—
SheffU 1964—
UCL **

AMERICAS; PORTUGUESE EDITION. Pan American Union. Washington, D.C.
1, Mr 1949—

BM 7 (1), Ja 1955—
HispLBC **

AMERICAS; SPANISH EDITION. Pan American Union. Washington, D.C.
1, Mr 1949—

BM 7 (9), S 1955—
HispLBC **

ANNALS OF THE ORGANIZATION OF AMERICAN STATES. Washington, D.C. 1, 1949
10 (2), 1958.//

BhmPL
HispLBC **
RIIA [W 1 (1)]

BANK & PUBLIC HOLIDAYS IN SOUTH & CENTRAL AMERICA . . . Bank of London & South America. London.

> BoLSA
> RIIA (current file only)
> SheffU 1965—

BELGIQUE-AMERIQUE LATINE. Maison de l'Amerique Latine (Brussels). Brussels. [Suspended My 1940— S 1945.]

> BoLSA **

BOLETIN, ASOCIACION LATINOAMERICANA DE LIBRE COMERCIO. See ALALC BOLETIN.

BOLETIN, COMISION INTERAMERICANA DE MUJERES. (Inter-American Commission of Women). Buenos Aires. 1, 1943—

BOLETIN ECONOMICO DE AMERICA LATINA; SUPLEMENTO ESTADISTICO. United Nations; Economic Commission for Latin America. Santiago de Chile.

> EssexU 5, 1960— 6, 1961.

BOLETIN DE LA REVISTA INTERAMERICANA DE CIENCIAS SOCIALES. Pan American Union. Washington, D.C. 1, Je 1961—

> LSE

BOLSA REVIEW. Bank of London & South America. London. 1 (1), Ja 1967— [Unites the Bank's prev.: Fortnightly Review, (&) Quarterly Review.]

> BoLSA ·
> HispLBC **
> RIIA
> SouU
> SwUC

BULLETIN, CHAMBRE DE COMMERCE FRANCE-AMERIQUE LATINE. Paris. [1], D 1946—

CARTA INFORMATIVA, CONSEJO INTERAMERICANO DE COMERCIO Y PRODUCCION; SERIE ALALC. Montevideo. 1, JE 1964— [ALALC = Asociacion Latinoamericana de Libre Comercio.]

CIENCIAS SOCIALES. Notas e informaciones. Pan American Union; Department of Intercultural Affairs; Social Science Section. Washington, D.C. 1, Ja 1950— ?1956. [Subs.: Revista interamericana de Ciencias Sociales.]

> LSE

CIRCULAIRE, CHAMBRE DE COMMERCE FRANCE-AMERIQUE LATINE. Paris.

COMERCIO INTERAMERICANO. Pan American Union; Office of Foreign Trade Advisers & Special Publications. Washington, D.C. (S 1946)— [S-OC 1946 actually titled: Noticiero Suspended 1952.]

COMPENDIO ESTADISTICO CENTROAMERICANO. Secretaria Permanente del Tratado General de Integracion Economica Centroamericana (SIECA). Guatemala? 1, [1957] — [1-2, 1962 issued by: United Nations Committee on Economic Cooperation in Central America.]

> BoLSA

12

CONSUMER PRICE (COST-OF-LIVING) INDEXES FOR THE AMERICAN NATIONS. =
Indices de Precios al Consumidor (Costo de la Vida) de las Naciones Americanas.
Pan American Union; Department of Statistics. Washington, D.C.
(No. 1, 1959)—
[Covers statistics from 1955. Title and text of nos. 1—5 in Spanish only.
No.6, first with title in English, contains all information published in
nos. 1—5.]

   Bodl. *7, Je 1961—
   BoLSA **
   LSE

CTAL NEWS.
   see NOTICIERO DE LA CTAL.

DOCUMENTOS OFICIALES DE LA ORGANIZACION DE LOS ESTADOS AMERICANOS;
INDICE Y LISTA GENERAL. Organization of American States. Pan American
Union. Washington, D.C. 1, 1960—

   LSE
   RIIA

ECONOMIA LATINOAMERICANA. Pan American Union; Department of Economic
Affairs. Washington, D.C. 1, 1963—
[3/A. Engl., Span., Port., Fr.]

   Bodl.
   BM
   LSE
   NLL
   RIA

ECONOMIC BULLETIN FOR LATIN AMERICA. United Nations; Economic Commission
for Latin America. Santiago de Chile. 1, 1956—

   BhmPL
   Bodl
   BoLSA
   EssexU *2 (2), 1957—
   ExU
   GlasU
   HispLBC
   IBank (one year file)
   LdsU 3, 1958—
   LivU 9 (2), 1964—
   MarshallL
   NottU *
   NuffCollOx
   OxIES
   RIIA
   SheffU *3, 1958—
   TropProdl
   UCL
   WarU 8, 1963—

ECONOMIC SURVEY OF LATIN AMERICA. United Nations; Department of Economic
Affairs. Lake Success (&c). 1948 (1949)—
[Not publ. 1950, 1961.]

   BhmPL
   Bodl
   BoLSA
   EdinU 1948- 1958.
   EssexU [W 1959, 1960.]

[Contd..]

ExU
GlasU
HispLBC **
IBank **
LdsU
LondU   1948 — 1958.
MarshallL   1948—   1955.
NottU
OxIES   1948 — 1966
RIIA   1948—
SheffU   1948–9.   1953.   1955—
TropProdl *
UCL **
WarU   ? 1965—

ESTADISTICA.   Journal of the Inter-American Statistical Institute.
Washington, D.C.   1, 1943—

Bodl   *18 (69), 1960—
BoLSA   1952—
HispLBC **
LivPL   Je-D 1957. D 1958— 1959. Je & D 1960.   1961—
LivU   *1944— 1950.

EVOLUTION DE L'ECONOMIE DES PAYS SUD—AMERICAINS.   Banque Francaise et
Italienne pour l'Amerique du Sud.   Paris.

BoLSA **

EXTENSION EN LAS AMERICAS.   Instituto Interamericano de Ciencias Agricolas.
Turrialba, Costa Rica.   1, Mr/Ap 1956—
[Issued by the Inst. in co-op. with the International Co-operation Admini—
stration of the U.S. Body in Engl.: Inter-American Institute of Agricultural
Sciences.]

TropProdl   1958—

FORTNIGHTLY REVIEW, BANK OF LONDON & SOUTH AMERICA.   London. 1(1), 1936—
31 (788), D 1966.
[Subs. part of: BOLSA Review. (with the Bank's 'Quarterly Review.')]

BelfPL   (Five year file)
BhmPL   (One year file)
BoLSA
Courtaulds Ltd 1939—
Guildhall   (Five year file)
HispLBC **
IBank   (Three month file)
LivPL   1937—
NuffCollOx   16 (373), Ja 1951—
OxIES
PrudAssurCo (2-3 year file)
RIIA   11 (255), J1 1946—
SheffU   29, 1964—
SouU   30, 1965—
TropProdl   1963—

HISPANIC AMERICAN REPORT.   Hispanic American Society. Stanford University;
Institute of Hispanic American & Luso-Brazilian Studies. Stanford, Calif.
3, 1950— 17 (9), 1964.//
["Analysis of developments in Spain, Portugal & Latin America." Prev.:
Hispanic World Report.]

Bodl
BoLSA   [Contd.]

14

EdinU
ExU   17(1),   1964—
GlasU   [W   12(2)— 13.]
HispLBC **
LdsU   17 (3),   1964—
LivU   3-4. 5(4). 7-12, 1960
LondU
LSE   16 (1), Mr 1963—
NottU   13(11), 1961—
RIIA
SheffU   17, 1964—
UCL **

HISPANIC WORLD REPORT.   Stanford University; Hispanic Work Affairs Seminar.
     Stanford, Calif.   1, Oc 1948—2, D 1949 ...
     [Subs.: Hispanic American Report.]

     Bodl   2, 1949.
     BoLSA   2,   1949
     LivU   2,   1949.
     LondU   ?
     RIIA   1,   1968 - 2 (12), 1949

INDEX TO LATIN AMERICAN PERIODICALS; HUMANITIES & SOCIAL SCIENCES. =
     Indice general de Publicaciones periodicas latinoamericanas; Humanidades y Ciencias
     sociales.   New York Public Library.   Pan American Union; Columbus Memorial
     Library.   [G.K. Hall & Co.]   Boston, Mass.   1, Ja/Mr 1961 —
     [Q, cumulated A.]

     BelfPL
     LSE
     SheffU

INDICE GENERAL DE PUBLICACIONES PERIODICAS LATINOAMERICANAS;
     HUMANIDADES Y CIENCIAS SOCIALES.
     see INDEX TO LATIN AMERICAN PERIODICALS; HUMANITIES & SOCIAL
     SCIENCES.

INDICES DE PRECIOS AL CONSUMIDOR (COSTO DE LA VIDA) DE LAS NACIONES
     AMERICANAS. see CONSUMER PRICE (COST-of-LIVING) INDEXES OF THE
     AMERICAN NATIONS.

INFORMATIONES ECONOMICAS. Pan American Union; Department of Economic
     & Social Affairs.   Washington, D.C.   1, Ag 1956—
     ["A monthly summary of current economic events in Latin America . . ."]

INFORMATION LATINE. Paris.

     EssexU   No. 4055,   5/J1 1966—   [W no. 4056]

INFORMATIVO ALALC.   Asociacion Latinoamericana de Libre Comercio. Santiago de
     Chile.   1,   1961—
     ["Revista semanal de actualidades economicas latinoamericanas." Published for
     ALALC by the Chilean Chamber of Commerce.]

     BoLSA **

INTER-AMERICAN BULLETIN.   International Federation of Commercial, Clerical &
     Technical Employees.   Lima (&c).

INTER-AMERICAN ECONOMIC AFFAIRS.   Institute of Inter-American Studies.
     Washington, D.C.   1(1), Je 1947—

     Bodl
     BoLSA Winter 1951—
     EdinU   16, 1962—   [contd.]

15

EssexU   19, 1965–
ExU *
HispLBC **
LeicU
LivPL   Autumn   1956–
LivU
LondU
LSE
NottU   15, 1961–   [W 15 (2-3).]
NuffCollOx
RIIA   [W 15 (1-3), 1961]
UCL **
UEAnglia   18,   1964–
WarU   ? 1965–

INTER-AMERICAN FOREIGN TRADE. Chamber of Commerce for Latin America (New York).
    New York.   No.1. 1953–

INTER-AMERICAN LABOR BULLETIN.   Inter-American Regional Organization of Workers.
    Washington, D.C.   1,   F 1951–
    [Also issued in Spanish.]

INTERNATIONAL TRADE OF THE AMERICAN STATES. Pan American Union; Department
    of Social & Economic Affairs. Washington, D.C.   Bulletin no.1, Ag 1954.–

JOURNAL OF INTER-AMERICAN STUDIES. Pan American Foundation. University of
    Florida; School of Inter-American Studies. Gainesville, Fla.   1, 1959–
    [Published Q. by the Foundation for the School.)

    EdinU   5, 1963–
    EssexU   [W 5-6.]
    ExU   6,   1964–
    HispLBC**
    LeicU   5, 1963–
    RIIA
    UCL **
    WarU   ? 1965–

LATIN AMERICA IN PERIODICAL LITERATURE. University of California; Center of
    Latin American Studies.   Los Angeles   1, 1962 - 2 (6), 1963.//
    [Separately numbered special issues also published, nos. 1-7.]

    HispLBC **
    SouU

LATIN AMERICAN BUSINESS HIGHLIGHTS.   Chase Manhattan Bank.   New York.
    1, N 1950–

    EssexU *6, 1956–
    HispLBC **
    HullU 9, 1959–
    IBank   (One year file)
    RIIA   6 (4), D 1956–

LATIN AMERICAN REPORT (NEWSLETTER). New Orleans. No.1, 14/S 1946–
    ["Newsletter" added to original title from 1956, when the same publisher
    also began to issue: Latin American Report Magazine.]

LATIN AMERICAN RESEARCH REVIEW. Austin, Tex.   1 (1), Fall 1965–

    BhmU
    LondICS
    LSE
    SouU

16

LATIN AMERICAN TIMES. New York. 1, 1965–
["International Daily of Latin America."]
UCL

LATIN AMERICA & THE WORLD. [Foreign News Service.] New York.
BoLSA **

LETTERS & REPORTS FROM FOREIGN COUNTRIES; EAST COAST SOUTH AMERICA
SERIES. American Universities Field Staff. New York. 1 (1), 1952–

LETTERS & REPORTS FROM FOREIGN COUNTRIES; MEXICO & CARIBBEAN SERIES.
American Universities Field Staff. New York.

LETTERS & REPORTS FROM FOREIGN COUNTRIES; WEST COAST SOUTH AMERICA
SERIES. American Universities Field Staff. New York. 1(1), 1954–

LIBRE COMERCIO. Asociacion Latinoamericana de Libre Comercio. Montevideo.
1 (1), 1964–

LIST OF BOOKS ACCESSIONED & PERIODICALS INDEXED IN THE COLUMBUS
MEMORIAL LIBRARY. Pan American Union; Columbus Memorial Library.
Washington, D.C. 1951– (Prev., Ag 1950– F 1951: Accessions ...]
UCL *My 1961–

MEMORIA DE LABORES, BANCO CENTROAMERICANA DE INTEGRACION ECONOMICA
Tegucigalpa. 1, 1961/62–
BoLSA

MUNDO NUEVO. Instituto Latinoamericano de Relaciones Internacionales. Paris
1, 1966–
EssexU
NLL
ReadU

NEWS BULLETIN, INTER-AMERICAN COMMISSION OF WOMEN. Washington, D.C.
No.1, J1 1953–
[Eng. ed. of: Noticiero de la Comision Interamericana de Mujeres.
Nos. 7-11 never published.]

NOTICIAS. Weekly digest of hemispheric reports. National Foreign Trade
Council (U.S.). New York.

NOTICIAS DE LA CEPAL. United Nations; Economic Commission for Latin America.
Santiago de Chile. 1954 (no.1)–
[Issues numbered from 1 within each year. "CEPAL" represents name of the
Commission in Spanish.]
HispLBC **
RIIA 1966 (1) [W1966 (6)]
UCL 1963 (1) –

NOTICIAS, COMISION INTERAMERICANA DE ARBITRAJE COMERCIAL. Inter-
American Commercial Arbitration Commission. New York. 1, 1960–

NOTICIAS ECONOMICAS INTERAMERICANAS. Chase National Bank. New York.
1, 1964–

NOTICIERO DE LA COMISION INTERAMERICANA DE MUJERES. Inter-American
Commission of Women. Washington, D.C. No.1, D 1951/Ja 1952 –
[Published for the Commission by the Pan American Union. Also issued in
Engl. ed. 1953-57 as: News Bulletin, Inter-American Commission of Women.)
HispLBC **

NOTICIERO DE LA CTAL. = CTAL News. Confederacion de Trabajadores de America
Latina. Mexico, D.F. 1, 23/Jl 1945–
[Span. & Engl. Body in Engl.: Latin American Federation of Labor.
Prev.: Mexican Labor News.]

OAS CHRONICLE. Organisation of American States. Pan American Union.
Washington, D.C. 1, Ag 1965·–
[Published for the OAS by the PAU.]

HispLBC **
LSE
RIIA

PROVISIONAL LISTING OF ALLIANCE FOR PROGRESS PROJECTS. Alliance for
Progress Information Team. Washington, D.C.
[Kept up to date with Q. supplements.]

LSE Mr 1963–

QUARTERLY REVIEW, BANK OF LONDON & SOUTH AMERICA. London. 1, Jl 1960–
6 (4), 1966.
[Subs. part of: BOLSA REVIEW. (With the Bank's 'Fortnightly Review.')]

Bodl
BoLSA
BoT 1961–
Guildhall (Five year file)
HispLBC
HullU 2, 1962–
MarshallL
NuffCollOx 3, 1963–
OxIES
Prud AssurCo
RIIA [W5 (1), Ja 1965]
SheffU 4 (3), 1964–
SouU 5, 1965–
TropProdI 1964–
UCL

REPORT OF THE DIRECTORS & STATEMENT OF ACCOUNTS, BANK OF LONDON
& SOUTH AMERICA. London.

BoLSA
HispLBC **
HullU 1959 (1960)–
RIIA 1962 (1963)–

REVIEW BY THE CHAIRMAN, BANK OF LONDON & SOUTH AMERICA. London.

BoLSA
HispLBC **
HullU 1959–
RIIA 1962–
SheffU 1964–

REVISTA INTERAMERICANA DE CIENCIAS SOCIALES. Pan American Union; Department of Intercultural Affairs; Social Science Section. Washington, D.C. 1, 1961–
[Called "2. epoca" of prev.: Ciencias Sociales.]

Bodl. *
EssexU 2, 1963– 3 (2), 1965.
HispLBC **
LSE
UCL

18

REVISTA INTERAMERICAN DE CIENCIAS SOCIALES; BOLETIN.
see BOLETIN DE LA REVISTA . . .

REVISTA LATINOAMERICANA DE SOCIOLOGIA.   Instituto Torcuato di Tella.
Buenos Aires.   1, 1965—
[3/A.]
WarU ?

SERVICIO SOCIAL INTERAMERICANO.   Inter-American Economic & Social Council.
Pan American Union; Division of Labor & Social Affairs.   Washington, D.C.
1, Mr 1955—
[Issued by the Council and prepared by the PAU.]

SINTESIS MENSUAL, ASOCIACION LATINOAMERICANA DE LIBRE COMERCIO.
see ALALC SINTESIS MENSUAL.

STATISTICAL ABSTRACT OF LATIN AMERICA.   University of California; Center of
Latin American Studies.   Los Angeles.   1955—
[Not published 1958-59.   To 1957, Center preceded by the
University's Committee on Latin American Studies.]

EssexU   1955.   1957.   1960.   1962.   1964.
GlasU   1957.
HispLBC **
LSE   1955-57.   1960.   1962—
RIIA   1956.   1961.   1963.
SouU   1955—
UCL **

STATISTICAL BULLETIN FOR LATIN AMERICA.   United Nations; Economic
Commission for Latin America.   New York.   1, Mr 1964—

BedCollLond   11, 1965—
BhmU
Bodl
BoLSA
EssexU
ExU
HispLBC
LdsPL
LdsU
LivU   11,   1965—
MancPL
MarshallL   1 (1).
NuffCollOx
NottU
RIIA
SheffU
SouU
UCL
WarU
YorkU

STATISTICAL BULLETIN FOR LATIN AMERICA; STATISTICAL SUPPLEMENT.   United
Nations;   Economic Commission for Latin America.   Santiago de Chile.

VIVIENDA Y PLANEAMIENTO.   Pan American Union; Division of Labor & Social Affairs.
Washington, D.C.   no. 1, Ag 1952—
[Name of subordinate body varies.]

BM No.3,   Ja/F   1953—

CARIBBEAN AREA

ACCESSIONS LIST, CARIBBEAN REGIONAL LIBRARY. Hato Rey, P.R. No.1,
Mar 1966—
[Library part of: Caribbean Economic Development Corporation]

    LondICS

BULLETIN DU COMMERCE. Caribbean Commission.
see COMMODITY BULLETIN.

BULLETIN, MINISTRY OF TRADE & INDUSTRY (WEST INDIES, FEDERATION),
Port-of-Spain. No.1, Jan 1959—

    LSE

CADORIT INFORMATION BULLETIN. Inter-American Regional Organization of
Workers (Caribbean Area Division). Port-of-Spain. ?1955— 1960.
["Cadorit" = Caribbean Area Division of the "Organizacion Regional
Interamericana de Trabajadores". Issues unnumbered. Subs: Caribbean
Labour.]

    LondICS   Dec 1957— Jan 1958; Sep 1958; Christmas 1958; Mar/Ap 1959— Aug 1959;
              Ap 1960; July 1960.

CARIB. A (monthly) periodical owned and published by Caribbean and Latin
American Workers. Caribbean Workers' Movement. London. 1 (1), Oct 1964—

    LondICS
    LSE

CARIBBEAN. (1955) Caribbean Commission. Port-of-Spain. 8 (6), 1955—
14 (4), 1960.
[Prev titles, from 1, Aug 1947: (1) Monthly bulletin, . . . (2) Monthly
Information Bulletin . . . Body originally: Anglo-American Caribbean
Commission]

    BhmU
    BM
    BodI
    CambU
    EdinU
    HullU
    LondICS
    LONDIEd
    LondU
    LSE
    RhodesHQx
    RIIA
    TropProdI

CARIBBEAN. (1960) Caribbean Commission. Hato Rey, P.R. 1 (1), May/Nov
1960—1 (10), Aug 1961.
[Prev: Caribbean. (1955). Subs: Caribbean. (1961).]

    LondICS
    LSE
    RIIA

CARIBBEAN. (1961) Caribbean Organization. Hato Rey, P.R. 1, Sep 1961—
4 (5), Dec 1964.//
[Prev: Caribbean. (1960).]

    LondICS

20

CARIBBEAN AFFAIRS (New Series).   University of the West Indies; Department
of Extra-Mural Studies.   Mona,   Jamaica.   1, May 1962—
BM (NH)

CARIBBEAN AGRICULTURE.   Caribbean Organization.   Hato Rey, P.R.   1, Dec 1962—
3 (1),   Dec 1964.//   Q.

BangUCSci   1 (2),   1963—
CSA   1 (2),   1963—
LondICS   1 (2),   1963—
TropProdl   1 (2),   1963—

CARIBBEAN ECONOMIC ALMANAC.   [Economic & Business Research Information &
Advisory Service]   Port-of-Spain.

LondICS 1962— 1963/4.
SouU   1964/66   (1964)—

CARIBBEAN ECONOMIC REVIEW.   Caribbean Commission; Central Secretariat.
Port-of-Spain.   1, Dec 1949— 6, 1954.//

BM   BhmU   2—
Bodl
BoT
CambU
EdinU
GlasU
HullU
LondICS
LondlEd   1—5, 1953.
LondU
LSE
MinAg
NLS *
OxfAgEconResl
OxfDepFor
OxfICS
OxfSchGeog
RhodesHOxf
TropProdl   1950-

CARIBBEAN LABOUR.   Information Bulletin of the Caribbean Congress of
Labour.   Port-of-Spain.   No.1, Oct 1960—
[Prev: CADORIT Information Bulletin]
LondICS   *No. 1—50, Oct/Dec 1964.

CARIBBEAN MARKET SURVEY.   Caribbean Commission.   Port-of-Spain.
1,   1955— 3, 1956.//
LondICS   1—2.

CARIBBEAN MONTHLY BULLETIN.   University of Puerto Rico; Institute of
Caribbean Studies.   Rio Pedras, P.R.   1, Nov 1963—
LondICS

CARIBBEAN PLAN; ANNUAL REPORT.   Caribbean Organization.   Hato Rey, P.R.
1962—
LondICS   1962— 1963.

CARIBBEAN QUARTERLY.   University [College] of the West Indies; Extra—
    Mural Department.   Mona, Jamaica.   1, Ap/June   1949—

    BhmU   2(4)—
    BM
    BodI
    BrU
    EdinU   4, 1955/6— 5 (2/3),   1958.
    LdsU
    LondICS
    LondIEd
    LondU
    MancPL
    OxfICS
    RhodesHOxf
    SellyOakC
    YorkU   2 (3-4).   3—

CARIBBEAN SOCIALISTS' REVIEW.   Caribbean Socialist Party.   [Carib
    Publications]   London.   1(1),   1966—
    [2M]

    LondICS

CARIBBEAN STATISTICAL DIGEST.   Caribbean Commission.   Port-of-Spain.
    1, Sep 1951—

    BhmU
    BM
    LondICS   2—
    RhodesHOxf

*CARIBBEAN STUDIES.   University of Puerto Rico; Institute of Caribbean
    Studies.   Rio Piedras, P.R.   1, Ap 1961—

    LondICS
    LSE
    UCL
    WarwickU   4(4), 1965—

CARIBBEAN WORKERS' WEEKLY.   Caribbean Workers' Movement.   London
    No.1, 3-10/July 1965—
    [Suppl. to: Carib]

    LondICS

CCL NEWSLETTER.   Caribbean Congress of Labour.   Port-of-Spain.
    No.1, 19/Oct 1963—

    LondICS*

CHRONICLE OF THE WEST INDIA COMMITTEE.   London.   74 (1333), Jan 1959—
    [M. Prev: West India Committee Circular]

    LondICS
    LondIEd
    NLS
    OxfICS

COMMODITY BULLETIN. = BULLETIN DU COMMERCE.   Caribbean Commission.
    Port-of-Spain.   1, 1953— 8, 1958.//
    [Prev: External Trade Bulletin]

    LondICS

22

COOPERATIVE NEWSLETTER. Caribbean Organization; Central Secretariat.
Hato Rey, P.R. 1, Aug 1962– 2(4), Dec 1964.//
[Q]

LondICS 2 (1), Mar 1964–

CROP ENQUIRY SERIES. Caribbean Commission; Committee on Agriculture,
Nutrition, Fisheries & Forestry. Port-of-Spain. 1, 1946– 6, 1947.//

BM
CambU
CSA
EdinU 4-6.
Rothamsted
SL

CURRENT CARIBBEAN BIBLIOGRAPHY. Caribbean Commission. Port-of-Spain.
1, 1951–
["An alphabetical list of publications issued in the Caribbean territories of France, Great Britain, the Netherlands, and the U.S."]

Aslib
BhmU
GlasU 7, 1957– 8, 1958.
LdsU
LondICS 1, 1951– 9, 1961.
SL
TropProdl 1958–

DEVELOPMENT & WELFARE IN THE WEST INDIES; BULLETIN. Development &
Welfare Organization in the West Indies. (British West Indies).
No.1, 1940/42 (1943)–
[Place varies. Organization part of: (G.B.) Colonial Office]

BM*
CambU 2–4, 6–22. 24. 26.
EdinU *19A–
LondICS 1–40, 1958.
SL 22–

DEVELOPMENT & WELFARE IN THE WEST INDIES; REPORT. Development &
Welfare Organization in the West Indies. (British West Indies).
[Place varies]

BM 1940/42 (1943)–

ESTIMATES OF REVENUE & EXPENDITURE (WEST INDIES, FEDERATION).
(Port-of-Spain).
[A. Includes: Supplementary Estimates of Expenditure]

LSE 1959–

FINANCIAL STATISTICS (WEST INDIES, FEDERATION). (West Indies, Federation)
Federal Statistical Office. Port-of-Spain.

BM 1959–

FISHERIES SERIES. Caribbean Commission; Committee on Agriculture,
Nutrition, Fisheries & Forestry. Port-of-Spain. 1, 1945–

BM 3–
CambU 1–2.
LondICS 2–3.
OxfSchGeog 3–
SL

INFORMATION BULLETIN, CARIBBEAN AREA DIVISION, INTER-AMERICAN
REGIONAL ORGANIZATION OF WORKERS.
    see CADORIT INFORMATION BULLETIN.

INTER-CARIBBEAN TRADE STATISTICS. = STATISTIQUES DU COMMERCE
INTERCARAIBE. Caribbean Organization; Central Secretariat. Hato Rey, P.R.
    BoT   1964

MONTHLY JOURNAL, CLEARING HOUSE ON TRADE & TOURISM INFORMATION,
CARIBBEAN ORGANIZATION. Hato Rey, P.R. 1, 1962—3 (6), Nov/Dec 1964.//
    LondICS   3 (1/2), Jan/Ap 1964—
    LSE   (Temporary file)

MONTHLY TRADE STATISTICS (WEST INDIES, FEDERATION). (West Indies,
Federation) Federal Statistical Office. Port-of-Spain. 1, 27/July 1959—
    LSE   *No.2, Aug 1959—

NEW HOPE CHRONICLE.   The official organ of the West Indies New Hope
Fund.   London.
[M]
LondICS   2 (1), Feb 1965—2 (2), Mar 1965.

NEWSLETTER, CARIBBEAN CONGRESS OF LABOUR.
    see CCL NEWSLETTER.

NIEUWE WEST-INDISCHE GIDS.   The Hague.   40 (1), July 1960—
[6/A. Prev: West-Indische Gids., from 1, 1919/20]
    BM
    LondICS

PROGRESS REPORT, INSTITUTE OF SOCIAL & ECONOMIC RESEARCH, UNIVERSITY
OF THE WEST INDIES. Mona, Jamaica. (1948/55)—
[First issue (1948/55) actually titled; Research Programme and Progress
Report, . . . Body originally as: University College of the West Indies.]
LondICS

QUARTERLY TRADE STATISTICS (WEST INDIES, FEDERATION). (West Indies,
Federation) Federal Statistical Office. Port-of-Spain. No.1, Mar 1959—
    LSE

RESEARCH PROGRAMME & PROGRESS REPORT, INSTITUTE OF SOCIAL &
ECONOMIC RESEARCH, UNIVERSITY (COLLEGE) OF THE WEST INDIES.
    see PROGRESS REPORT, INSTITUTE.

SELECTIVE LIST OF RECENT ADDITIONS, LIBRARY, CARIBBEAN COMMISSION.
Port-of-Spain.   No.1, Jan 1958— 19/20, Oct 1959.
[Subs as above but with changed name of parent body: Caribbean Organization.]
LondICS

.SELECTIVE LIST OF RECENT ADDITIONS, LIBRARY, CARIBBEAN ORGANIZATION.
Hato Rey, P.R.   1(1), Ap/June 1962— 3(3), Oct 1964.//
[Prev as above but with earlier name of parent body: Caribbean Commission]
LondICS

SELECTIVE LIST OF RECENT ADDITIONS TO THE (CARIBBEAN REGIONAL) LIBRARY
Hato Rey, P.R.   1 (1), Mar 1966—
[Actual title ends with phrase: . . . to the Library.   Library part of:
Caribbean Economic Development Corporation]
LondICS

STATISTIQUES DU COMMERCE INTERCARAIBE.
see INTER-CARIBBEAN TRADE STATISTICS.

WEEKLY, CLEARING HOUSE ON TRADE & TOURISM INFORMATION, CARIBBEAN
ORGANIZATION. Hato Rey, P.R. No.?1, , 1962—22/26, 28/Dec 1964.//

LondICS   No.3,   19/Feb 1964—

WEST INDIES & CARIBBEAN YEAR BOOK.   London.   1953/54—
[Prev from 1926/27:   (1) Year Book of the Bermudas, the Bahamas, British
Guiana, British Honduras & the British West Indies. (2) West Indies Yearbook.
(3) Yearbook of the West Indies & Countries of the Caribbean.]

BhmPL
BM
Bodl
BoT   1957/58—
BrU
CambU
HackneyPL
HispLBC **
LdsPL
LivPL
LondICS 1954/55 — 1958/59. 1961—
LondU   1954/55.   1958/59—
LSE

WEST INDIES FISHERIES BULLETIN.   (West Indies, Federation) Ministry of
Natural Resources & Agriculture.   Port-of-Spain.   1, 1959—   Mar/Ap 1962.//

BM
TropProdl

WEST INDIES YEARBOOK.   London.   1936— 1947/48.
[Prev: Year Book of the Bermudas, the Bahamas, British Guiana, British
Honduras & the British West Indies.   Subs: Yearbook of the West Indies
& Countries of the Caribbean.]

BhmPL
BM
Bodl
BrU   1939—
CambU
HackneyPL   1938. 1046—
KensingtonPL   1940. 1944— 1948.
LdsPL   1937. 1940— 1945.   1947—
LivPL   1943—
LSE
MancPL
OxfSchGeog   1937—1938.   1941/42.

WEST-INDISCHE GIDS.   The Hague (etc).   1, 1919/20— 39(4), Dec 1959 . . .
[Subs: Nieuwe West-Indische Gids]

BM   36, July 1955—
LondICS   32 (1), Ap 1951—   [W 39(1).]

YEAR BOOK OF CARIBBEAN RESEARCH.   Caribbean Commission; Central Secretariat;
Research Branch.   Port-of-Spain.   1948.//
["Survey of Research & Investigation in the Caribbean & Adjoining Countries"]

LondICS
LSE
RhodesHOxf

YEARBOOK OF THE WEST INDIES & COUNTRIES OF THE CARIBBEAN.
London. 1948/49—1952.
[Prev: 1926/27— 1935 as: Year Book of the Bermudas, the Bahamas,
British Guiana, British Honduras & the British West Indies. Then 1936—
1947/8 as: West Indies Yearbook. Then as above. Subs: West Indies &
Caribbean Year Book.]

BhmPL
BM
BodI
BrU
CambU
HackneyPL
LdsPL
LivPL
LondICS   1948.   1952.
LondU   1950.
LSE
MancPL

ARGENTINA

AGRO. Publicacion tecnica. (Argentina) Ministerio de Asuntos Agrarios.
La Plata. 1(1), Aug 1959–

BM

AHORRO (Y SEGURO). Caja Nacional de Ahorro Postal (Argentina). Buenos
Aires. No. 1, Aug 1948–
[To 7, 1954 actually titled: Ahorro]

NCL No 106, Sep/Oct 1963 (as specimen issue).

ANALES DE LA ACADEMIA DE CIENCIAS ECONOMICAS. Buenos Aires.
(2S) 1, 1943– 6, 1948; (3S) 1, 1956–
[Original series (1, 1927– 4, 1938) titled: Bibliotheca de la
Academia ...]

ANUARIO DEL COMERCIO EXTERIOR DE LA REPUBLICA ARGENTINA. (Argentina)
Direccion Nacional de Estadistica y Censos. Buenos Aires. 1915–
[Name of issuing body varies]

BM   1915– 1917; 1925; 1940–
Bodl   1935–
LSE   1916–
OxfIES 1937–
RIIA   1927– 1938; 1940– 1943.
TropProdl 1959.

ANUARIO ESTADISTICO DE LA REPUBLICA ARGENTINA. (Argentina) Direccion
Nacional de Estadistica y Censos. Buenos Aires. 1, 1950–

Bodl   1949/50.

ANUARIO SOCIALISTA. Partido Socialista (Argentina). Buenos Aires.
1928–

LSE   1929; 1930; 1935– 1939; 1941; 1946.

ARGENTINA AUSTRAL. Buenos Aires.

ScottPolarRI   21(217), 1949–

ARGENTINA FINANCIERA. Buenos Aires.

ARGENTINE LAW BULLETIN. Buenos Aires. 1, Mar 1962–

UCL

ARGENTINE WEEKLY NEWS BULLETIN
London.

BoLSA **

BALANCE ENERGETICO ARGENTINO. Consejo Nacional de Desarollo (Argentina).
Buenos Aires.
[A]

LSE   1961–

BANCOS ANDINOS. Revista de finanzas. Mendoza, Arg. 1, Dec 1955–

BIBLIOTHECA DE LA ACADEMIA DE CIENCIAS ECONOMICAS. Buenos Aires.
1, 1927– 4, 1938.
[Subs (called "2S"): Anales de la Academia ...]

27

BIEN RAIZ.   Revista mensual de la propriedad immueble.   Buenos Aires.

BOLETIN ADMINISTRATIVO DEL MINISTERIO DE SALUD PUBLICA DE LA NACION
(ARGENTINA).   Buenos Aires.
   (Prev: Boletin Admin. de la Secretaria de Salud ...; from 1, 1946)
   LSH

BOLETIN ADMINISTRATIVO DE LA SECRETARIA DE SALUD PUBLICA DE LA
NACION (ARGENTINA).   Buenos Aires.   1, 1946—
   [Subs: Boletin Admin. del Ministerio de Salud ...]
   LSH

BOLETIN BIBLIOGRAFICO, BANCO CENTRAL DE LA REPUBLICA ARGENTINA.
   Buenos Aires.
   BM No.174, May/June 1964; 178, Jan/Feb 1965—
   UCL **

BOLETIN DE LA BOLSA DE COMERCIO DE BUENOS AIRES.   Buenos Aires.
   BM No.1547, 3/Dec 1934.
   BoLSA **

BOLETIN DE LA CAMARA DE COMERCIO ARGENTINO-ALEMANA.   Buenos Aires.

BOLETIN DE LA COMISION PERMANENTE, ASOCIACION DEL CONGRESO
PANAMERICANO DE FERROCARRILES. Buenos Aires. 1, 1917—

   BM   29(93) — 30 (95).
   SL   20—

BOLETIN DE COMUNICACIONES.   (Argentina) Ministerio de Educacion Nacional.
   Buenos Aires.   1, 1949—
   DurhamU 2 (106-108, 110-124), 1950—
   LdsU   2 (106),   1950—
   RadclSL   2 (106), 1950—
   SwUC   *2 (106), 1950—

BOLETIN DE LA DIRECCION GENERAL IMPOSITIVA (ARGENTINA).   Buenos Aires.
   1, Jan 1954—

BOLETIN DE ESTADISTICA (ARGENTINA).   (Argentina) Direccion Nacional de
   Estadistica y Censos.   Buenos Aires.   1963—
   [Prev (from 1, 1956) : Boletin Mensual de Estadistica]
   BoLSA
   EssexU   1964—
   HispLBC
   OxfIES
   RIIA
   UCL

BOLETIN DE ESTADISTICA (Y JURISPRUDENCIA), POLICIA DE LA CAPITAL
FEDERAL (BUENOS AIRES).   Buenos Aires.

   BM   19(79), 1932—   (Also "Anuario" to above from 1932).
   Bodl   *1932— 1946.
   LdsU   19 (84), 1933.

BOLETIN ESTADISTICO, BANCO CENTRAL DE LA REPUBLICA ARGENTINA. (1937)
   Buenos Aires.   No.1,   Aug 1937-113, Aug 1948.
   [Prev: Revista Economica, Banco Central . . .;   Suplemento Estadistico.
   Again under above title from 1, Jan 1958]
   NuffCollOxf   No. 110, 1946—
   OxfIES 1938 — Ap 1948.

BOLETIN ESTADISTICO, BANCO CENTRAL DE LA REPUBLICA ARGENTINA. (1958)
Buenos Aires.   1, Jan 1958—

Bodl   *6 (1), 1963—
BoLSA
BoT 1958—
IBank   (selected articles only kept)
MarshallL   *4, 1961— 7, 1064.
NuffCollOxf
OxfIES   1958—

BOLETIN DE LA FACULTAD DE DERECHO Y CIENCIAS SOCIALES, UNIVERSIDAD
NACIONAL DE CORDOBA.   Cordoba, Arg.   1, 1937—

BM   9 (4/5), 1945 — 10 (1/3), 1946.

BOLETIN DE INFORMACIONES PETROLERAS.   (Argentina) Direccion General de
Yacimientos Petroliferos Fiscales.   Buenos Aires.   1, Sep 1924—
26 (301), 1949 . . .
[Subs: Revista YPF]

Bodl   13, 1936— 24, 1947.
BM   11 (115-119); 22 (254)—
RadclSL   11 (115)—
SL   25 (281)—

BOLETIN INFORMATIVO, BANCO DE LA PROVINCIA DE BUENOS AIRES.   Buenos
Aires.   1, Oct 1959—

UCL **

BOLETIN INFORMATIVO, JUNTA NACIONAL DE GRANOS (ARGENTINA).

BoLSA   1958—

BOLETIN DEL INSTITUTO DE ESTUDIOS ECONOMICOS Y FINANCIEROS,
UNIVERSIDAD NACIONAL DE LA PLATA. (La Plata)   1, June 1958—

BOLETIN DEL INSTITUTO DE SOCIOLOGIA.   Buenos Aires.

BM   10 (7), 1958—

BOLETIN MENSUAL DE ESTADISTICA (ARGENTINA). (Argentina) Direccion
Nacional de Estadistica y Censos. Buenos Aires.   1, Jan 1956—
[Subs (from 1963); Boletin de Estadistica (Arg.)]

Bodl
BoT
EssexU   *1-2, 1957.
HispLBC
NLS
OxfIES
RIIA

BOLETIN, MINISTERIO DE HACIENDA (ARGENTINA).   Buenos Aires.
1,   30/Mar 1946—
[W]

BM

BOLETIN DE PRODUCCION Y FOMENTO AGRICOLA. (Argentina) Direccion General
de Agricultura y Defensa Agricola.   Buenos Aires.   1, July 1949—

BM   [W 1(5)]
CSA
Rothamsted

BOLETIN DEL TRABAJO. (Argentina) Ministerio de Trabajo y Seguridad
    Social. Buenos Aires.

BUSINESS CONDITIONS IN ARGENTINA. Buenos Aires.   1884—
    (Q)

    Bodl *199—
    BoLSA   1931—
    BoT   * 1952—
    EssexU   *282, 1954—
    HispLBC **
    LivU   1929—
    LSE   144, 1919— [W 147; 150]
    RIIA   *1939— 1946; no. 253, 1947—

CAMOATI. Revista de economia y estadistica. Buenos Aires.   June 1940—

    BM   16 (185), 1955—

CLARIN ECONOMICO.   Buenos Aires.

    BoLSA   1961—

COMERCIO EXTERIOR (ARGENTINA); (ANNUAL). (Argentina) Direccion Nacional
    de Estadistica y Censos. Buenos Aires.   1951/54—
    [Part of the Direccion's: Informe C]

    Bodl
    BoLSA
    BoT
    EssexU   1961 - 1964.
    LSE   1951/4; 1955/7; 1958—
    RIIA   1951/4; 1955/7; 1957—

COMERCIO EXTERIOR (ARGENTINA); (MONTHLY).   (Argentina) Direccion Nacional
    de Estadistica y Censos.   Buenos Aires.
    [Part of the Direccion's: Informe C]

    BoISA   1957—
    BoT   1956-1958*; 1963—
    EssexU   *1956—
    HispLBC **
    LSE   May 1964—
    OxfIES   1945—
    RIIA   Sep 1956

COMERCIO MINORISTA, PRECIOS AL POR MAYOR (ARGENTINA).   (Argentina)
    Direccion Nacional de Estadistica y Censos.   [Buenos Aires]
    [Part of the Direccion's: Informe C]

    BoLSA   1963—
    BoT **
    EssexU   * 1963—
    HispLBC **
    LSE   Ap 1964—
    UCL **

COMMENTS ON ARGENTINE TRADE. Chamber of Commerce of the United States of
    America in the Argentine Republic. Buenos Aires.   1, 1958—
    ["Directory of American business in Argentina"]

COSTO DE VIDA, PRECIOS MINORISTAS, SALARIOS INDUSTRIALES (ARGENTINA).
(Argentina) Direccion Nacional de Estadistica y Censos. Buenos
Aires. Mar 1963—
[Part of the Direccion's: Informe E.S. Mar 1963 = Informe E.S.1]

    BolSA
    BoT   1968—
    EssexU*
    HispLBC **
    LSE*

CUADERNOS, CENTRO DE ESTUDIOS ARGENTINOS. Buenos Aires. 1, Oct 1957—
BhmU

DERECHO FISCAL. Buenos Aires. 1, July 1951—

DESARROLLO ECONOMICO.   Institute de Desarrollo Economico y Social.
Buenos Aires. 1, Ap/June 1961—

    EssexU   4(13), 1964—
    MarshallL *1-3.
    OxfIES 1961—
    RIIA   2 (3), 1962—

DINAMICA SOCIAL. Centro de Estudios Economico Sociales. Buenos Aires.
No. 1, Sep 1950—

    BM   No.112/133, 1960—

ECA. Revista del Instituto Superior de Ciencias Administrativas,
Universidad Nacional de la Plata. [La Plata] 1, 1959—
[Name of body (and subtitle) vary. Orig.: ECA. Revista de la
Escuela Superior de Ciencias . . .]

*ECONOMICA. Revista de la Facultad de Ciencias Economicas, Universidad
Nacional de la Plata. Buenos Aires. 1, July/Sep 1954—

    GlasU
    MarshallL   *5-8.

EDICAMER. Camara Argentina de Sociedades Anonimas. Buenos Aires.
1, Ap 1954—

EDIFICACION. (Argentina) Direccion Nacional de Estadistica y Censos.
Buenos Aires.
[Part of the Direccion's: Informe E]

    BoLSA 1964—
    BoT 1963—
    EssexU   *Mar 1963—
    HispLBC **
    LSE Mar 1964—

EMBARCACIONES DE BANDERA ARGENTINA EN NAVIGACION COMERCIAL.
(Argentina) Direccion Nacional de Estadistica y Censos. Buenos Aires.
BM 1959-1960.

ESTADISTICA INDUSTRIAL (ARGENTINA). (Argentina) Direccion Nacional de
Estadistica y Censos. Buenos Aires.

    BodI *1937— 1942.
    BM 1941—

ESTADISTICA SOBRE TRANSITO TURISTICO (ARGENTINA). (Argentina)
Direccion Nacional de Turismo.　　Buenos Aires.　　1, 1958—
[M]

　　LSE

ESTUDIOS ECONOMICOS.　　Universidad Nacional del Sur (Argentina); Instituto
de Economia.　　Bahia Blanca.　　1, Jan/June 1962—

　　BM

EXPORTACION DE CUEROS LANARES.　Federacion Lanera Argentina.　Buenos
Aires.

FRANCE-ARGENTINE.　　Chambre de Commerce Argentine-France.

　　BoLSA **

GUIA PRACTICA DEL EXPORTADOR E IMPORTADOR.　Buenos Aires.　1, Jan 1957—
[M] . -

　　BoLSA

HERALDO MERCANTIL.　　Cordoba, Arg.　1, 1960—
[M]

INFORMACION.　　Revista mensual.　　Buenos Aires.

　　BM　*18, 1947—

INFORMACIONES ESTADISTICAS AGROPECUARIAS (ARGENTINA).　(Argentina)
Ministerio de Agricultura; Direccion de Estadistica.　Buenos Aires.　1, 1937—

　　BM　　3(3)—
　　LdsU　*2-6.
　　LivU　*2-6.
　　OxfIES
　　SL

INFORME, DIRECCION NACIONAL DE ESTADISTICA Y CENSOS (ARGENTINA).
Buenos Aires.　　1, 1923—

　　BodI　　1951—
　　BM　　*1933— 1936.

INTERCAMBIO COMERCIAL ARGENTINO CON LOS PAISES DE LA (ALALC).
(Argentina)　Direccion Nacional de Estadistica y Censos.　Buenos Aires.
["ALALC" in title actually as　A.L. de L.C.]

　　BoLSA　1962—
　　BoT　1962—
　　EssexU　*4, 1962— 15, 1965.
　　LSE　　1964—

INVESTIGACIONES DEL SEMINARIO (DE CIENCIAS JURIDICAS Y SOCIALES),
UNIVERSIDAD DE BUENOS AIRES.　Buenos Aires.　　No.1, 1927—

LEGISLACION DEL TRABAJO.　Revista mensual de legislacion, jurisprudencia y
doctrina.　Buenos Aires.　　1, Jan 1953—

LIBERALIS.　　Idea, accion.　Buenos Aires.　No.1, May/June 1949—
[Subtitle varies: Una tribuna por el hombre libre]

　　BM　　38/39, Jan/Mar 1957—

MEMORIA ANUAL, BANCO CENTRAL DE LA REPUBLICA ARGENTINA. Buenos Aires.
1, 1935 (1936)—

BhmPL (Current issue only)
Bodl 2, 1936—
BoLSA
HispLBC **
IBank (Two year file)
MarshallL 1953—1954; 1960-1961; 1963
NuffCollOxf 10, 1944—
RIIA 1947— 1964.
UCL **

MEMORIA ANUAL, BANCO HIPOTECARIO NACIONAL (ARGENTINA). Buenos Aires.
Bodl 46, 1931— 63, 1948.

MEMORIA Y BALANCE GENERAL, BANCO DE LA NACION ARGENTINA. Buenos Aires.
1, 1891—
Bodl 1934— 1948

MEMORIA . . ., BOLSA DE COMERCIO, BUENOS AIRES. Buenos Aires.
(Actual title: Memoria correspondiente al Ejercicio del Ano . . .)
UCL 1961 (1962)—

MEMORIA DE LA CONTADURIA GENERAL DE LA NACION (ARGENTINA).
Buenos Aires.
Bodl *1931— 1940
RIIA 1940

MEMORIA, INSTITUTO MOVILIZADOR DE INVERSIONES BANCARIAS. Buenos Aires.
1, 1936 (1937)—
Bodl 1—8, 1943.

MEMORIA, JUNTA NACIONAL PARA COMBATIR LA DESOCUPACION (ARGENTINA).
Buenos Aires:
LSE 1937.

MEMORIA, MINISTERIO DE AGRICULTURA Y GANADERA DE LA NACION
(ARGENTINA) Buenos Aires.
[Name of Ministerio varies. To 1941, actually titled: Memoria presentada al
Honorable Congreso de la Nacion]
Bodl 1935— 1942.

MEMORIA, MINISTERIO DE COMERCIO Y INDUSTRIA (ARGENTINA). Buenos Aires.
1957—

MEMORIA, MINISTERIO DE HACIENDA (ARGENTINA). Buenos Aires.
Bodl 1932— 1943.
BoLSA 1951—
RIIA 1937— 1943; 1944 (Vol. 1).

MEMORIA, MINISTERIO DE OBRAS PUBLICAS (ARGENTINA). Buenos Aires.
Bodl 1936— 1942.

MEMORIA, MINISTERIO DE TRABAJO Y PREVISION DE LA NACION (ARGENTINA).
Buenos Aires.
[Name of Ministerio varies]

MERCURIO.   Camara Argentina de Comercio   Buenos Aires.

MONTHLY JOURNAL, BRITISH CHAMBER OF COMMERCE IN THE ARGENTINE
REPUBLIC.   Buenos Aires.   1, Sep 1920—
BM   1 (3)— 2 (4).
BoLSA   1959—
HispLBC **
LivPL   *27, 1947—

MUNDO AGRARIO.   Revista mensual de ganaderia, agricultura e industrias.
Buenos Aires.   1, June 1949—

MUNDO INDUSTRIAL.   Buenos Aires.   1, 1948—

SL   2 (7, 9)—

NACION; WEEKLY AIRMAIL EDITION.   Buenos Aires.

BoLSA**

NAVEGACION COMERCIAL ARGENTINA.   (Argentina) Direccion Nacional de
Estadistica y Censos.   Buenos Aires.
UCL   Informe no.2,   1964—

PANORAMA DE LA ECONOMIA ARGENTINA.   Asociacion de Dirigentes de Ventas de
Buenos Aires.   Buenos Aires.   1, 1957—
BoLSA   1957—
EssexU   4(25),   1964—
OxfIES   4 (28),   1965

PRODUCTIVIDAD Y BIENESTAR SOCIAL.   Congreso Nacional de Productividad y
Bienestar Social (Argentina).   Buenos Aires.

QUARTERLY ECONOMIC REVIEW; ARGENTINA.   Economist Intelligence Unit.
London.   No.1, 1952—
LSE   *No.2, May 1952—

REVIEW OF THE RIVER PLATE.   Buenos Aires.   1, 1892—
[Subtitle (varies slightly): Revista del Rio de la Plata, with which is
incorporated the Times of Argentina.   A journal dealing with financial,
economic, and shipping affairs]
BM   1 (31)— 3 (126); 27 (833)— 29 (888); 35 (1004)— 57 (1795).
BoLSA   1945—
BoT **
EssexU   *111, 1952— 132, 1962; *137, 1965—
HispLBC **
OxfIES   133, 1963—
RIIA   135 (3518),   1964—

REVISTA AGRONOMICA DEL NOROESTE ARGENTINO.   Universidad Nacional de
Tucuman; Facultad de Agronomia.   Tucuman.   1, May 1953 —
EMall 2, 1956—

REVISTA ARGENTINA DE CIENCIA POLITICA. Asociacion Argentina de Ciencia
Politica. Buenos Aires. 1, Jan/June 1960—

LSE   2 (3), Jan/June 1961—

REVISTA DEL BANCO CENTRAL DE LA REPUBLICA ARGENTINA. Buenos Aires
1, Jan/Mar 1965—
[Q]
BoLSA

REVISTA DEL BANCO DE LA NACION ARGENTINA. Buenos Aires. 1, 1937—

Bodl   1— 9, 1945.
OxfIES   1—9 (1), 1945.

REVISTA DE CIENCIAS ECONOMICAS. Universidad de Buenos Aires; Facultad de
Ciencias Economicas. Buenos Aires. 1, July 1913—
BoLSA   1959—
LSE *9—
OxfIES 27, 1939—

REVISTA DE CIENCIAS JURIDICAS Y SOCIALES. Universidad Nacional de
Litoral (Argentina). Santa Fe. 1, 1930—
Bodl   1943— 1954.
LivU   Nos. 18—22; 40-49; 54-85. (1936— 1955).

REVISTA DEL COMERCIO EXTERIOR ARGENTINO. (Argentina) Ministerio de
Comercio. [Buenos Aires] No.1, June 1953— 9, Jan/Feb 1955.//
[To 7, 1954, name of body was: Ministerio de Comercio Exterior]

REVISTA DE DESARROLLO ECONOMICO. Junta de Planificacion de la Provincia
de Buenos Aires. La Plata. 1, Oct/Dec 1958— 2 (4). 1959.//

LSE

REVISTA DE LA DIRECCION GENERAL DE ESTADISTICA, CENSOS Y
INVESTIGACIONES (CORDOBA). Cordoba, Arg. 1, 1940—

BM   7 (72)—

REVISTA DE ECONOMIA. Banco de la Provincia de Cordoba (Argentina);
Departamento de Coordinacion y Estudios. Cordoba, Arg. No.1,
Jan/June 1949—
[Suspended 1955]
BoLSA   No.14, 1956/57—
MarshallL**
OxfIES Jan/June 1949 — July/Dec 1954

REVISTA DE ECONOMIA ARGENTINA. Buenos Aires. 1, July 1918—

OxfIES   18, 1935— 30, 1947.

REVISTA DE ECONOMIA Y ESTADISTICA.   Universidad Nacional de Cordoba (Arg.);
Facultad de Ciencias Economicas. Cordoba, Arg. 1, 1939—8, 1946;
(NS) 1, 1957—
[To 1946, issued by the Universidad's Escuela de Ciencias Economicas]
MarshallL**
OxfIES   6, 1962—

REVISTA ECONOMICA, BANCO DE LA REPUBLICA ARGENTINA. Buenos
    Aires.   1, Aug 1937—

REVISTA ECONOMICA, BANCO CENTRAL DE LA REPUBLICA ARGENTINA;
SUPLEMENTO ESTADISTICA. Buenos Aires. No.1, Aug 1937— 105,
    [Subs: Boletin Estadistica, Banco Central . . .]

    OxfIES   1938—

REVISTA DE LA ESCUELA SUPERIOR DE CIENCIAS ADMINISTRATIVAS,
UNIVERSIDAD NACIONAL DE LA PLATA.
    see ECA

REVISTA DE LA FACULTAD DE CIENCIAS ECONOMICAS, COMERCIALES Y
POLITICOS, UNIVERSIDAD NACIONAL DEL LITORAL (ARGENTINA). Santa Fe.
    1, (Dec 1926— 1927); (2S)   1, 1928; (3S) 1, Sep 1930—

    Bodl **
    LivU **
    LSE **

REVISTA DE LA FACULTAD DE CIENCIAS ECONOMICAS, UNIVERSIDAD DE
BUENOS AIRES.   Buenos Aires.   1, Mar 1948—
    [Prev: Revista de Ciencias Economicas]

    LSE
    OxfIES   Sep 1949— Dec 1953.

REVISTA DE LA FACULTAD DE DERECHO Y CIENCIAS SOCIALES, UNIVERSIDAD
DE BUENOS AIRES.   Buenos Aires.   1, 1946—

    Bodl

REVISTA DEL INSTITUTO DE ESTUDIOS COOPERATIVOS, UNIVERSIDAD NACIONAL
DE LA PLATA.   La Plata.   1, July/Sep 1958—

REVISTA DEL INSTITUTO DE INVESTIGACIONES ECONOMICAS, UNIVERSIDAD
NACIONAL DEL LITORAL (ARGENTINA).   Rosario (Santa Fe). 1, Oct/Dec 1957

REVISTA DEL INSTITUTO SUPERIOR DE CIENCIAS ADMINISTRATIVAS,
UNIVERSIDAD NACIONAL DE LA PLATA.
    see ECA.

REVISTA DEL MINISTERIO DE TRABAJO Y SEGURIDAD SOCIAL (ARGENTINA).
    Buenos Aires.   1, May 1957—
    [1—2 (15), July 1958 actually titled: Revista del Ministerio de Trabajo
    y Prevision. Prev: Revista de Trabajo y Prevision.]

REVISTA DE TRABAJO Y PREVISION. (1944)   (Argentina) Secretaría de
    Trabajo y Prevision. Buenos Aires.   1, 1944— 3(10), 1946.
    [Publ. again under above title from 1953]

REVISTA DE TRABAJO Y PREVISION. (1953) (Argentina) Ministerio de
    Trabajo y Prevision.   Buenos Aires. 1, Feb 1953—
    [Subs: Revista del Ministerio . . . (From 1958 as :Revista del Ministerio
    de Trabajo y Seguridad Social]

REVISTA DE LA UNION INDUSTRIAL ARGENTINA. Buenos Aires.
[Prev from 1, 1887: (1) Boletin de la Union . . . (2) (Nov 1925– Dec
1936) Anales de la Union . . . Then as above]

SL   58 (921), 1945–

SEGUROS Y BANCOS. Buenos Aires.   1, 1912–

BM 234, July 1933–

SINTESIS ESTADISTICA MENSUAL DE LA REPUBLICA ARGENTINA. (Argentina)
Direccion Nacional de Estadistica y Censos.   Buenos Aires.   1, Jan 1947–
[Suspended Ap 1948– Jan/Dec 1949]

SINTESIS ESTADISTICA MENSUAL DE LA REPUBLICA ARGENTINA; SUPLEMENTO.
Buenos Aires.   No.1, 1947–
[Actual title: Suplemento de la Sintesis . . .]

OxfIES   1947– 1955.

SITUATION IN ARGENTINA.   First National Bank of Boston. Boston, Mass.

BoLSA **

TECNICA Y ECONOMIA. Revista del Instituto Tecnologico del Sur. Bahia
Blanca. No.1, Sep 1949–

SL   No.4/5, 1950–

TRABAJOS DEL SEMINARIO, FACULTAD DE CIENCIAS ECONOMICAS.
COMERCIALES Y POLITICAS, UNIVERSIDAD NACIONAL DEL LITORAL
(ARGENTINA). Rosario (Santa Fe).   1, 1924–

BodI   4, 1928– 22, 1948.

VERITAS ARGENTINA. Buenos Aires.   1, 15/Jan 1931–
[Actual title to Mar 1950: Veritas. Suspended Ap 1950– Dec 1955]

BM 17 (196), Ap 1947–
EssexU 35, 1965–

WEEKLY LETTER, BRITISH CHAMBER OF COMMERCE IN THE ARGENTINE
REPUBLIC. Buenos Aires.

BoLSA **

BAHAMAS

(BAHAMAS).   Report.   (Great Britain) Colonial Office / Commonwealth
     Relations Office.   London.

     BM   1947 − 1965
     HullU   1949−
     LondICS   1933−1938;   1946−1951;   1952/3−

BAHAMAS HANDBOOK & BUSINESSMANS ANNUAL.   Nassau.   1, 1960−

     Bodl   1966/67−

CUSTOMS ADMINISTRATIVE REPORT & TRADE RETURN (BAHAMAS).

     BM 1940;   1952;   1957−
     BoT **
     LondICS   1956−

PRINCIPAL ITEMS OF DOMESTIC EXPORTS (BAHAMAS).

     BoT **

PRINCIPAL ITEMS IMPORTED (BAHAMAS).

     BoT **

[Also certain items available at the Board of Trade Library, not in published
form: Monthly and quarterly returns of imports and exports by direction;
Monthly return of statistics: imports of textiles.]

BARBADOS

ABSTRACT OF STATISTICS (BARBADOS).   (Barbados) Statistical Service.
Bridgetown.   No.1, 1956–
BM
BoT   1956–1957;   1960–1963
LondICS

ADMINISTRATION REPORT OF THE COMPTROLLER OF CUSTOMS (BARBADOS).
Bridgetown.
BM   1940;   1948–
Bot   1957–
LondICS   1948–

(BARBADOS).   Report. (Great Britain) Colonial Office / Commonwealth.
Relations Office.   London.
BM
HullU   1949–
LondICS   1933– 1939;   1947– 1952; 1952/3–

BEACON.   Barbados Labour Party.   Bridgetown.
[W]
LondICS   19(28, 29, 34, 35, 37–55), 1965, 20 (1), 1966–

CENSUS OF TOURISM (BARBADOS).   Barbados Statistical Service.   Bridgetown.
[A]
BM   1958
BoT   1956 –
LSE   1958 –

COMMERCIAL JOURNAL.   Barbados Chamber of Commerce.   Bridgetown.
1,   1951– 6, 1958.
[Subs: Journal, Barbados Chamber of Commerce]

"CRASH" ESTIMATES OF GROSS DOMESTIC PRODUCT AT FACTOR COST
(BARBADOS).
[A]
BoT**

JOURNAL, BARBADOS CHAMBER OF COMMERCE.   Bridgetown.   Jan 1959–
[Prev: Commercial Journal]
Lond ICS
TropProdI*

MONTHLY NEWSLETTER, BARBADOS EMPLOYERS CONFEDERATION.   Bridgetown
LondICS   No.82, 1964–

OVERSEAS TRADE (BARBADOS).   Barbados Statistical Service.   (Bridgetown)
1957–
[Prev: Report of the Comptroller of Customs . . .]
BM   1960–
BodI
BoT
LondICS
LSE

OVERSEAS TRADE (BARBADOS); QUARTERLY REPORT. Barbados statistical Service. Bridgetown.

    BM   S1962;   D1965—
    Bodl   Jan 1957—
    BoT **
    LondICS   (retained until annual vol. received)

QUARTERLY DIGEST OF STATISTICS (BARBADOS). Barbados Statistical Service. Bridgetown. No.1, Dec 1956—

    BM   No.36; No.39 —
    Bodl
    BoT   1956—
    LondICS   No.17, 1961—

REPORT ON REVENUE, TRADE & SHIPPING (BARBADOS).   (Barbados) Comptroller of Customs.   Bridgetown.

    LondICS   1942— 1956;   1957—

SELECTED MONTHLY INDICATORS (BARBADOS).

    BM   D1965—
    BoT 1957—

SERIES OF ECONOMIC SURVEYS.   Economic Planning Unit (Barbados). (Bridgetown)   1, 1962—

    BM
    LondICS   1962;   1964—

[Also certain items available at the Board of Trade Library, not in published form: Monthly or quarterly returns of imports and exports by direction; Monthly return of statistics: imports of textiles; Statement of imports and exports by countries of origin and destination; (Sugar return).]

BERMUDA

(BERMUDA).   Report   (Great Britain) Colonial Office / Commonwealth
Relations Office.   London.

BM   1946 – 1964.
LondICS   1933 – 1938; 1946–1952;   1953/4–

IMPORTS & EXPORTS (BERMUDA).

BM   1940; 1957 – 1958.
LondICS   1952–

REPORT OF THE TRADE DEVELOPMENT BOARD (BERMUDA).

BM   1946 – 1949; 1953 –
LondICS   1947

BOLIVIA

ANUARIO DEMOGRAFICO (BOLIVIA). (Bolivia) Direccion Nacional de
Estadistica y Censos. La Paz.

LSE 1946/50—

ANUARIO INDUSTRIAL (BOLIVIA). (Bolivia) Direccion Nacional de
Estadistica y Censos. La Paz. 1950/57 [1962] —
LSE
UCL

BALANZA COMERCIAL DE BOLIVIA; COMERCIO EXTERIOR. (Bolivia) Direccion
Nacional de Estadistica y Censos. La Paz.
[A]
BoT **
LSE [2nd], 1951/59 —

BOLETIN DEL BANCO CENTRAL DE BOLIVIA. La Paz. (1, Sep 1929) —
[1929 — Jan 1931 actually titled: Boletin Mensual . . .]

BOLETIN DEL BANCO CENTRAL DE BOLIVIA; SUPLEMENTO ESTADISTICO.
La Paz. No.1, May 1943 —
[Issued by the Banco's: Seccion Estudios Economicos y
Estadistica. (Name varies). Parent title not mentioned
in this publ?]

BOLETIN ESTADISTICO (BOLIVIA). (Bolivia) Direccion Nacional de
Estadistica y Censos. La Paz. ?1, 1945 —
[2/A]
BoT **
UCL **

COMERCIO EXTERIOR (BOLIVIA). (Bolivia) Direccion Nacional de Estadistica
y Censos. La Paz.

OxfIES 1936—1938. 1941.
BoT **

GACETA OFICIAL DE BOLIVIA. (Bolivia) Secretaria General de la
Presidencia de la Republica; Departamento de Publicidad. La Paz.
1, Jan/June 1957 —

NRL (Holb) 3 (194), 1964—

INDICE DEL COSTO DE VIDA EN LAS CIUDADES DE LA PAZ, COCHABAMBA, ORURO.
(Bolivia) Direccion Nacional de Estadistica y Censos; Seccion
Estadisticas Financieras. La Paz.

BoT **
LSE No.23, 1961 —

MEMORIA ANUAL DEL BANCO CENTRAL DE BOLIVIA. La Paz.

BoLSA 1943 —
BoT 1960 —

MEMORIA ANUAL, YACIMIENTOS PETROLIFEROS FISCALES BOLIVIANOS. La Paz.
LSE 1948; 1949; 1954—1956; 1958—

MEMORIAS ANUALES, BANCO MINERO DE BOLIVIA. La Paz.

BoT 1955/59—

42

PLANEAMIENTO. Junta Nacional de Planeamiento (Bolivia). La Paz.
 1, Oct/Dec 1960 –
 [Q]
 HispLBC

REVISTA ECONOMICA. Universidad Tecnica de Oruro; Centro de Estudiantes
 de Ciencias Economicas. Oruro, Bolivia.
 [2 nos. (in 1) p.a.]
 HispLBC **
 LSE No.21/22, Sep 1958/June 1959–

SEGURIDAD SOCIAL. Caja Nacional de Seguridad Social (Bolivia).
 La Paz.
 LSE 21 (237/239), Jan/Mar 1960 –

SUPLEMENTO ESTADISTICO (Bolivia). (Bolivia) Direccion Nacional de
 Estadistica y Censos. La Paz. 1, Sep 1963 –
 [2M]
 LSE

SUPLEMENTO ESTADISTICO. Banco Central de Bolivia.
 see BOLETIN DEL BANCO CENTRAL DE BOLIVIA; SUPLEMENTO ESTADISTICO.

BRAZIL

AGRICULTURA E PECUARIA.　Rio de Janeiro.　1, 9/Mar 1938—

AGRICULTURA EM SAO PAULO.　(Sao Paulo, Estado) Departamento da Producao
Vegetal; Divisao de Economia Rural.　Sao Paulo.　1, Ap 1951—
　BoLSA　1963—
　LSE　4, 1954—
　MinAg　9 (2),　1962—
　OxfIES　Jan 1960— Oct 1963;　Dec 1963

*AMERICA LATINA.　Centro Latino-Americano de Pesquisas em Ciencias Sociais.
Rio de Janeiro.　5, 1962—
　[Prev: Boletim do Centro . . . . from 1,　1958]
　EssexU　8, 1965—
　LSE
　RAnthrol　9, 1966—
　UCL　5(3), 1962—

ANALISE E PERSPECTIVA ECONOMICA.
see APEC.

ANHEMBI.　Sao Paulo 1(1), Dec 1950— 48 (144), Nov 1962.//

ANNUAL REPORT, BRAZILLIAN CHAMBER OF COMMERCE & ECONOMIC AFFAIRS
IN GREAT BRITAIN.　London.
　GlasU　1957— 1959.

ANUARIO DE ESTATISTICA E INFORMACOES, COMISSAO EXECUTIVA DE DEFESA
DA BORRACHA (BRAZIL).　Rio de Janeiro.　14(15), Jan/Dec　1962—
　[Prev: Boletim de Estatistica e Informacoes, . . .]

ANUARIO ESTATISTICO DO BRASIL.　Rio de Janeiro.　1, 1908/12 —
　BoLSA　1956—
　BoT **
　EdinU　3, 1937. 7,　1946— 22, 1961.
　GlasU　8, 1947—
　LondU　6, 1941/5 (1946)—
　MarshallL　1954— 1961.
　StAndU　3,　1937— 22, 1961.

ANUARIO ESTATISTICO DA RFFSA.　Rede Ferroviaria Federal S.A. (Brazil).
Rio de Janeiro.
　EssexU　1965.

APEC.　A Brazilian fortnightly economic letter.　Rio de Janeiro.
　[APEC = Analise e perspectiva economica]
　BoLSA　1962—

ARCO IRIS.　Centro Nacional de Estudos Cooperativos (Rio de Janeiro).
Rio de Janeiro.

ARQUIVOS ECONOMICOS.　Banco do Brasil.　Rio de Janeiro.　1, 1955—
　[Port., Engl., Fr.]
　Bodl

BANAS INFORMA.　Servico Banas (Sao Paulo).　Sao Paulo.
　[Port.　Also issued in Engl.]
　BoLSA **

44

BIBLIOGRAFIA, CENTRO LATINO-AMERICANO DE PESQUISAS EM CIENCIAS
SOCIAIS. Rio de Janeiro. 1, Sep/Oct 1962
[2M]
LSE

BOLETIM DO BANCO CENTRAL DO BRASIL. Rio de Janeiro. 1, 1965—
BoLSA

BOLETIM DE BIOESTATISTICA E EPIDEMIOLOGIA (BRAZIL). (Brazil) Ministerio
de Saude. Rio de Janeiro.

BOLETIN DE BIOESTATISTICA (PERNAMBUCO). (Pernambuco) Divisao de Epidemiologia
e Bioestatistica do Estado de Pernambuco. Recife? 1, 1960—
[Issued by the Divisao jointly with: (Brazil) Servico Federal de Bioestatistica,
(&) Fundacao Servico Especial de Saude Publica]

BOLETIM DA CAMARA DE EXPANSAO ECONOMICA DO PARANA.
see PARANA.

BOLETIM CAMBIAL. Rio de Janeiro.
BoLSA **

BOLETIM DA CARTEIRA DE EXPORTACAO E IMPORTACAO (BRAZIL). Banco do Brasil.
Rio de Janeiro. 1, Dec 1948— ? 1951.
[Subs: Comercio Internacional]
OxfIES

BOLETIM DO CENTRO LATINO—AMERICANO DE PESQUISAS EM CIENCIAS SOCIAIS.
Rio de Janeiro. 1, 1958—4, 1961 . . .
[Subs: America Latina]
LSE 3, 1960—

BOLETIM DAS CLASSES DIRIGENTES. Instituto Brasileiro de Opiniao Publica e
Estatistica. Rio de Janeiro. 1, 1950—

BOLETIM DA CONTADORIA GERAL DA REPUBLICA (BRAZIL). Rio de Janeiro. 1, 1925—

BOLETIM DE CPE. Comissao de Planejamento Economico do Estado da Bahia.
Salvador, Brazil.

BOLETIM DO DEPARTAMENTO DE ESTATISTICA DO ESTADO DE SAO PAULO. Sao
Paulo.
UCL **

BOLETIM DE ESTATISTICA E INFORMACOES, COMISSAO EXECUTIVA DE DEFESA DA
BORRACHA (BRAZIL). Rio de Janeiro.
[Subs: Anuario de Estatistica e Informacoes, . . .]

BOLETIM ESTATISTICO (BRAZIL). Conselho Nacional de Estatistica (Brazil).
Rio de Janeiro. 1943—
[Material prepared by: Instituto Brasileiro de Geografia e Estatistica]
BoLSA 1956—
OxfIES no 15, 1946.
RIIA 1961—

BOLETIM ESTATISTICO, INSTITUTO BRASILEIRO DO CAFE. Rio de Janeiro.
No.1, 1953—
BoLSA 1964—
OxfIES Ap 1955 — Feb 1958

BOLETIM ESTATISTICO, INSTITUTO NACIONAL DO MATE (BRAZIL).   Rio de Janeiro.
July 1940—

BOLETIM ESTATISTICO (PARAIBA).   (Paraiba) Departamento Estadual de
Estatistica.   Joao Pessoa.

UCL   1962—

BOLETIM DO ESTUDOS DE PESCA.   Superintendencia do Desenvolvimento do
Nordeste (Brazil).   Recife.   1, Oct 1961—
[Publ. by the Divisao de Pesca (of the) Departamento de Estudos Especiais
(of the) Superintendencia. Main body also known by abbreviation: SUDENE]

BM (NH)   4, 1964—
HispLBC **

BOLETIM DE IMPOSTO DE CONSUMO, IMPOSTO DE RENDA E TRIBUTAS EN GERAL
(BRAZIL).   Rio de Janeiro.   1, N 1949—

BOLETIM DE INDUSTRIA ANIMAL.   Sao Paulo. 4, 1941—
[Prev: Revista de Industria Animal (New Series), from 1, 1938]

BMA
NIRD
WelshPlant   7, 1944. 14/17, 1954/59—

BOLETIM DO INFORMACOES, MINISTERIO DA VIACAO E OBRAS PUBLICAS (BRAZIL).
Rio de Janeiro.   1, 1909—

MancU   1—3
RGS

BOLETIM INFORMATIVO, CENTRO E FEDERACAO DAS INDUSTRIAS DO ESTADO
DE SAO PAULO.   Sao Paulo.   1, Oct 1949—

HispLBC **   [Title varies]

BOLETIM INFORMATIVO DA CODEPE.   Comissao de Desenvolvimento Economico de
Pernambuco.   Recife.   1, 1954—

BOLETIM INFORMATIVO (E ESTATISTICO), INSTITUTO BRASILEIRO DO CAFE.
Rio de Janeiro.   1(1), 1958—
["E Estatistico" inserted into title from 1 (23), Feb 1959, after absorbing
the Instituto's: Boletim Estatistico . . .]

OxfIES   Jan 1958 — Jy 1961

BOLETIM INFORMATIVO, FEDERACAO E CENTRO DAS INDUSTRIAS DO ESTADO
DE SAO PAULO see BOLETIM INFORMATIVO, CENTRO E FEDERACAO . . .

BOLETIM INFORMATIVO DO INSTITUTO DE CACAU DA BAHIA. Salvador, Brazil.
1, Jan 1954—

BOLETIM DO INSTITUTO DE ECONOMIA "GASTAO VIDIGAL". Sao Paulo. 1, Oct 1951—
[Suppl. to: Digesto Economico.   Publ. for the Inst. by: Associacao Comercial
de Sao Paulo]

BOLETIM DO INSTITUTO JOAQUIM NABUCO DE PESQUISAS SOCIAIS.   Recife.
1, 1952 —
RAnthrol

BOLETIM MENSAL DE INFORMACOES DO INSTITUTO BAHIANO DO FUMO. Salvador,
Brazil.   1,   1952—

BOLETIM MENSAL DO SERVICO FEDERAL DE BIOESTATISTICA (BRAZIL). Rio de Janeiro.

BOLETIM DO MINISTERIO DE AGRICULTURA (BRAZIL)

UCL **

BOLETIM DO MINISTERIO DO TRABALHO, INDUSTRIA E COMERCIO (BRAZIL). [Rio de Janeiro] 1, 1934– 165, May 1948; (NS) 1, 1951–

BM 4, 193?–

BOLETIM DO SERVICO SOCIAL DOS MENORES (BRAZIL). Sao Paulo. 1, 1941–

BOLETIM SUMOC. Superintendencia da Moeda e do Credito (Brazil). Rio de Janeiro. 1, 1955– 11(3), Mar 1965.
[Subs: Boletim, Banco Central da Republica do Brasil]
BM 2 (7), July 1956–
BoLSA 1955–
BoT **

BOLETIM DA SUPERINTENDENCIA DOS SERVICOS DO CAFE (BRAZIL). Sao Paulo.
EMall *22, 1947– 33, 1958. [W 24, 1949]

BOLETIM TRIMESTRIAL, BANCO DO BRASIL. Rio de Janeiro. 1, 1966–
BoLSA
OxfIES Jan-Mar 1966

BOLSA. Bolsa de Valores do Rio de Janeiro. Rio de Janeiro.
Guildhall Aug 1963 –(will maintain 5 year file)

BORRACHA. (Brazil) Ministerio de Fazenda. Rio de Janeiro. 1, 1952–

BRASIL. (Brazil) Ministerio das Relacoes Exteriores. Rio de Janeiro.
BM 1955–

BRASIL. Revista dos Bancarios. Rio de Janeiro.

BRASIL CONSTROI. (Brazil) Ministerio de Viacao e Obras Publicas; Servico de Documentacao. Rio de Janeiro. 1, Oct 1948–
BM *1952– (4 (8); 5 (9-11); 6 (12)–)
Bodl *4 (8), 1952–
NLS 4 (7), 1950–

BRAZIL. An economic, social and geographic survey. (Brazil) Ministerio das Relacoes Exteriores. Rio de Janeiro.

BRAZIL. American Brazilian Association. New York. 1, 1927– Oct/Dec 1959.//

BRAZIL JOURNAL. Brazilian Chamber of Commerce & Economic Affairs in Great Britain. London. 10, 1952–
[Prev: Journal of the Brazilian Chamber . . ., from 1, 1943]
BM
BoLSA 1960–
GlasU
HispLBC **
LivPL

BRAZIL, LAND & PEOPLE. Brazilian Government Trade Bureau. London.
No.1, (1954)–
Bodl

47

*BRAZILIAN AMERICAN SURVEY.   Rio de Janeiro.   1, 1953/54—
   ["Editorial cooperation by Brazilian Government Trade Bureau" (Ministerio
   do Trabalho, Industria e Comercio)]

BRAZILIAN BULLETIN.   Brazilian Government Trade Bureau.   London.   1, 1951—
   BhmU   5—   [W 5(23—25)]
   BM   6(35),   1954—   [W 6(37, 41)]
   Bodl   *5 (26),   1953—
   HispLBC **
   NCL   [One issue as specimen]
   SouU   7 (45),   1955—

*BRAZILIAN BUSINESS.   American Chamber of Commerce in Rio de Janeiro. Rio
   de Janeiro.   1, Ap 1921—
   [Prev: Weekly Bulletin, American Chamber . . .]
   BoLSA   1960—

BRAZILIAN LETTER.   American Chamber of Commerce in Sao Paulo.   Sao Paulo.
   BoLSA **

BRAZILIAN NEWS.   (Brazil) Embassy; Great Britain. London
   Bodl   No.5, June 1962—
   EdinPL   (One year file)
   HispLBC **
   IBank (Selected articles only kept)
   LivPL   No.5, June 1962—
   NLS   No.5, 1962—
   ScotCollComm   No.5, June 1962
   Wimbledon PL   (one year file)

BULLETIN, BRITISH CHAMBER OF COMMERCE IN SAO PAULO. Sao Paulo.
   HispLBC **
   LivPL   1953—

CACAU ATUALIDADES.   Centro de Pesquisas do Cacau (Itabuna).   Itabuna,
   Brazil.   1, Jan 1964—
   EMall

CADERNOS DE NOSSO TEMPO.   Instituto Brasileiro de Economia, Sociologia e
   Politica.   (Rio de Janeiro]   1 (1), Oct/Dec 1953— 1(5), Jan/Mar 1956.
   ["Publication suspended"]

CAPES.   Boletim informativo da Campanha Nacional de Aperfeicoamento de
   Pessoal de Nivel Superior (Brazil).   Rio de Janeiro.   1952—
   HispLBC **

CARNES, DERIVADOS E SUBPRODUTOS.   (Brazil) Servico de Estatistica da
   Producao.   Rio de Janeiro.
   BoT **

CARTA ECONOMICA BRASILEIRA.   (Brazil) Servico de Pesquisa e Divulgacao
   Socio-economica Limitada. Rio de Janeiro (etc).
   [M. Body also known by initials: SPED]
   BoLSA   1965—

CARTA MENSAL, CONSELHO TECNICO CONSULTIVO, CONFEDERACAO NACIONAL
DO COMERCIO (BRAZIL).   Rio de Janeiro.   1, 1955—
   BoLSA   1961—
   OxFIES   July 1955— Dec 1959

CNC.   Confederacao Nacional do Comercio (Brazil).   Rio de Janeiro.
No.1,   June 1961—

COMENTARIO COMERCIAL ANGLO-BRASILEIRO.   British Chamber of Commerce
in Brazil.   Rio de Janeiro.   No.1, May 1945 —
(NS) [1] (1), 1949—
[New series numbered from 1-43, then from Vol.5]
BM   *(NS)

COMERCIO EXTERIOR DO BRASIL. (Brazil) Servico de Estatistica, Economia
e Financeira.   Rio de Janeiro.
RIIA 1919/23 —   1930/31.
UCL   1958/69 (1960) —

COMERCIO EXTERIOR DO BRASIL POR MERCADORIAS, SEGUNDO OS PORTOS.
BhmPL   (Current issue only)
Bodl   1916— 1920.
BoLSA **
BoT**

COMERCIO INTERNACIONAL (BRAZIL).   Banco do Brasil.   Rio de Janeiro.
1,   1951—
["Boletim mensual da carteira de exportacao")
OxfIES   Aug 1951— Dec 1959

CONJUNTURA ECONOMICA.   Fundacao Getulio Vargas; Centro de Analise da
Conjuntura Economica.   Rio de Janeiro.   1, Nov 1947—
BoLSA   1948—
BoT**
EAnglU   19, 1965—
MarshallL   *1961; 1962; 1964.
OxfIES 1950 - 1955; 1956 — May 1963; 1964 — Aug 1967
RIIA   7 (12),   1953—

COOPERAMINAS.   (Minas Gerais) Secretaria da Agricultura, Industria,
Comercio e Trabalho; Divisao de Assistencia ao Cooperativismo.
Belo Horizonte.

*DESENVOLVIMENTO E CONJUNTURA. Confederacao Nacional da Industria (Brazil).
Rio de Janeiro.   1, July 1957—
BoLSA   1962—
BoT **
EssexU   9, 1965—
OxfIES

DIGESTO ECONOMICO.   Associacao Comercial de Sao Paulo (&) Federacao do
Comercio do Estado de Sao Paulo.   Sao Paulo.   No.1, Dec 1944—
(Suppl.   to: Boletim do Instituto de Economia "Gastao Vigidal"]

DIRIGENTE INDUSTRIAL.   Revista de administracao, produtividade, equipamentos
e procesos.   Sao Paulo.   1, 1959—

ECONOMIA E FINANCAS.
Consultoria tecnica de Asuntos Economicos e Financeiros
(Sergipe).   Aracaju.   1, ?1953—

ECONOMICA BRASILEIRA.   Clube de Economistas.   Rio de Janeiro.   1, Jan/Mar
1955—

ECONOMICS & BUSINESS IN BRAZIL. Instituto Brasileiro de Economia; Centro
de Analise da Conjuntura Economica. Rio de Janeiro. 1, Ap 1954—
["International ed." of: Conjuntura Economica. Prev: Brazilian Economy . . .]

ECONOMISTA. Universidade de Bahia; faculdade de Ciencias Economicas.
Salvador, Brazil. 1, ? 1957—

ESTATISTICA DO COMERCIO EXTERIOR (BRAZIL). (Brazil) Servico de Estatistica
Economica e Financeira. Rio de Janeiro.
[Each issue contains cumulative statistics as from Jan. of each year]

ESTUDOS ECONOMICOS. Confederacao Nacional de Industria (Brazil); Departamento
Economico. Rio de Janeiro. 1, 1950—

    BhmU
    LSE

ESTUDOS ECONOMICOS, POLITICOS E SOCIAIS. Universidade de Minas Gerais;
Faculdade de Ciencias Economicas. Belo Horizonte. [No.] 1, 1959—

    BodI
    GlasU   1—23, 1961.
    MarshallL 1—7, 1961   [W 3].   23, 1961.

ESTUDOS SOCIAIS. Rio de Janeiro.   1, May/June 1958—

EXPORTACAO DE PRODUTOS DO ESTADO DA BAHIA. Bolsa de Mercadores da Bahia.
Bahia, Brazil.

FINANCAS PUBLICAS (RIO GRANDE DO SUL). (Rio Grande do Sul) Departamento
Estadual de Estatistica.   Porto Alegre. 1946—
[Issued with cooperation of: Instituto Brasileiro de Geografia e Estatistica]

FOLHA DO COMERCIO. Associacao Comercial do Parana.   Curitiba. 1 (1),
20/Feb 1960—

IDORT. Revista da organizacao e produtividade. Instituto de Organizacao
Racional de Trabalho. Sao Paul. 1, 1932—
[Title varies.   10, 1941 (only?): Revista de Organizacao Cientifica]

INDUSTRIARIOS. Instituto de Aposentadoria e Pensoes dos Industriarios.
Rio de Janeiro.   No.1, Feb 1948—

INFORMACOES TRIMESTRAIS, COMISSAO EXECUTIVA DE DEFESA DA BORRACHA
(BRAZIL). Rio de Janeiro.   1, Jan/Mar 1952—

INFORMATION CIRCULAR, BRITISH CHAMBER OF COMMERCE OF SAO PAULO &
SOUTHERN BRAZIL.
see SAO PAULO INFORMATION CIRCULAR.

INTERCAMBIO.   Cultural, turistico, comercial. Rio de Janeiro. 1, 1939—

JOURNAL OF THE BRAZILIAN CHAMBER OF COMMERCE & ECONOMIC AFFAIRS IN
GREAT BRITAIN. London. 1, 1943— 9, 1951 . . .
[Subs: Brazil Journal]

    BM
    GlasU
    HispLBC **

JUSTICA DO TRABALHO.   Rio de Janeiro.   1, 1937—

LAVOURA.   Sociedade Nacional de Agricultura (Brazil).
UCL **

LEGISLACAO AGRICOLA DO BRASIL.   Sociedade Nacional de Agricultura (Brazil).
Rio de Janeiro.   1, 1960—
UCL

LEGISLACAO DO TRABALHO.   Sao Paulo   1, 1937—

LEI FISCAL.   Orgao de divulgacao da legislacao federal.   Rio de Janeiro.

LINGOTE.   Companhia Siderurgica Nacional (Brazil); Servico de Relacoes Publicas.
Rio de Janeiro.

MENSAGEM ECONOMICA.   Federacao da Associacoes Comerciais de Minas Gerais.
Belo Horizonte.   1, 1952—
[Body as indicated from 3, 1954/55. Originally as: Associacao Comercial
de Minas Gerais.]

MENSARIO ESTATISTICO (BRAZIL).   (Brazil) Servico Estatistica Economica e
Financeira.   Rio de Janeiro.   No.1, July 1951—
BM   no.10, 1952—
BoLSA   1959—
BoT **
OxfIES   195
UCL   no. 127, 1962—

MONTHLY BULLETIN, BRITISH CHAMBER OF COMMERCE IN BRAZIL.   Rio
de Janeiro.   1, 1919—
BoLSA   1956—
HispLBC **
LivPL   1948—49.   1951—
LSE *

MOVIMENTO BANCARIO DO BRASIL.   Segundo as pracas.   (Brazil) Servico de
Estatistica Economica e Financeira.   Rio de Janeiro.   Dec 1956—
BhmPL   (Current issue)
BoLSA   1952—

MOVIMENTO BANCARIO (ESPIRITO SANTO).   (Espirito Santo)   Departamento Estadual
de Estatistica.   Vitoria, Brazil.   1, ? 1938—
[Publ. with the cooperation of: Conselho Nacional de Estatistica (Brazil)]

OBSERVADOR ECONOMICO E FINANCIERO.

HispLBC **

OLEOS E GORDURAS VEGETAIS (E SUBPRODUTOS).   (Brazil) Servico de Estatistica
da Producao.   Rio de Janeiro.
[Title extended from 1956 (1958)]
BoT **

PARANA.   Boletim de Camara de Expansao Economica do Parana.   Curitiba.
1,   1952—

PARANA ECONOMICA.   Associacao Comercial e Federacao das Industrias do Estado
do parana.   Curitiba.   1, 1955—

PECURIA E AVICULTURA, APICULTURA E SERICICULTURA.   (Brazil) Servico de
Estatistica da Producao. Rio de Janeiro.
BoT **

PESCA. (Brazil) Servico de Estatistica da Producao. Rio de Janeiro.

BoT **

PESQUISAS. Instituto Anchietano de Pesquisas. Porto Alegre. 1, 1957– 3, 1959.
[Vol. 3 in two sections: Seccao A (Ciencias Historicas; (&) Seccao B (Ciencias
Naturais). From 1960 issued in five series with new numbering: Antropologia;
Botanica; Historia; Zoologia; Communications]

Bodl
LondU   1–2, 1958.
RAnthrol

PESQUISAS; COMMUNICATIONS. Instituto Anchietano de Pesquisas. Porto Alegre.
No.1, 1960–

LondU

PESQUISAS; HISTORIA. Instituto Anchietano de Pesquisas. Porto Alegre.
No.12, 1960–
[Numbering as from number of articles on the subject in the prev. publ.]

LondU

PREVISAO AGRICOLA. (Brazil) Servico de Estatistica da Producao. Rio de
Janeiro. 1, 1958–

BoT **

PRODUCAO AGRICOLA. (Brazil) Servico de Estatistica da Producao. Rio de
Janeiro.

BoT **

PRODUCAO ANIMAL. (Brazil) Servico de Estatistica da Producao. Rio de
Janeiro.

BoT**

PRODUCAO INDUSTRIAL BRASILEIRA. Conselho Nacional de Estatistica (Brazil).
Rio de Janeiro (etc.)   1955–
[A]

BoT **
LSE

PRODUCAO MINERAL. (Brazil) Servico de Estatistica da Producao.   Rio de
Janeiro. 1954–
[(Prev) 1947-1948 as: PRODUCAO Brasileira dos Principais Productos
Minerais. Then 1949-1953 as: Producao Extrativa Mineral.   Then as above]

BoT **

PRODUCTIVIDADE. Rio de Janeiro. 1, Jan 1960–

PROGRAMA DE METAS. Conselho do Desenvolvimento (Brazil). Rio de Janeiro.
[A]

LSE   1959–

PUBLICACAO ESPECIAL, DEPARTAMENTO NACIONAL DA PRODUCAO MINERAL
(BRAZIL). Rio de Janeiro. 1, 1959–

BM (NH)

52

QUARTERLY ECONOMIC REVIEW: BRAZIL.   Economist Intelligence Unit.
London.   (No.1, 1952)—
[Title varies]
LSE *No. 3, Sept 1952—

RELATORIO . . ., BANCO DO BRASIL.   Rio de Janeiro.   1905 (1907) —
(Actual title: Relatorio apresentado a Assembleia Geral Ordinaria dos
Acionistas; 1940 (1941) — 1950 (1951): . . . a Assembleia Geral dos Acionistas
no Sessao Ordinaria]
BoLSA   1934—
BoT **
HispLBC **
RIIA   1949— 1961.
UCL   1961 (1962)—

RELATORIO . . .,MINISTERIO DE FAZENDA (BRAZIL).   Rio de Janeiro.
[Actual title: Relatorio apresentado ao Presidente da Republica dos
Estados Unidos do Brasil]

RELATORIO SUMOC.   Superintendencia da Moeda e do Credito (Brazil).   Rio de
Janeiro.
BoLSA   1956—

REPORT ON ECONOMIC CONDITIONS IN BRAZIL.   (Great Britain) Board of Trade;
Commercial Relations & Exports Dept.   London.
BoT

RESENHA ECONOMICA MENSAL, BANCO DO BRASIL.   Rio de Janeiro.   1, Sept 1948—
OxfIES   1948— Jan 1951.

RESENHA INFORMATIVA. SUPERINTENDENCIA DO PLANO DE VALORIZACAO
ECONOMICA DA AMAZONIA.
see SPVEA.   Resenha informativa.

REVISTA DE AGRICULTURA.   Piracicaba, Brazil.   1, 1926—
CSA   9, 1934—
GrasslandRI   1941—

REVISTA AGRONOMICA.   Sindicato Agronomico de Rio Grande do Sul.   Porto
Alegre.   1, 1937—
GrasslandRI

REVISTA BANCARIA BRASILEIRA.   Rio de Janeiro.
BoLSA   1955—
UCL   31(359), 1962—

REVISTA DOS BANCARIOS.   Instituto de Aposentadoria e Pensoes dos
Bancarios (Rio de Janeiro).   Rio de Janeiro.   1, Jan/Feb 1958—

REVISTA DO BNDE.   Banco Nacional do Desenvolvimento Economico (Brazil).
Rio de Janeiro.   1, Jan/Mar 1964—
BoLSA

REVISTA BRASILEIRA DE CIENCIAS SOCIAIS.   Universidade de Minas Gerais;
Faculdade de Ciencias Economicas.   Belo Horizonte.   9 (1), Nov 1961—
LSE

*REVISTA BRASILEIRA DE ECONOMIA. Fundacao Getulio Vargas. Rio de Janeiro.
1, Sep 1947–

BM 19 (1), 1965–
Bodl
BoLSA
LondU 1-10 (3), 1956.
OxfIES 1950–

*REVISTA BRASILEIRA DE ESTATISTICA. Conselho Nacional de Estatistica (Brazil),
(&) Sociedade Brasileira de Estatistica. Rio de Janeiro. 1, Jan/Mar 1940–
["Orgao oficial do Conselho . . . e da Sociedade . . ." Q.]

BelfU
Bodl
GlasU 1, 1940. 2 (5), 1941. 8, 1947–
LondU 8 (30/31), 1947–
OxfIES 1956–
StAndU 8, 1947–
UCL **

*REVISTA BRASILEIRA DE ESTUDOS POLITICOS. Minas Gerais. 1, 1956–

EssexU *7, 1959–
GlasU 22, 1956–
HispLBC **
LSE

*REVISTA BRASILEIRA DOS MUNICIPIOS. Rio de Janeiro. 1, 1948–
[Q]

UCL **

*REVISTA BRASILEIRA DE POLITICA INTERNACIONAL. Instituto Brasileiro de
Relacoes Internacionais. Rio de Janeiro. 1, Jan 1955.

HispLBC **
RIIA

REVISTA BRASILIENSE. Sao Paulo. No.1, Sep/Oct 1955–

EssexU 2, 1955– 5, 1956. 8, 1956–

REVISTA DE CIENCIAS ECONOMICAS. (1939) Ordem dos Economistas de Sao Paulo.
Sao Paulo. 1, 1939– [18] , 1957.
[Not publ. 1953. In new numbering series from 1960]

LSE

REVISTA DE CIENCIAS ECONOMICAS. (1960) Ordem dos Economistas de Sao Paulo.
Sao Paulo. No.1, 1960–2, 1962.//

LSE

REVISTA DE CIENCIAS JURIDICAS, ECONOMIÇAS E SOCIAIS. Universidade do Para:
Departamento de Educacao e Ensino. Belem. 1, 1963–
["Publicacao semestral do Departamento . . ."]

LdsU
LSE

REVISTA DO CONSELHO NACIONAL DE ECONOMIA (BRAZIL). Rio de Janeiro.
1, May 1952–

OxfIES nos 1, 2, 4, 1963; no.1, 1965.

UCL **

54

REVISTA DO CONSELHO DE TERRAS DA UNIAO (BRAZIL). Rio de Janeiro. 1, 1952—

*REVISTA DE DIREITO PUBLICO E CIÊNCIA POLITICA. Instituto de Direito Publico
e Ciencias Politica (Rio de Janeiro.) Rio de Janeiro. 1, 1958—
[2/A]
EssexU

REVISTA FERROVIARIA. Rio de Janeiro.

*REVISTA DE FINANCAS PUBLICAS (BRAZIL). (Brazil) Ministerio da Fazenda.
Rio de Janeiro.

REVISTA GOIANA DE ECONOMIA. Federacao do Comercio do Estado de Goias.
Goiania.
[Prepared by the Fed. and other commercial organizations of the state]

REVISTA DE IMIGRACAO E COLONIZACAO. Conselho de Imigracao e Colonizacao.
Rio de Janeiro. 1, 1940—
LondU 2—9 (2).

REVISTA DO IRB. Instituto de Resseguros do Brasil. Rio de Janeiro.
1, 1940—
HispLBC **

REVISTA DOS MERCADOS (SAO PAULO). Bolsa de Mercadorias de Sao Paulo
Sao Paulo. 1 Sep 1950—
[Prev: Boletim de Informacoes, Bolsa . . .]

REVISTA DE ORGANIZACAO CIENTIFICA. Sao Paulo.
see IDORT.

REVISTA DE ORGANIZACAO E PRODUTIVIDADE. Sao Paulo.
see IDORT
REVISTA PARAENSE DE ESTUDOS SOCIAIS. Escola de Servico Social do Para.
Belem. 1, Sep 1952—

REVISTA PAULISTA DE INDUSTRIA. Sao Paulo.

*REVISTA DO SERVICO PUBLICO (BRAZIL). (Brazil) Departamento Administrativo
do Servico Publico. Rio de Janeiro. 1, Nov 1937—
BM 11 (3)—
CambU *8—
HispLBC **

REVISTA DO TRABALHO. Rio de Janeiro. 1, 1933—

SAO PAULO INFORMATION CIRCULAR. British Chamber of Commerce of Sao Paulo
and Southern Brazil. Sao Paulo.
BoLSA 1947—
HispLBC **
RIIA 4/Ap 1944—

SERIE ESTUDOS E ENSAIOS. Campanha Nacional de Aperfeicoamento de Pessoal de
Nivel Superior (Brazil). Rio de Janeiro. 1, 1953—

SERIE LEVANTAMENTOS E ANALISES. Campanha Nacional de Aperfeicoamento de
Pessoal de Nivel Superior (Brazil). Rio de Janeiro. 1, 1954—

SERVICO SOCIAL.   Revista de cultura superior.   Sao Paulo.   1, 1941—
(Suntotle varies slightly)

*SINTESE POLITICA, ECONOMICA, SOCIAL.   Pontificia Universidade Catolica do
Rio de Janeiro; Instituto de Estudos Politicos e Sociais.   Rio de
Janeiro.   1, Jan/Mar 1959—

EssexU   *1 (2), 1959—

*SOCIOLOGIA.   Sao Paulo.   1, 1939—

SPVEA.   Resenha informativa.   Superintendencia do Plano de Valorizacao
Economica da Amazonia.   Belem.   1, 30/Ap 1955—

SUL-COOP. Boletim cooperativismo. (Rio Grande do Sul) Secretaria de
Agricultura, Industria e Comercio; Seccao de Assistencia ao Cooperativismo.   Porto Alegre.   1 (1), June 1946—
[Not publ. May 1951— Ap 1952, Jan 1953— June 1955. Issues numbered
continuously together with vol. numbering]

SURVEY OF THE BRAZILIAN ECONOMY.   (Brazil) Embassy: United States.
Washington, D.C.   1957—

BoT

TENDENCIAS ECONOMICAS-FINANCEIRAS. Organizacoes Novo Mundo; Assessoria de
Assuntos Economicos.   Sao Paulo   1, Feb 1953—

TRABALHO E SEGURO SOCIAL. Rio de Janeiro.   1, 1943—

VIDA INDUSTRIAL.   Federacao das Industrias do Estado de Minas Gerais.
Belo Horizonte.   1, 1951—

WEEKLY SUPPLEMENT OF THE BRITISH CHAMBER OF COMMERCE IN BRAZIL.
Rio de Janeiro.

BoLSA **

BRITISH HONDURAS

ANNUAL ABSTRACT OF STATISTICS (BRITISH HONDURAS).   (British Honduras)
Ministry of Finance & Development.   Belize.   1961—

    LondICS
    LSE

BELIZE WEEKLY NEWSLETTER.   (British Honduras) Department of Information.
Belize.

    BM 1962—
    LondICS   (Current year only)

(BRITISH HONDURAS).   Report.   (Great Britain) Colonial Office / Commonwealth
Relations Office.   London.

    BM   1946—1963
    HullU   1949 —
    LondICS   1933—1938;   1946—1961;   1962/3—

CHAMBER OF COMMERCE BULLETIN.   Bellize.   [M]

    LondICS   Feb 1965—

SUPPLEMENTARY ABSTRACT OF STATISTICS (BRITISH HONDURAS).
·(British Honduras)   Ministry of Finance & Development.   Belize.

    LondICS   May 1961.

TRADE REPORT (BRITISH HONDURAS).   (British Honduras)   Department of
Customs.   Belize.

    BM   1953—
    BoT **
    LondICS   1946— 1955; 1957—

[Also certain items available at the Board of Trade Library, not in published form:
Monthly and quarterly returns of imports and exports by direction; Monthly return of
statistics; imports of textiles]

CAYMAN ISLANDS

(CAYMAN ISLANDS).   Report.   (Great Britain) Colonial Office / Commonwealth
Relations Office.   London.

    BM   1946 — 1960
    LondICS   1933—1937; 1953/4—

CHILE

AGRICULTURA Y GANADERIA. (Chile) Direccion General de Produccion Agraria y
    Pesquera.   Santiago de Chile.

    EMall   3 (8), 1957—

ANALES DE LA FACULTAD DE CIENCIAS JURIDICAS Y SOCIALES, UNIVERSIDAD DE
CHILE.   Santiago de Chile.   1, Jan/June 1935—

    BodI   1—14, 1950/1.

BALANZA DE PAGOS DE CHILE.   Banco Central de Chile.   Santiago de Chile.

    BoLSA   1943—
    BoT **
    HullU   1958—
    RIIA   1963

BOLETIN ESTADISTICO (CHILE).   (Chile) Direccion de Estadistica. y Censos.
Santiago de Chile.

    BoLSA **
    OxfIES   34, 1961—
    UCL **

BOLETIN INFORMATIVO, INSTITUTO DE ECONOMIA, UNIVERSIDAD DE CHILE.
Santiago de Chile. No.1, (1958) — 4, 1960.//

    BodI

BOLETIN INFORMATIVO, INSTITUTO LATINOAMERICANO DEL FIERRO Y EL
ACERO.   see ILAFA.   Boletin Informativo.

BOLETIN MENSUAL DEL BANCO CENTRAL DE CHILE.   Santiago de Chile.   1, 1928—

    BodI   14, 1929—
    BoLSA   1957—
    BoT **
    HispLBC **
    HullU   33, 1960—
    IBank   (Selected articles only kept)
    LdsU   29 (329, 333), 1955.
    LivPL   Mar 1951— Nov 1955. Mar 1956—
    OxfIES   No.108, 1937—
    RIIA   [Current copy only]
    UCL **

CHILE INDUSTRIAL.   Santiago de Chile.   1, June 1947—

COMERCIO EXTERIOR (CHILE).   (Chile) Direccion de Estadistica y Censos.
Santiago de Chile.

    BoLSA **
    BoT**
    LdsU   1953.
    UCL   1960 (1962)—

DESDE CHILE.   Compania Salitrera Anglo-Lautaro.   Santiago de Chile.
    [Approx. 2/W]

    BoLSA **

*ECONOMIA. Universidad de Chile; Facultad de Ciencias Economicas. Santiago de
Chile

EssexU   *10,   1949–
MarshallL   Nos.41, 45, 48 , 51, 53, 55-5; , 64, 65.
OxfIES   21–

ERCILLA. Santiago de Chile.
(Newspaper)
BoLSA **   (Subscription discontinued with 32(1648), 4/Jan 1967)

ESTADISTICA BANCARIA (CHILE).   Superintendencia de Bancos (Chile).
Santiago de Chile.   No.1, 1936–
[Q. (Varies).   "Resumen de los balances generales"]
BoLSA   No.86, 1943–

ESTADISTICA CHILENA.   (Chile) Direccion General de Estadistica. Santiago de
Chile.
[Subs (1961): Boletin Estadistico (Chile).   (Chile) Direccion de Estadistica
y Censos]

BoLSA   1957–
HispLBC**
LdsU   28 (1–4, 9–10), 1955.
UCL **

ESTADISTICAS, SERVICIO DE SEGURO SOCIAL (CHILE).   Santiago de Chile.

Bodl   1952/56–

ILAFA.   Boletin informativo.   Instituto Latinoamericano del Fierro y el
Acero.   Santiago de Chile.   1, May   1960–   Aug 1962.
[Subs: Revista Latinoamericana de Siderurgia]

MEMORIA ANUAL . . ., BANCO CENTRAL DE CHILE.   Santiago de Chile.
[Actual title: Memoria Anual presentada a la Superintendencia de Bancos]

Bodl   3, 1928–
BoLSA   1940–
HispLBC **
HullU   1959 (1960)–
IBank   (Two year file)
RIIA   1944; 1954–
UCL **

MEMORIA DE LA CONTRALORIA GENERAL (DE LA REPUBLICA) (CHILE).
Santiago de Chile.
[Actual title: Memoria de la Contraloria General correspondiente al ano
(Date)   y Balance General de la Hacienda Publica al (Date)]
BoLSA   1956–

MEMORIA, CORPORACION DE FOMENTO DE LA PRODUCCION (CHILE). [Santiago]
de Chile] 1961–
[A]
BoLSA

PANORAMA ECONOMICO.   Santiago de Chile.   1, 1947–

BhmU   7–
BoLSA   1958–
OxfIES   14, 1960–

59

POLITICA Y ESPIRITU.   Santiago de Chile.   1 (1), July 1945—

    EssexU   19 (289), 1965—

PRODUCCION Y CONSUMO DE ENERGIA EN CHILE.   Empresa Nacional de
Electricidad (Chile); Departamento de Produccion; Seccion Movimento de Energia
Santiago de Chile.
[A]

    LSE   1957—

PUBLICACIONES, INSTITUTO DE ECONOMIA, UNIVERSIDAD DE CHILE. Santiago de
Chile.   No.1, 195 —

    Bodl   *2, 1956—   (very imperfect)

REVISTA LATINOAMERICANA DE SIDERURGIA.   Instituto Latinoamerican del Fierro
y el Acero.   Santiago de Chile.
[Prev: ILAFA; from 1, May 1960]

    BoLSA **

SINTESIS ESTADISTICA (CHILE).   (Chile) Direccion de Estadistica y Censos.
Santiago de Chile.

    BoLSA **
    BoT **
    EssexU   1966—
    UCL   1962—

COLOMBIA

ACCION LIBERAL. Bogota. 1, 1965—
[Called "segunda etapa" of earlier serial of same title, 1, Jan 1960—]

EssexU

ALGODON Y OLEAGINOSAS. Economia y estadisticas. Instituto de Fomento
Algodonero. Bogota.

UCL 1960—

ANNUAL REPORT, BANCO DE LA REPUBLICA (COLOMBIA). Bogota.

BoLSA 1939—
IBank (Two year file)

ANUARIO DE COMERCIO EXTERIOR (COLOMBIA). (Colombia) Departamento
Administrativo Nacional de Estadistica. Bogota.

BoLSA 1945—
BoT**
EssexU 1959.
HispLBC**
OxfIES 1935— 1937.
UCL 1960 (1961)—

ANUARIO ESTADISTICO (COLOMBIA). (Colombia) Departamento Administrativo
Nacional de Estadistica. Bogota.

Guildhall (Current issue)
UCL**

ANUARIO GENERAL DE ESTADISTICA DE COLOMBIA. (Colombia) Departamento
Administrativo Nacional de Estadistica. Bogota.

BoLSA 1951—
BoT 1952—1955; 1957—
EssexU 1963.
HispLBC **
OxfIES 1934—1938
RIIA 1938; 1940; 1953—1961. [W 1959]
UCL **

APUNTES ECONOMICOS. Bogota. Ano 1, 1965—

EssexU 1965 (Nos. 10, 24—25, 27)—

ARCHIVO DE LA ECONOMIA NACIONAL (COLOMBIA). Banco de la Republica de
Colombia. Bogota.

GlasU 5, 1952. 7. 11—

BANCOS Y BANCARIAS DE COLOMBIA. Bogota. No.1, 1957—
[Q]

BoLSA

BOLETIN ESTADISTICA DE LA FEDERACION NACIONAL DE CAFETEROS DE
COLOMBIA. Bogota. No. 1, Mar 1932—

BM 18 (39), 1963—
BoLSA **

BOLETIN, FEDERACION NACIONAL DE COMERCIANTES (COLOMBIA).
see BOLETIN FENALCO.

BOLETIN FENALCO.   Federacion Nacional de Comerciantes (Colombia). Bogota.

BoLSA   1959—

BOLETIN MENSUAL DE ESTADISTICA (COLOMBIA).   (Colombia) Departamento
Administrativo Nacional de Estadistica.   Bogota.

BoLSA   1956—
BoT
EssexU   14 (176),   1965.
HispLBC**
RIIA   No.118,   1961—
UCL**

BOLETIN DE PETROLEOS.   (Colombia) Ministerio de Minas y Petroleos.
Bogota.
[Issued by the Ministerio's "Office of Economic Research"]

BOLETIN SEMANAL, CAMARA DE COMERCIO DE BARRANQUILLA. Barranquilla.

HispLBC**

BOLETIN, SUPERINTENDENCIA BANCARIA (COLOMBIA).   Bogota.

BoLSA   1957—
UCL **

CARTA AGRARIA.   Caja de Credito Agrario (Colombia); Departamento de
Investigaciones Economicas.   Bogota.
[2W]

BoLSA **
TropProdl   *1960—

CONTADOR PUBLICO.   Instituto Nacional de Contadores Publicos (Colombia).
Bogota.
[Q]

IChartAccScot   Mar/June 1963—

DISPOSOCIONES ECONOMICAS (COLOMBIA).   Banco de la Republica (Colombia).
Bogota.
[Actual title contains year; e.g.; Disp. Econ. de 1963]

BM   1963 (1964)—

*ECONOMIA.   Bogota.   1, [1963] —
[Prev; Economia Grancolombiana]

EssexU

*ECONOMIA COLOMBIANA.   (Colombia) Contraloria General de la Republica.
Bogota. 1,   — 5, Oct 1958.
["Revista de la Contraloria . . .".   Subs: Economia Grancolombiana]

UCL**

ECONOMIA Y ESTADISTICA (COLOMBIA).   (Colombia) Departamento Administrativo
Nacional de Estadistica.   Bogota.

UCL **

ECONOMIA GRANCOLOMBIANA.   Bogota.   1, Aug 1959— 21, 1963.
[Prev: Economia Colombiana.   Subs: Economia]

EssexU

62

FERROCARRILES EN CIFRAS (COLOMBIA).   Ferrocarriles Nacionales (Colombia).
   Bogota.
   [M]
   LSE   Jan 1963–

INDUSTRIA COLOMBIANA.

   BoLSA**

INFORMACION ESTADISTICA, INSTITUTO DE FOMENTO ALGODONERO.   Bogota.

   BoT**

INFORME DE ACTIVIDADES, INSTITUTO COLOMBIANO DE LA REFORMA AGRARIA.
   Bogota [A]
   LSE   1962–

INFORME ANUAL, BANCO DE LA REPUBLICA (COLOMBIA).   Bogota.
   Bodl   *26, 1948/49–
   BoLSA **
   NuffCollOxf   1953/54–
   RIIA   1953– 1963   [W 31st–33rd]

INFORME ANUAL, SUPERINTENDENCIA BANCARIA (COLOMBIA).   Bogota.
   UCL **   BoLSA**

INFORME FINANCIERO DEL CONTRALOR GENERAL (COLOMBIA).   Bogota.
   BoLSA **

INFORME DEL GERENTE DE LA CAJA DE CREDITO AGRARIO INDUSTRIAL
(COLOMBIA).   Bogota.
   BoLSA**

INFORME REFERENTE, BANCO DE COLOMBIA.   Bogota.
   BoLSA **

INFORME, SUPERINTENDENCIA BANCARIA (COLOMBIA).   Bogota.
   UCL   1959 (1960)–

LEGISLACION ECONOMICA (COLOMBIA).
   BoLSA   1959–

MEMORIA DE HACIENDA.   (Colombia) Ministerio de Hacienda.   Bogota.
   BoLSA**
   UCL**

MEMORIA DE MINISTERIO DE AGRICULTURA . . . (COLOMBIA).   Bogota.
   [Actual title continues: . . . al Congreso Nacional]
   UCL   1960–

NEWSLETTER, BANCO DE COLOMBIA.   Bogota.
   [M]
   BoLSA**

QUARTERLY ECONOMIC REVIEW; COLOMBIA.   Economist Intelligence Unit.   London.
   No. 1, Ap 1960–
   [Prev part of: Q. Econ. Rev.; Colombia, Venezuela]
   LSE

REPORT ON ECONOMIC CONDITIONS IN COLOMBIA. (Great Britain) Board of Trade; Commercial Relations & Exports Dept. London. 1921– 1938; 1949

    BoT

REVISTA DEL BANCO DE LA REPUBLICA (COLOMBIA). Bogota. 1, 1927–

    Bodl   Feb 1955–
    BoLSA   1953–
    BoT   1953– (earlier issues incomplete)
    EssexU   *27 (327), 1955–
    HispLBC**
    UCL   35 (414), 1962–

REVISTA CAFETERA DE COLOMBIA. Federacion Nacional de Cafeteros (Colombia). Bogota. 1, Nov 1928–

    BM   1937–
    EMall   12 (129); 13, 1957–

REVISTA DE CIENCIAS ECONOMICAS.

    UCL**

REVISTA DE LA FACULTAD DE CIENCIAS ECONOMICAS, UNIVERSIDAD NACIONAL DE COLOMBIA. Bogota 1, 1965–
    [2/A]

    LSE

*REVISTA JAVERIANA; (NS). Publicacion mensual catolica de interes general. Universidad Javeriana; Facultad de Ciencias Economicas y Juridicas. Bogota. 1, Fev 1934–
    [Prev "series" issued 1933]

COSTA RICA

ALLGEMEINE STATISTIK DES AUSLANDES; LANDERBERICHTE; COSTA RICA.
Wiesbaden. 1966—
BM
LSE

BALANZA DE PAGOS, BANCO CENTRAL DE COSTA RICA.   San Jose.
BM   17,1965—
BoT   1953; 1955—1960;   1963—1965.

BOLETIN ESTADISTICO MENSUAL, BANCO CENTRAL DE COSTA RICA. San Jose.
No.1,   Jan 1950—
[Prev: Resumen Estadistico Mensual,   . . .]
BM   no6, 1967—
BoLSA 1957—
BoT   1953— (earlier issues incomplete)
RIIA   (Current year only)
UCL **

BOLETIN TECNICO, OFICINA DEL CAFE (COSTA RICA).   San Jose.   1, 1964—
CSA

COMERCIO EXTERIOR DE COSTA RICA.   (Costa Rica) Direccion General de
Estadistica y Censos. San Jose. 1953—
BM   1955—1965.
BoT   1953—
UCL   1961 (1962)—

ENCUESTA INDUSTRIAL (COSTA RICA).   (Costa Rica) Direccion General de
Estadistica y Censos. San Jose.   1959—
BM   1959—1960; 1965.
LSE

INDICE DE PRECIOS AL POR MENOR (COSTA RICA).
BM   1960—
BoT   1955—

INFORME DEL DEPARTAMENTO DE PLANES ANUALES, OFICINA DE
PLANIFICACION (COSTA RICA).   [San Jose]
[A]
BM   1963—
LSE   1963—

INFORME DE LA OFICINA DEL PRESUPUESTO (COSTA RICA).   [San Jose]
[A]
LSE   1955—1957;   1960—

MEMORIA ANUAL, BANCO CENTRAL DE COSTA RICA.   San Jose.
BM   1950— 1965.
BoLSA   1950—
IBank (Two year file)
RIIA 1950—1963.
UCL 1961—

MEMORIA ANUAL, INSTITUTO DE TIERRAS Y COLONIZACION.   San Jose?
EssexU   1963.

MEMORIA ANUAL, MINISTERIO DE ECONOMIA Y HACIENDA (COSTA RICA). San Jose.

BM 1954—
BoT 1952—
EssexU 1959—1960; 1964.
UCL 1961—

MEMORIA DE LAS LABORES REALIZADAS EN LOS MINISTERIOS DE GOBERNACION Y POLICIA, JUSTICIA Y GRACIA . . . (COSTA RICA).
San Jose
[Actual title ends: . . . presentada a la Asamblea Legislativa]

BM 1953—1960
LSE 1915; 1959/60—

REPORT ON ECONOMIC CONDITIONS IN COSTA RICA. (Great Britain) Board of Trade; Commercial Relations & Exports Dept. London. 1929— 1933; 1950— 1954.

BM
BoT

RESUMEN ESTADISTICO MENSUAL, BANCO NACIONAL DE COSTA RICA. San Jose.

[Subs: Boletin Estadistico Mensual, . . .]

REVISTA, BANCO CENTRAL DE COSTA RICA. San Jose.

BM 1955—
BoLSA 1957—
UCL**

REVISTA DE CIENCIAS JURIDICO-SOCIALES. Universidad Nacional (Costa Rica). San Jose. 1(1), Mar 1956—2(3), 1958 . . .
[Issues numbered continuously 1—3 together with vol. numbering. Latter dropped with subs title: Revista de Ciencias Sociales]

EssexU*

REVISTA DE CIENCIAS SOCIALES. Universidad de Costa Rica. San Jose (etc).
No.4, Sep 1959—
[Prev: Revista de Ciencias Juridico-sociales. Body (and place) changed from "Universidad Nacional" after beginning of this title]

BM 1963—

REVISTA DE ESTUDIOS Y ESTADISTICA. (Costa Rica) Direccion General de Estadistica y Censos. San Jose. No.1, July 1961—
[Also numbered in the Direccion's "Serie Demografica". No.1 above also as No.1 of the Serie]

BM
LSE

*TEMAS SOCIALES. (Costa Rica) Ministerio del Trabajo y Prevision Social. San Jose. 1, Nov/Dec 1954—
[Organo cultural e informativo del Ministerio . . ." Name of body varies; orig. (for this title): Secretaria del Trabajo . . .]

BM 1959—1964.
UCL **

66

CUBA

AGRO.   Organo de los trabajadores agricolas.   [Havana]

    BM   No.30,   1963—

ANUARIO AZUCARERO DE CUBA. = CUBA SUGAR YEAR BOOK.   Havana.
[1], 1937—
    BoT   1952-1953; 1958; 1960
    LSE   [1], 1937; 12, 1948; 16, 1952; 23, 1959.

ANUARIO DEMOGRAFICO DE CUBA.   (Cuba) Direccion General de Estadistica.
Havana.   1961—
[Supplemented by: Resumen de Estadisticas de Poblacion (Cuba)]
    LSE

ANUARIO ESTADISTICO DE CUBA.   (Cuba) Direccion General de Estadistica.
Havana.   1952—
    BM   1952; 1956-1958
    BoT   1952; 1956, 1957

BALANZA COMERCIAL DE CUBA.   (Cuba) Direccion General de Estadistica.
Havana.   1952—
    BoT   1955—1956

BOLETIN DE DIVULGACION, INSTITUTO NACIONAL DE REFORMA AGRARIA (CUBA)
Havana.   1, 1959— 2 (8), 1960.
[Cover title: Divulgacion. INRA]
    BM

BOLETIN DE DIVULGACION, INSTITUTO NACIONAL DE REFORMA AGRARIA (CUBA);
SUPLEMENTO SEMANAL.   Havana.   1, Dec 1959—

BOLETIN DE DIVULGACION TECNICA.   Centro de Investigaciones Pesqueras
(Cuba).   Havana.   No.1, 1963—
[Centro subord. to: Instituto Nacional de la Pesca (Cuba).   Centro located
at Bauta, Cuba]
    BM
    BM (NH)

BOLETIN DE ESTADISTICAS (CUBA).   (Cuba) Direccion General de Estadistica.
Havana.   1, 1945—
[M from 1945—1954, then Q or 2/A]
    BM   1945;   1953—1955

BOLETIN INFORMATIVO, CONSEJO NACIONAL DE ECONOMIA (CUBA).   Havana.
1, May 1952—
    BM   1952— (1), 1958.

BOLETIN INTERNACIONAL DE LA FEDERACION NACIONAL DE TRABAJADORES
AZUCAREROS (CUBA).   Havana.   1, Aug 1954—

BOLETIN OFICIAL DE LA ASOCIACION DE TECNICOS AZUCAREROS DE CUBA.
Havana.   1, Mar 1942—

    CSA   *1(3), 1942—
    EMall   *11, 1952— 18, 1959.

BOLETIN OFICIAL, DIRECCION DE LA OPINION PUBLICA (CUBA).   Havana. 1, 1960—

BOLETIN OFICIAL DE LA PROPRIEDAD INDUSTRIAL (CUBA)
    HispLBC**

CAPITAL Y HOGAR. Havana. 1, 1951—

COMERCIO EXTERIOR DE CUBA. Revista mensual del Ministerio del Comercio
    Exterior. Havana. 1, Mar 1963—
    [Prev: Revista de Ministerio de Comercio (Cuba)]
    BhmPL   (Current edition)
    BM   1963—1964
    Bodl   (Also from 1956/7 of earlier title)
    BoLSA **
    BoT**
    LSE
    MarshallL   1(3)

COMERCIO EXTERIOR DE CUBA; IMPORTACIONES, EXPORTACIONES.

    BM   1962—1964.
    BoT   1961—May 1962

CONTABILIDAD Y FINANZAS. Havana. 1, 1928—
    LSE

CUBA. Revista Mensual. Instituto Nacional de Reforma Agraria (Cuba).
    Havana. 1, Ap 1962—
    (Prev: INRA)

    BM   1962—1965.

CUBA ECONOMIC NEWS. Camara de Comercio de la Republica de Cuba. Havana.
    1(1), July 1965—
    ["Monthly Bulletin edited by the Chamber of Commerce of the Republic of
    Cuba"]
    BM 1965 —
    BoT* W May 1966, Feb 1967—
    HispLBC **
    LSE

CUBA ECONOMICA Y FINANCIERA. Havana. 13, Nov 1937—
    [(Prev) 1, 1926— 2 (17), 1927 as: Cuba Foodstuff Record. Then 2 (18), 1927—
    12, 1937 as: Cuba Importadora (y Industrial). Then as above]

    OxfIES

CUBA FOREIGN TRADE. Camara de Comercio de la Republica de Cuba. Havana.
    No.1, 1964—
    [Also in Spanish ed.]

    BM
    BoT   (5-6), 1965; (1,3,4), 1966.

CUBA SOCIALISTA. Distribuidora Nacional de Publicaciones (Cuba). Havana.
    1, 1961—
    BM
    EssexU   *1963—
    HispLBC**
    LSE   1(2), 1961—
    RIIA   1 (2), 1961—

CUBA SUGAR YEAR BOOK.
    see ANUARIO AZUCARERO DE CUBA.

CUBAN INFORMATION SERVICE. Coral Gables, Fla. 1, 1960–
   RIIA   1(38), 1961–

CUBAZUCAR. Asociacion Nacional de Hacendados de Cuba. Havana. 1, Nov 1955–
   61(1/3), Jan/Mar 1961.//

DIVULGACION. Instituto Nacional de Reforma Agraria (Cuba).
   see BOLETIN DE DIVULGACION, INSTITUTO . . .

EXPORTACION (CUBA). (Cuba) Direccion General de Estadistica; Seccion de
   Comercio. Havana. Sep 1950–

INFORME ESTADISTICO SEMESTRAL (CUBA). (Cuba) Oficina de Coordinacion, de
   Estadisticas e Investigaciones. [Marianao] July/Dec 1959–
   BM   No.2, 1960.
   LSE

INRA. Revista mensual ilustrada. Instituto Nacional de Reforma Agraria
   (Cuba). Havana. 1, Jan 1960–
   [Subs: Cuba. Revista mensual]
   BM
   HispLBC**

LEGISLACION BANCARIA Y ECONOMICO-FINANCIERA (CUBA). Banco Nacional de
   Cuba; Departamento Legal. Havana. 1, 1954–
   BM

MEMORIA ANUAL, BANCO NACIONAL DE CUBA. Havana.
   BM   1954–1959.
   BoLSA   1950-1959.
   IBank   (Two year file)
   RIIA   1952/3– 1958/9.

METAS. (Cuba) Direccion de Relaciones Publicas. Havana. 1, [1960] –
   [Prev: Revista de Servicio Social. Name taken from: Metas Cubanas. Organo
   de orientacion revolucionaria. (Three issues published, in Mexico)]

MOP. Boletin oficial. (Cuba) Ministerio de Obras Publicas. Havana.
   1, Aug   1955–

NEWS FROM CUBA. (Cuba) Embassy: Great Britain. London. No.1, 1962–
   BM
   BodI
   HispLBC**

NUESTRA INDUSTRIA (CUBA); REVISTA ECONOMICA. (Cuba) Ministerio de Industrias.
   Havana.
   [Companion publ. to: Nuestra Industria (Cuba); Revista Tecnologica]
   BM   1962–1964.
   LSE   *No.6,   1964–

OBRERO PANADERO. Sindicato de Obreros Panaderos de la Provincia de la
   Habana. Havana. 1, 1931– 16(9), Sep 1947.//

PANORAMA ECONOMICO LATINOAMERICANO. Havana.
   (M)
   BodI   No.2.
   EssexU   3(27), 1961–
   HispLBC**
   LSE   1960– 1961.

ECUADOR

ANUARIO DE COMERCIO EXTERIOR (ECUADOR).   (Ecuador) Direccion del
   Presupuesto; Seccion de Estadistica Fiscal.   Quito.
   LSE   (2nd)   1958–

ANUARIO DE ESTADISTICAS VITALES (ECUADOR).   (Ecuador) Direccion General
   de Estadistica y Censos. Quito.   1954–
   LSE

BOLETIN DEL BANCO CENTRAL DEL ECUADOR.   Quito.

   BoLSA   1957–
   BoT **
   EssexU   *33(392/395),   1960–
   HispLBC**
   IBank (selected articles only kept)
   OxfIES   1937– 1957; 1964–
   UCL**

BOLETIN DE INFORMACION ECONOMICA.
   see ECONOMIA Y ADMINISTRACION.

BOLETIN TRIMESTRIAL DE INFORMACION ECONOMICA.
   see ECONOMIA Y ADMINISTRACION.

COMERCIO EXTERIOR ECUATORIANO.   Banco Central del Ecuador. Quito.
   No.1, 1947–
   [Nos. 1–4 (also called Ano 1) as suppl. to: Boletin del Banco . . .]
   BoLSA   1956–
   BoT   1952– 1964*
   EssexU   Nos. 202–208, 1964
   HispLBC **
   UCL   No.169, 1961–

COMERCIO EXTERIOR ECUATORIANO.   (Ecuador) Direccion del Presupuesto.
   Quito.   1957–
   BoT   1957– 1959.

COMERCIO EXTERIOR ECUATORIANO.   (Ecuador) Direccion de Financiamento y
   Asesoria Fiscal.   Quito.   1964–
   [Cover title: Anuario de Comercio Exterior]
   BoT   1964–
   HispLBC**

ECONOMIA Y ADMINISTRACION. Universidad Central del Ecuador; Instituto
   de Investigaciones Economicas. Quito.   1, 1950–
   [Title varies; Jan/Mar 1951 as: Boletin de Informacion Economica.
   Sep/Nov 1951–Ap/Dec 1960 as: Boletin Trimestrial de Informacion
   Economica. Numbering irregular; to Sep 1954 as Ano 1-4; then as
   from Ano 10. Oct 1954/Mar 1955.]
   LSE   1(11/12), 1951–

INFORME ANUAL DE LABORES, BANCO NACIONAL DE FOMENTO (ECUADOR). Quito
   UCL   1960 (1961)–

INFORME DEL GERENTE, COMISION NACIONAL DE VALORES (ECUADOR). Quito.
   [A]
   LSE   1957/8–

74

INFORME A LA NACION, MINISTERIO DEL TESORO (ECUADOR). Quito.
[A]
LSE   1957–

MEMORIA DEL GERENTE GENERAL DEL BANCO CENTRAL DEL ECUADOR. Quito.
BoLSA   1952–
Bot**
EssexU   1961; 1963–
HispLBC**
RIIA   1961–1962.
UCL   1961 (1962)–

PLANIFICACION.   Junta Nacional de Planificacion y Coordinacion Economica
(Ecuador).   Quito.   1(1), Sep/Dec 1962–

FALKLAND ISLANDS

(FALKLAND ISLANDS & DEPENDENCIES).   Report.   (Great Britain) Colonial
Office / Commonwealth Relations Office.   London.
BM   1947 –
HullU   1947–

COMERCIO Y PRODUCCION (DOMINICAN REPUBLIC).

    BM   169, 1960–
    HispLBC **

ESTADISTICA BANCARIA (DOMINICAN REPUBLIC). (Dominican Republic)
    Direccion General de Estadistica.   Santo Domingo.

    BM 1943– 1957.
    GlasU 9 (2), 1944– 26, 1961. [W 11; 17]
    HispLBC**
    RIIA 1948– 1961.

ESTADISTICA DEMOGRAFIA (DOMINICAN REPUBLIC). (Dominican Republic)
    Direccion General de Estadistica. Santo Domingo. 1, 1943–

    BM 1943– 1956.
    BoT
    GlasU
    UCL**

ESTADISTICA INDUSTRIAL DE LA REPUBLICA DOMINICANA. (Dominican Republic)
    Direccion General de Estadistica. Santo Domingo. No.1, 1950–

    BM 1954– 1960.
    BoT
    GlasU 1(1), 1950. 2, 1951–
    HispLBC**

ESTADISTICA DE LOS NEGOCIOS DE SEGUROS (DOMINICAN REPUBLIC). (Dominican
    Republic) Direccion General de Estadistica. Santo Domingo.

    BM 1942– 1957
    GlasU 1942– 1961.

EXPORTACION DE LA REPUBLICA DOMINICANA. (Dominican Republic) Direccion
    General de Estadistica. Santo Domingo.

    BM   6 (1/13), 1945–
    GlasU   13, 1944– 21, 1952.
    RIIA Jan/Mar 1949–

IMPORTACION DE LA REPUBLICA DOMINICANA. (Dominican Republic) Direccion
    General de Estadistica. Santo Domingo.

    BM   6 (1/13), 1945–
    GlasU   4(7), 1943– 12, 1951.

INFORME ECONOMICO, BANCO CENTRAL DE LA REPUBLICA DOMINICANA. Santo
    Domingo.
    [Prep. by the Banco's: Departamento de Estudios Economicos]

    BM   1, 1963–
    BoLSA   1963–

MEMORIA DEL ANO, SECRETARIA DE ESTADO DE JUSTICIA Y TRABAJO
(DOMINICAN REPUBLIC). Santo Domingo.

    LdsU   1958.

MEMORIA, BANCO CENTRAL DE LA REPUBLICA DOMINICANA.

    BM   1947–
    IBank   (Two year file)

MEMORIA, SECRETARIA DE ESTADO DEL TESORO (DOMINICAN REPUBLIC).

BM   1946– 1953
Bodl   1947– 1948.

POBLACION DE LA REPUBLICA DOMINICANA.   (Dominican Republic) Direccion
General de Estadistica.   Santo Domingo.

GlasU   1935– 1945; 1950.

REGISTRO PUBLICO (DOMINICAN REPUBLIC).   (Dominican Republic) Direccion
General de Estadistica.   Santo Domingo.

BM   1944– 1957.
GlasU   1943–

REVISTA DE LA SECRETARIA DE ESTADO DE ECONOMIA NACIONAL (DOMINICAN
REPUBLIC).   Santo Domingo.   No.   –25, 1952 ...
[Subs: Revista de la Secretaria de Estado de Trabajo, Economia y
Comercio (Domin. Repub.)]

Bodl   *No.6, 1949–
GlasU   No.6, 1949– [W No.8]
LdsU   No.6, 1949– 14.

REVISTA DE LA SECRETARIA DE ESTADO DE TRABAJO, ECONOMIA Y COMERCIO
(DOMINICAN REPUBLIC). Santo Domingo.   No.26, 1953– 37, 1954 . . .
[Prev as preceding entry.   Subs: Revista de la Secretaria de Estado de
Industria y Comercio]

Bodl*
GlasU
LdsU

REVISTA DE LA SECRETARIA DE ESTADO DE INDUSTRIA Y COMERCIO
(DOMINICAN REPUBLIC).   Santo Domingo.   No.38, 1955–
[Prev as preceding entry]

BM   1955– 1958.
Bodl*
GlasU   No.38–50, 1958.

REVISTA DE TRABAJO (E INDUSTRIA).   (Dominican Republic) Secretaria de Estado
de Trabajo e Industria.   Ciudad Trujillo.   1, Jan/Mar 1956–
[Called "2S".   Title extended as indicated after vol.1.

BM   1956– 1959.
Bodl
LdsU   4 (13/14), 1959.

SACRIFICIA DE GANADA (DOMINICAN REPUBLIC).   (Dominican Republic) Direccion
General de Estadistica.   Santo Domingo.

BM   1944– 1957
GlasU   1943–

PUBLICACIONES JUCEPLAN (CUBA).   Junta Central de Planificacion (Cuba).
Havana.   No.1, 1962–

LSE

REPORT ON ECONOMIC CONDITIONS IN CUBA.   (Great Britain) Board of Trade;
Commercial Relations & Exports Dept.   London.   1922– 1937; 1949– 1954.

BM
BoT

RESUMEN ANALITICO DE LAS EXPORTACIONES DE TOBACO Y SUS PRODUCTOS
(CUBA)
Bot   1954;   1956– 1958

REVISTA DE AGRICULTURA, [COMERCIO Y TRABAJO].   (Cuba) Secretaria de
Agricultura.   Havana.   1, Jan 1918–
[Title reduced as indicated after 14(21), Mar 1934. Publ. suspended July 1921–
Feb 1922]

EMall   35, 1951–
MinAg   1939–
Rothamsted 1919–
TropProdl   *1931–

REVISTA DEL BANCO NACIONAL DE CUBA.   Havana.   1, Jan 1955–

BM   1956– 1960.
BoLSA 1957– Mar 1960.
RIIA

REVISTA DEL INRA.   Instituto Nacional de la Reforma Agraria (Cuba).
Havana.

HispLBC**

REVISTA, MINISTERIO DE COMERCIO (CUBA).   Havana.   No.1, Jan/Mar 1959–
[Q]

LSE

REVISTA NACIONAL DE LA PROPIEDAD URBANA (CUBA).   Federacion Nacional
de la Propriedad (Cuba).   Havana.   1, 1934–

REVISTA DE SERVICIO SOCIAL (CUBA).   Patronato de Servicio Social de Cuba.
Havana.   1, 1949–

SBB.   Seguros, Banca y bolsa.   Havana.
["Revista mensual informativa"]
ChartInsl   5(5), 1944–   [W 5(10)– 8(4)]

SBB; EDICION SUPLEMENTARIA SEMANAL. Havana.   1, 1944– 9 (52), 1952.//
ChartInsl   *4 (21)–

TRABAJO.   (Cuba) Ministerio de Trabajo.   Havana.   1, June 1960–
BM   1960– 1964.
HispLBC**

TRIMESTRE SUPLEMENTO DEL DIRECTORIO FINANCIERO (CUBA).
BM   1, 1962– 7, 1964.
Bodl   6, 1964–
BoT   1–3, 1962.

DOMINICAN REPUBLIC

ACCIDENTES DE TRABAJO (DOMINICAN REPUBLIC). (Dominican Republic) Direccion
General de Estadistica. Santo Domingo. 1, 1944–
GlasU 1–2, 1945; 4, 1947– 9, 1952: 11, 1954–

ALLGEMEINE STATISTIK DES AUSLANDES; LANDERBERICHTE; DOMINIKANISCHE
REPUBLIK. Wiesbaden (etc). 1965–
BM
LSE

ANUARIO ESTADISTICO DE LA REPUBLICA DOMINICANA. (Dominican Republic)
Direccion General de Estadistica. Ciudad Trujillo (etc). 1936–
BhmU 5, 1940– 19, 1954 (1957).
BM 1936–1954
Bodl 1948/49.
GlasU 1940– 1945; 1948–1954.
Guildhall (Current issue only)
RIIA 1943; 1944/5; 1946/7; 1948/9; 1950– 1954.

BOLETIN ESTADISTICO, BANCO AGRICOLA DE LA REPUBLICA DOMINICANA.
Santo Domingo.

BOLETIN MENSUAL, BANCO CENTRAL DE LA REPUBLICA DOMINICANA.
Santo Domingo
BM 1960–
BoLSA **
BoT 1952–
UCL **

CENSO NACIONAL DE INDUSTRIAS Y DE COMERCIO (DOMINICAN REPUBLIC).
(Dominican Republic) Direccion General de Estadistica. Santo Domingo.
GlasU 1955.

CENSO NACIONAL DE POBLACION (DOMINICAN REPUBLIC). (Dominican Republic)
Direccion General de Estadistica. Santo Domingo.
BM 1946; 1950.
GlasU 1950; 1960.
HispLBC**
RIIA 1961–1962.

COMERCIO EXTERIOR DE LA REPUBLICA DOMINICANA ... (Dominican Republic)
Direccion General de Estadistica. Ciudad Trujillo. 1, 1953–
BM 1 (3)–
BoLSA**
BoT 1953–
GlasU [W 1(8); 2 (10,11)]
HispLBC **
TropProdl 1963–
UCL **

COMERCIO EXTERIOR DE LA REPUBLICA DOMINICA ...; RUSEMEN DEL ANO.
(Dominican Republic) Direccion General de Estadistica. Ciudad Trujillo.
1, 1953–
[Consists of December issues of previous publ.]
BoLSA
BoT
HispLBC**
TropProdl 1956– 1960.
UCL**

GUATEMALA

ALMANAQUE AGRICOLA DE GUATEMALA.
EMall No.1, 1949—

ANUARIO DE COMERCIO EXTERIOR (GUATEMALA). (Guatemala) Direccion General
de Estadistica y Censo. Guatemala.

BM 1956—1962
BoLSA 1952—
BoT 1952—1962
EssexU 1962.
UCL**

APUNTES ECONOMICOS (GUATEMALA). Publicacion del Consejo Nacional de
Planificacion Economica (Guatemala). Guatemala.

BM 8(6), 1962—

BALANZA DE PAGOS INTERNACIONALES DE GUATEMALA. Banco de Guatemala.
Guatemala.

BoT 1952—1953; 1955—1958.
StAndU 1953; 1957; 1958.

BOLETIN DE AGRICULTURA. (Guatemala) Secretaria de Agricultura. Guatemala
1, Jan 1921— 10, 1931.
[Not publ. 1932. Subs: Revista Agricola]

SL 4, 1925—

BOLETIN DE LA DIRECCION GENERAL DE ESTADISTICA Y CENSO (GUATEMALA).
Guatemala.

BoLSA**
UCL**

BOLETIN DE ESTADISTICAS BANCARIAS (GUATEMALA). (Guatemala)
Superintendencia de Bancos. Guatemala.

BoLSA**
HispLBC**
StAndU 1954—56; 1958; 1960—63.

BOLETIN DE ESTADISTICAS DE SEGUROS (GUATEMALA). (Guatemala)
Superintendencia de Bancos. Guatemala.

StAndU 1958; 1961; 1962.

BOLETIN ESTADISTICO, ASOCIACION NACIONAL DEL CAFE (GUATEMALA).
Guatemala. (M)

LSE No.4, S 1961—

BOLETIN ESTADISTICO DEL BANCO DE GUATEMALA. Guatemala.
[M]

BM 13, 1960—
BoLSA 1957—
BoT**
HispLBC**
RIIA 19 (4th q.), 1966—
StAndU 7(3), 1954—
UCL 15, 1962— [W 15(11/12)]

76

BOLETIN MENSUAL, DIRECCION GENERAL DE ESTADISTICA (GUATEMALA).
Guatemala. No.1, 1957—
BM 1—12, 1957.

CARTA SEMANAL DE CAFE. Banco de Guatemala. Guatemala.
BM ano 3(5), 1960 — ano 5 (6), 1962.

ESTADISTICAS DE SEGUROS Y FINANZAS (GUATEMALA). (Guatemala)
Superintendencia de Bancos. Guatemala
StAndU 1961 (1962)—

ESTADISTICO DEL CAFE (GUATEMALA).
BoT 1954—1959.

ESTUDIOS CENTROAMERICANOS. Guatemala. 1, 1965—

GUATEMALA EN CIFRAS.
BM 1957—
BoLSA**
BoT 1955—

GUATEMALA INDIGENA. Instituto Indigenista Nacional (Guatemala). Guatemala.
1, 1961—
BodI 2 (1), 1962—
RAnthroI

INDUSTRIA. Organo oficial de la Camara de Industria (Guatemala). Guatemala.
BM (4 epoca) No.12, 1961—

INFORME ECONOMICO, BANCO DE GUATEMALA. Guatemala.
[2M]
BM 1, 1958—12, 1964.
BoLSA**
BoT 1959—1962.
StAndU 11(1,3), 1963—

INVESTIGACIONES AGROPECUARIAS. Instituto Agropecuario Nacional (Guatemala);
Division de Investigaciones. La Aurora. 1, Jan/Ap 1960—
CSA 1 (2)—
GrasslandRI

MEMORIA ANUAL, DIVISION DE INVESTIGACIONES AGROPECUARIAS, INSTITUTO
AGROPECUARIO NACIONAL (GUATEMALA). Guatemala.
EMalI 1963.

MEMORIA ANUAL Y ESTUDIO ECONOMICO, BANCO DE GUATEMALA. Guatemala.
BM 1952; 1956—
BoLSA 1946—
BoT**
HispLBC**
IBank (Two year file)
RIIA 1962.
StAndU 1950—1961.
UCL 1960 (1961)—

MEMORIA DE LAS LABORES, MINISTERIO DE TRABAJO Y BIENESTAR SOCIAL
(GUATEMALA).   Guatemala.
   [A]

   BM   1957/58.
   LSE 1958/59—

REPORT ON ECONOMIC CONDITIONS IN GUATEMALA. (Great Britain) Board of Trade;
   Commercial Relations & Exports Dept.   London.   1922— 1937; 1951— 1956.

   BM
   BoT

REVISTA AGRICOLA.   (Guatemala) Secretaria de Agricultura.   Guatemala.
   1933—
   [Prev: Boletin de Agricultura; 1, 1921— 10, 1931. Not publ.   1932]

   SL
   TropProdl

REVISTA CAFETALERA.   Asociacion Nacional del Cafe (Guatemala.) Guatemala.
   (2S) 1, 1956   ; (3S) 1, 1959—   ;(4S) 1, 1961—

   [Prev (1S): Revista Cafetalera de Guatemala]

   EMall (3S) 1 (1/3), 1959.   (4S) 1 (1), 1961— (36), 1064.

REVISTA CAFETALERA DE GUATEMALA.   (Guatemala) Oficina Central del Cafe.
   Guatemala.   1, Dec 1944—   ?1955.
   [Subs: Revista Cafetalera]

   BM   7 (56), 1951.

REVISTA DE LA FACULTAD DE CIENCIAS JURIDICAS Y SOCIALES . . . .,
UNIVERSIDAD DE GUATEMALA.   Guatemala.
   [Actual title: Rev. Fac. Cienc. Jurid. y Soc. de Guatemala]

   Bodl   *1938/39—

REVISTA, MINISTERIO DE TRABAJO Y BIENESTAR SOCIAL (GUATEMALA).
   Guatemala.   1, 1958—

   BM   1 (2—12), 1958.
   LSE 1(2), 1958—

TRIMESTRE ESTADISTICO (GUATEMALA).   (Guatemala) Direccion General de
   Estadistica   Guatemala.   1, July/Sep 1963—

   BM   1963—
   UCL 1964—

GUYANA (ex BRITISH GUIANA)

ANNUAL ACCOUNT RELATING TO EXTERNAL TRADE (BRITISH GUIANA). (British Guiana) Department of Customs & Excise.   Georgetown.

BM   1956–1961.
BoT   1954– 1955; 1957; 1959; 1961–1962
LondICS   1954–

ANNUAL REPORT OF THE CONTROLLER OF CUSTOMS & EXCISE (BRITISH GUIANA). Georgetown.–

BM   1898–1927; 1939–1954; 1956–1960.
Bot**
LondICS   1946–

BACKGROUND TO GUYANA.   Guyana Information Services.   Georgetown.
No.1,   Oct 1966–

LondICS

BOOKER NEWS.   Georgetown.

LondICS   No.230, 21/Aug 1964–

(BRITISH GUIANA).   Report.   (Great Britain) Colonial Office / Commonwealth Office.   London.
[From 1962 as: Guyana.   Annual Report]

BM 1946–1961.
HullU 1949–
LondICS   1933– 1938; 1946–

COMMERCIAL REVIEW.   Bi-monthly journal of the Chamber of Commerce of the City of Georgetown. Georgetown.   1, 1918–
[Title varies slightly: to Nov 1923 as: Commercial Review Illustrated.
Then: Commercial Review, British Guiana]

Guildhall (Three year file)
LondICS   49(1), Jan/Feb 1966–

GUIANA TIMES NEWS MAGAZINE . . .   Georgetown.   [Q]
[Actual title ends: . . .. for British Guiana and the West Indies]

LondICS   13(1), 1964–

GUYANA.   Annual report.   Georgetown.   1962–
[Prev as: (British Guiana).   Report of the (G.B.) Colonial Office]

BM
LondICS
LSE

GUYANA YEAR BOOK.   [Guiana Graphic Ltd.]   Georgetown.

BoT   (Current volume)
LondICS   1964–

INTERNATIONAL AFFAIRS (QUARTERLY).   Guyana Institute of International Affairs.   Georgetown   [1(1)] , 1965–

LondICS

JOURNAL OF THE ROYAL AGRICULTURAL & COMMERCIAL SOCIETY OF BRITISH GUIANA.   see TIMEHRI

MONTHLY ACCOUNT RELATING TO EXTERNAL TRADE (BRITISH GUIANA).
(British Guiana) Department of Customs & Excise.   Georgetown.   1,? 1955—

BoT   1955—
TropProdl   1956—

NEW NATION.   Peoples National Congress (Guyana).   Georgetown.

LondICS   *1958;   *1959; *1964; *1966; 1967—

NEW WORLD (FORTNIGHTLY).   Georgetown.

LondICS   *No.2, 13/Nov 1964—

NEWS FROM GUYANA.   Guyana Information Services.   (Georgetown)
[W]

LondICS   23/June 1965—

QUARTERLY REVIEW OF FINANCIAL STATISTICS (GUYANA).   (Guyana) Ministry
of Economic Development: Statistical Bureau. Georgetown.   1965—

BoT

QUARTERLY STATISTICAL DIGEST (BRITISH GUIANA).

BM   1962;
BoT   1960—

SIMARA.   Committee for National Reconstruction (Guyana).   Georgetown.
[M]

LondICS   Feb 1966—

THUNDER.   Peoples Progressive Party (Guyana).   Georgetown.
[W]

LondICS   12(49), 1961— 13(3), 1962; 13(4), 1962— 1965 on microfilm;
17 (1), 1966—

TIMEHRI.   Journal of the Royal Agricultural & Commercial Society of British
Guiana. Georgetown.   1, 1882— 5, 1886, (NS)1, 1887— (15), 1902; (3S)
1, 1911— 7, 1921; (4S) 1, 1934—
[1900— 1902 (unnumbered, but in effect = (NS) vols. 13-15) actually as above
subtitle.]

(Several holdings in BUCOP, Vol. 4, 1958)
LondICS   No.27, July 1946— 40, Oct 1961.   [W no.33]

TRADE & ECONOMIC REPORT (BRITISH GUIANA).

BoT**

UG NEWSLETTER.   University of Guyana.   Georgetown.   1(1), Ap 1966—

LondICS

[Also certain items available in the Board of Trade Library, not in published form: Monthly
and quarterly returns of imports and exports by direction; [Sugar return] .]

80

HAITI

ALLGEMEINE STATISTIK DES AUSLANDES; LANDERBERICHTE; HAITI.
Wiesbaden (etc). 1965—

BM 1965.
LSE

BULLETIN D'INFORMATIONS, DEPARTEMENT DES AFFAIRES ETRANGERES (HAITI);
SERIE A. Port-au-Prince.
[2/W]
LSE (Current issues only)

BULLETIN TRIMESTRIEL DE STATISTIQUE (HAITI).

BM 24, 1957—
BoT**

RAPPORT ANNUEL DU DEPARTEMENT FISCAL, BANQUE NATIONALE DE LA
REPUBLIQUE D'HAITI. Port-au-Prince.

BM 1923/24; 1934/35 — 1954/55.
BoT**
IBank (Two year file)

RAPPORT ANNUEL, OFFICE DE CONTROLE ET DE DEVELOPPEMENT DES DENREES
D'EXPORTATION (HAITI). Port-au-Prince.

REPORT ON ECONOMIC CONDITIONS IN HAITI. (Great Britain) Board of
Trade; Commercial Relations & Exports Dept. London. 1921— 1938.
1957

BM
BoT

HONDURAS

ANUARIO ESTADISTICO (HONDURAS). (Honduras) Direccion General de
    Estadistica y Censos.   Tegucigalpa.
    BM 1958–
    BoLSA 1957–
    BoT**
    UCL**

BOLETIN ESTADISTICO (HONDURAS). (Honduras) Direccion General de
    Estadistica y Censos.   Tegucigalpa.
    [2/A]
    BoLSA 1965–
    BoT**
    LSE   Nov 1962–
    UCL 1962 (No.1)–

BOLETIN MENSUAL DEL BANCO CENTRAL DE HONDURAS. Tegucigalpa.
    BoLSA   1959–1964.
    BoT   1956–
    UCL**

COMERCIO EXTERIOR (HONDURAS).   (Honduras) Direccion General de Estadistica
    y Censos. Tegucigalpa.
    BM 1958–
    BoLSA**
    BoT   1953; 1956–
    LSE 1956–
    UCL**

ESTADISTICAS INDUSTRIALES (HONDURAS).   (Honduras) Direccion General de
    Estadisticas y Censos. Tegucigalpa.   1950–
    [1950 & 1951 issued by: Banco Central de Honduras]
    BM   1953/55.
    BoT   1953–1955
    LSE   !1953/1954/1955–

INDUSTRIA. Asociacion Nacional de Industria (Honduras). Tegucigalpa.

    BoLSA**

INFORMACION AGROPECUARIA (HONDURAS).   Promedios de precios e indices de
    precios y produccion.   (Honduras) Direccion General de Estadistica y
    Censos. Tegucigalpa.
    BM 1940/58; 1959.
    BoT**
    LSE   1940/48–

INFORME DE LABORES . . . ; MINISTERIO DE TRABAJO Y PREVISION SOCIAL
    (HONDURAS). Tegucigalpa.
    [A. Actual title: Inf. de Lab. presentada al Congreso Nacional]
    BM   1958/59–
    LSE   1958/59–

INFORME, SECRETARIA DE HACIENDA, CREDITO PUBLICO Y COMERCIO
    (HONDURAS). Tegucigalpa.
    BoLSA **

INVESTIGACION A LA INDUSTRIA MANUFACTURERA (HONDURAS). Consejo
    Nacional de Economia (Honduras) Tegucigalpa.   1962–
    BoT   1962

MEMORIA, BANCO CENTRAL DE HONDURAS.   Tegucigalpa.

    BM   1958/59—
    BoT
    IBank   (Two year file)
    RIIA   June 1950/Dec 1951.

MEMORIA, BANCO NACIONAL DE FOMENTO (HONDURAS),   Tegucigalpa.

    BoLSA**

REFORMA AGRARIA.   Instituto Nacional Agrario (Honduras).   Tegucigalpa.
    1, Mar 1962—

REPORT ON ECONOMIC CONDITIONS IN HONDURAS. (Great Britain) Board of Trade;
    Commonwealth Relations & Exports Dept. London. 1921— 1938; 1951— 1954.

    BM
    BoT

REVISTA TRIMESTRAL DEL BANCO CENTRAL DE HONDURAS. Tegucigalpa. 1(1),
    Jan/Mar   1965—

    BM
    BoLSA
    LSE

TRABAJO. (1955)   (Honduras) Ministerio de Trabajo.   Tegucigalpa.
    1, Dec 1955—
    [Subs from 1958 also under above title, with subtitle "Organo de
    publicidad del Ministerio de Trabajo y Prevision Social"]

TRABAJO.   (1958)   (Honduras) Ministerio de Trabajo y Prevision Social.
    Tegucigalpa.   1958—

    BM   1960—

JAMAICA

ABSTRACT OF STATISTICS (JAMAICA).   (Jamaica) Department of Statistics.
   Kingston.   No.18, 19   —
   [(Prev) No.1, 1947— 11, 1951 as: Quarterly Digest of Statistics. Then
   No.12, 1952— 17, 19 as: Digest of Statistics. Then as above.
   Subs: Annual Abstract of Statistics; (&) Quarterly Abstract of
   Statistics]

   BM   1961—
   Bodl
   BoT
   IBank (Selected articles only kept)
   LondICS

ANNUAL ABSTRACT OF STATISTICS (JAMAICA).   (Jamaica) Department of Statistics.
   Kingston.

   BM   1958—
   BoT   1960—

ANNUAL REPORT, BANK OF JAMAICA.   Kingston.

   IBanK   (Two year file)

ANNUAL REPORT, CENTRAL HOUSING AUTHORITY (JAMAICA).   Kingston.

   [Subs: Annual Report, Dept. of Housing (Jam.)]

   BM   1946 — 1956
   LSE   1944/5.

ANNUAL REPORT, DEPARTMENT OF HOUSING (JAMAICA).   Kingston.

   BM   1956—
   LondICS   1961/2—
   LSE   [2nd] 1957/8—

ANNUAL REPORT, JAMAICA TOURIST BOARD. Kingston.

   BM 1956 — 1963
   LondICS   1962/3—
   LSE   1958/9—

ANNUAL REPORT, SMALL BUSINESS LOAN BOARD (JAMAICA).   Kingston.

   BM   1956 — 1959.
   LSE   [3rd] 1958—

BALANCE OF PAYMENTS, JAMAICA.   (Jamaica) Department of Statistics;
   Financial Statistics Section.   Kingston.
   [A]

   BM   1961; 1964—
   BoT   1958—
   LSE   1958—

BULLETIN, BANK OF JAMAICA.   Kingston.   1(1), Mar 1962—
   [3/A]

   BM 1962—
   BoLSA
   Guildhall   Mar 1964—
   IBank   (One year file)
   LondICS

84

BULLETIN OF STATISTICS (JAMAICA); EXTERNAL TRADE OF JAMAICA.

BM   1961–1962; 1964–
Bodl   1952–
BoT   1961
LondICS 1958–

COMMODITY BULLETIN (Jamaica) Department of Agriculture. Kingston.
1, 1955–

CSA

DIGEST OF STATISTICS (JAMAICA).   (Jamaica) Department of Statistics.
Kingston.   No.12, 1952–17, 19 . . .
[Prev: Quarterly Digest of Statistics; from No.1, 1947.
Subs: Abstract of Statistics]

Bodl
BoT
LondICS

ECONOMIC SURVEY JAMAICA.   (Jamaica) Central Planning Unit. Kingston.

BM   1957–
BoT   1957–
LondICS 1957–
LondU   1963 (1) –

EXTERNAL TRADE (JAMAICA).   (Jamaica) Central Bureau of Statistics.   Kingston.
BM   no51, 1952–   [M]
Bot**
LondICS   (retained till receipt of annual vol.)

EXTERNAL TRADE OF JAMAICA.   (Jamaica) Central Bureau of Statistics. Kingston.
BM   1947–   [A]
Bodl   1939 –
BoT   1947–
IBank   (selected articles only kept)
LondICS   1947–
RIIA   1945– 1956.
TropProdl   1957–

FINANCE ACCOUNTS OF JAMAICA.   (Jamaica) Ministry of Finance. Kingston.
LondICS   1959/60–

HANDBOOK OF JAMAICA. (Govt. Printing Office)   Kingston.   1, 1881–
(See holdings in BUCOP, Vol. 2, 1956)

BM   1935–1936; 1939; 1946; 1948; 1950–
BoT
Guildhall (Current issue only)

HANDBOOK OF THE MINISTRY OF EXTERNAL AFFAIRS (JAMAICA). An official
yearbook. Kingston.   ? 1963–
LondICS   1964–

(JAMAICA). Report. (Great Britain) Colonial Office / Commonwealth Office.
London.
BM   1946–1961
HullU   1949– 1960.
LondICS 1932– 1938; 1946–

JAMAICA DIPLOMATIC & CONSULAR COURIER.   Kingston.
   [3/A]
   LondICS   2(2),   1964—

JAMAICA INDUSTRIAL & COMMERCIAL DIRECTORY.   Jamaica Industrial
   Development Corporation.   Kingston.

JAMAICA YEARBOOK OF INDUSTRY & AGRICULTURE. Kingston.   1956—
   [Title varies:Yearbook of Industry & Agriculture in Jamaica]
   LondICS   1965—

JOURNAL OF THE JAMAICA CHAMBER OF COMMERCE. KINGSTON.
   LondICS   19(6), Sep/Oct 1963—

MONETARY STATISTICS (JAMAICA).   (Jamaica) Department of Statistics.
   Kingston
   BM   1960—
   BoT   1952/56—
   LondICS   1958—
   PrudAssurCo   Sep 1963—

MONTHLY COMMENT.   Constant Springs, Jam.   1(1), Oct 1953— 5 (23/24),
   June/July 1964.//
   LondICS*

NATIONAL ACCOUNTS, INCOME & EXPENDITURE (JAMAICA).
   BM   1958—
   BoT**

NATIONAL PATRIOT.   Umemployed Workers Council (Jamaica).   Kingston.
   LondICS**   (?One issue only, Dec 1966)

NEW JAMAICA.   Kingston.   [Q]
   LondICS   Mar 1966—

NEW WORLD [QUARTERLY]. Mona, Jam.   1(1), Mar 1963—
   [First issue actually publ. in Georgetown, B.G.]
   LondICS
   UCL   [2(3), 1966] —

PUBLIC OPINION.   The national week-end review.   Kingston.
   LondICS   28 (53), 1/Jan 1965—

QUARTERLY ABSTRACT OF STATISTICS (JAMAICA).   (Jamaica) Department of
   Statistics.   Kingston.   No.1, Mar 1961—
   BM
   Bodl
   BoT
   LondICS
   LSE   No.2, June 1961—

QUARTERLY DIGEST OF STATISTICS (JAMAICA).   (Jamaica) Department of
   Statistics. Kingston.   No.1, June 1947— 11, Dec 1951 . . .
   [Subs: Digest of Statistics]
   BM   1947 — 1951; 1953; 1956; 1961
   Bodl
   BoT   [W no.4]
   LondICS
   86

REPORT, AGRICULTURAL DEVELOPMENT CORPORATION (JAMAICA).   Kingston.

LondICS   1952/3

REPORT, COCOA INDUSTRY BOARD (JAMAICA).   Kingston.
[Prev: Report, Cocoa Marketing Board; 1952/3– 1956/7]

LondICS   1963/4–

REPORT, COCOA MARKETING BOARD (JAMAICA).   Kingston.   1952/3– 1956/7

REPORT, JAMAICA AGRICULTURAL SOCIETY.   Kingston.

LondICS   1957/8–

REPORT OF THE RESEARCH DEPARTMENT, COCONUT INDUSTRY BOARD (JAMAICA)
Kingston.
BM   1960/61.
LongAshtonRS   1959/61–

REPORT & STATEMENT OF ACCOUNTS, BANK OF JAMAICA.   Kingston.
[A]

BM 1961–
LondICS   1961–

RETAIL PRICE INDEX (JAMAICA); KINGSTON AREA.
Kingston.
[M]
BM   1962–
Bodl   Jan 1963–
BoT   1956; 1962–

RURAL RETAIL PRICE INDEX (JAMAICA).

BM   1962–
Bodl   Mar 1958–
BoT   1952*

SOCIAL & ECONOMIC STUDIES.   University of the West Indies; Institute of
Social & Economic Research.   Mona, Jam.   No.1, Feb 1953–
[Q]

AbdU	LSE
BelfU	NottU
BhmU	NuffCollOxf
BM1953–	OxflES
Bodl	RIIA
BoT 2, 1953/4	SheffU 9, 1960–
BrU	SwUC*
EdinU	TropProdl *1957–
ExU	UCL
GlasU	WarwickU 12, 1963–
HullU	
LondICS	
LondU	

SPECIAL SERIES, INSTITUTE OF SOCIAL & ECONOMIC PLANNING, UNIVERSITY OF
THE WEST INDIES.   Mona, Jam.   1, 1956–

LondICS

TABLES OF NATIONAL INCOME & EXPENDITURE (JAMAICA).   (Jamaica) Department
of Statistics.   Kingston.
London   1950–

TRADE INDICES (JAMAICA).   (Jamaica) Department of Statistics.   Kingston.
   1948/58—
   [Base year: 1954. A.]

   BM   1948 — 1964
   BodI
   BoT
   LondICS
   LSE

UWI QUARTERLY.   University of the West Indies. Mona, Jam.   1(1), 1964—
   1(4), 1964 //

   LondICS

VOICE OF JAMAICA.   Kingston.

   LondICS   12(49-52), 1965.

WAGE RATES & HOURS IN SELECTED INDUSTRIES (JAMAICA).   (Jamaica)
   Department of Statistics.   Kingston.

   BodI   1957/9—
   BoT**
   LondICS   1957/9—

WAGE RATES IN SELECTED OCCUPATIONS (JAMAICA).   (Jamaica) Department of
   Statistics.   Kingston.   1957/9—

   BoT
   LondICS
   LSE

WEST INDIAN ECONOMIST.   Kingston. 1, June 1958— 5(4), Xmas 1962.//

   BoLSA
   LondICS
   TropProdI

YEARBOOK OF INDUSTRY & AGRICULTURE IN JAMAICA.
   see Jamaica Yearbook of Industry & Agriculture.

[Also the following, available at the Board of Trade Library, not in published form:
Monthly and quarterly return of imports and exports by direction.]

LEEWARD ISLANDS

[Antigua; St. Christopher-Nevis-Anguilla; Monserrat; British Virgin Islands]

ANNUAL REPORT OF THE DEPARTMENT OF LABOUR (ST. CHRISTOPHER . . .).
  (Basseterre)
  BM   1951– 1961
  Bodl   1951–
  BoT   1957–
  LondICS 1951–

ANNUAL REPORT, INDUSTRIAL DEVELOPMENT BOARD (Antigua). St. Johns, Antigua.
  BM   1958–1960.
  LondICS 1953; 1956–

ANNUAL TRADE REPORT (ANTIGUA).
  St.Johns, Antigua.
  BM 1957–1959; 1961 –
  BoT**
  LondICS 1962–

(ANTIGUA). Report. (Great Britain) Colonial Office / Commonwealth Office.
  London.
  BM   1955 – 1964.
  HullU 1955/56–
  LondICS 1955/56–

(BRITISH VIRGIN ISLANDS). Report. (Great Britain) Colonial Office /
  Commonwealth Office. London.
  BM   1955 – 1964.
  HullU 1955/56–
  LondICS 1955/56.

EXTERNAL TRADE OF ST.KITTS-NEVIS-ANGUILLA.
  Basseterre.
  Bodl   1955–
  BoT**
  LondICS 1955; 1959–

(LEEWARD ISLANDS). Report. (Great Britain)Colonial Office. London.
  BM   1947 – 1954.
  BoT 1947– 1950; 1953 – 1954.
  LondICS 1933– 1938; 1947– 1954.

(MONSERRAT). Report. (Great Britain) Colonial Office /Commonwealth
  Office. London.
  BM   1955 – 1064
  HullU 1955/56–
  LondICS 1955/56–

MONSERRAT MIRROR. Plymouth, Mons.   [W]
  LondICS *6 (26), 8/Jan 1966–

(ST.KITTS-NEVIS-ANGUILLA). Report. (Great Britain) Colonial Office /
  Commonwealth Office. London.
  BM   1955–1962
  LondICS 1955/56–

SOCIAL WELFARE REPORT (ANTIGUA). (Antigua) Social Welfare Dept. St.Johns,
  Ant.
  BM   1949 – 1953

SUMMARY OF IMPORTS & EXPORTS OF THE BRITISH VIRGIN ISLANDS. Tortola.

    Bodl   1954—
    BoT   1952—1962
    LondICS   1964—

WORKERS VOICE. Antigua Trades & Labour Union.   St. Johns, Ant.
    ["Organ of the working people of Antigua"]

    LondICS   *21 (146), Jan 1965—

[Also available at BoT Library, not in published form: (Monserrat) Monthly and quarterly
returns of imports and exports by direction; Monthly return of statistics: imports of textiles;
Value of imports and exports. (Antigua) Monthly or quarterly returns of imports and exports
by direction; Monthly return of statistics; imports of textiles; [Sugar return].
(British Virgin Islands) Monthly and quarterly returns of imports and exports by direction;
Monthly returns of statistics: imports of textiles. (St. Christopher-Nevis-Anguilla) Monthly and
quarterly returns of imports and exports by direction; Monthly return of statistics: Imports
of textiles; [Sugar statistics.)]

MARTINIQUE AND GUADELOUPE

ACTION.   Revue theorique et politique du Parti Communiste Martiniquaise.
Fort de France.
[Q]

LondICS   No.2, Dec 1963—

BULLETIN, CHAMBRE DE COMMERCE ET D'INDUSTRIE DE LA MARTINIQUE.
Fort de France.
[M]
LondICS   *Dec   1964—

BULLETIN DE STATISTIQUES (MARTINIQUE); (NS).   (Martinique) Service de Statistique.
Fort de France.
[Q. Service actually part of: Institut National de la Statistique et des
Etudes Economiques (Martinique)]

LondICS   No.10, Jan/July   1965—

CAHIERS, SOCIETE D'ETUDES DEMOGRAPHIQUES ET SOCIALES DE LA
MARTINIQUE; 1ERE SERIE.   [Fort de France]
LondICS   Feb 1963—

BULLETIN MUNICIPAL (POINTE A PITRE).   Pointe a Pitre.   No.1,   1965—
(Issued by "La Municipalite, Ville de Pointe a Pitre.   Q]
LondICS

MEXICO

ACTIVIDAD ECONOMICA EN LATINOAMERICA.   Mexico, D.F.   1, Aug 1960—

AGRICULTURA TECNICA EN MEXICO   (Mexico) Direccion General de Agricultura.
Mexico, D.F.   1, July 1955—
BM
CSA
GrasslandRI
SL

ALLGEMEINE STATISTIK DES AUSLANDES; LANDERBERICHTE;   MEXICO.
Wiesbaden.   1966—
BM
LSE

ANALES, SECRETARIA DE COMUNICACIONES Y OBRAS PUBLICAS (MEXICO).
Mexico.   D.F.   (3S)   1, 1920—
GlasU   1—4, 1924.

ANNUAL REPORT, BANCO NACIONAL DE MEXICO.   Mexico, D.F.
GlasU   29, 1951. 30, 1952.
LdsU   26, 1948— 30, 1952.

ANUARIO ESTADISTICO DEL COMERCIO EXTERIOR DE LOS ESTADOS UNIDOS
MEXICANOS. (Mexico) Direccion General de Estadistica. Mexico, D.F. 1940 (1942)—
BM   1940—1961, 1965—
BoLSA   1963—
BoT**
EssexU   1942—1950, 1952. 1958—1964.
Guildhall.   (Current issue)
HispLBC**

ANUARIO ESTADISTICO DE LOS ESTADOS UNIDOS MEXICANOS.   (Mexico) Direccion
General de Estadistica.   Mexico, D.F.   1920/22—
BM   1938—
BoT**
EssexU   1946—1952. 1955—1957. 1962—1963.
GlasU   1938.
Guildhall. (Current issue)
LdsU   1958.
RIIA   1940. 1954.
UCL**

ANUARIO FINANCIERO DE MEXICO.   Asociacion de Banqueros de Mexico. Mexico.
DF.   1, 1940—
BM   15, 1955 — 16, 1956.
BoLSA
EssexU   17, 1956— 24, 1963.

*ANUARIO INDIGENISTA.   Mexico, D.F.   22, 1962—
[Prev: Boletin Indigenista; from 1, 1941]
RAnthrol

ASPECTOS FINANCIEROS DE LAS ECONOMIAS LATINOAMERICANAS.   Centro de
Estudios Monetarios Latinoamericanos.   Mexico D.F.   1962—
[Prev: Aspectos Monetarios de las Economias . . . ; from 1956]
EssexU   1962—1964.

ASPECTOS MONETARIOS DE LAS ECONOMIAS LATINOAMERICANAS. Centro de Estudios Monetarios Latinoamericanos. Mexico, D.F. 1956– 1961.
[Subs: Aspectos Financieros de las Economias . . .]
BM   1958–
BoLSA   1957–
EssexU   1958–
LSE   1959–

BANCA Y COMERCIO. Escuela Bancaria y Comercial (Mexico). Mexico, D.F.
1,   Jan 1962–
[Called (2S) of prev: Revista Credito]

BANCOS Y EL MERCADO DE VALORES (MEXICO). Comision Nacional de Valores (Mexico). Mexico, D.F.
LSE   1958/59–

BIBLIOGRAFIA ECONOMICA DE MEXICO. Banco de Mexico; Departamento de Estudios Economicos; Biblioteca. Mexico, D.F. 1954/55–
[2A. (Also under same title as Q). Continues: Diez anos de literatura economica, 1943–53; by J. Bullejos]
BM   1954–1957; 1959; 1962.

BIBLIOGRAFIA ECONOMICA DE MEXICO. (Body and place as above). 1, Mar 1955–
[Q]
BM 1, 1955–
EssexU   *10, 1964– 11, 1965.

BOLETIN AZUCARERO MEXICANO. Union Nacional de Productores de Azucar (Mexico). Mexico, D.F. (etc). ?1949–
BM   No.186, 1964–

BOLETIN BIBLIOGRAFICO, BIBLIOTECA, BANCO DE MEXICO. [Mexico, D.F.]
1 Jan 1955–
["Lista de nuevas adquisiciones"]
BM 1, 1955–
EssexU   *1961–1963.

BOLETIN DE LA CAMARA NACIONAL DE COMERCIO DE LA CIUDAD DE MEXICO.
Mexico, D.F.

BOLETIN ESTADISTICO, COMISION NACIONAL BANCARIA (MEXICO). Mexico, D.F.
UCL**

BOLETIN DE ESTUDIOS ESPECIALES, BANCO NACIONAL DE CREDITO EJIDAL (MEXICO). Mexico, D.F. 1, Oct 1953–
BM no93, 1957 – no208, 1961.

BOLETIN INDIGENISTA. Mexico, D.F. 1, 1941– 21, 1961 . . .
[Subs: Anuario Indigenista]
RAnthroI

BOLETIN DE INDUSTRIAS. Mexico, D.F.
BM   1918–1921.
BodI *1918–1923.

BOLETIN MENSUAL, CENTRO DE ESTUDIOS MONETARIOS LATINAMERICANOS.
see CEMLA BOLETIN MENSUAL.

BOLETIN MENSUAL DE LA COMISION NACIONAL DE VALORES (MEXICO). Mexico, D.F. 1, Jan 1954–

BOLETIN MENSUAL DE LA DIRECCION DE ECONOMIA RURAL (MEXICO). Mexico, D.F. [Prev: Boletin Mensual de Estadistica Agricola]

    BM No.225, 1945–
    MinAg Nos. 122, 129–146 (1936–38).
    SL No.120, 1936–

BOLETIN MENSUAL DE INFORMACION, CONFEDERACION DE TRABAJADORES DE MEXICO. Mexico, D.F.   1, Jan/Mar 1955–
    [Title varies; also as: Boletin Trimestral de Informacion, . . .
    Prev: CTM.]

BOLETIN OFICIAL, SECRETARIA DE HACIENDA Y CREDITO PUBLICO (MEXICO). Mexico, D.F.   1, 1955–

    LSE

BOLETIN QUINCENAL, CAMARA NACIONAL DE COMERCIO DE LA CIUDAD DE MEXICO. Mexico, D.F.

BOLETIN QUINCENAL, CENTRO DE ESTUDIOS MONETARIOS LATINOAMERICANOS. Mexico, D.F.   1, 1955–

    BoLSA 2, 1956–
    EssexU   3, 1957– 11, 1965.
    IBank 1964–

BOLETIN QUINCENAL, INSTITUTO NACIONAL DEL CAFE (MEXICO). Mexico, D.F.
    1, Jan 1959–
    [Prev: Boletin Quincenal, Comision Nacional del Cafe (Mex.)]

BOLETIN, SECRETARIA DE COMUNICACIONES Y OBRAS PUBLICAS (MEXICO). Mexico, D.F.   1, 1955–

    Glas U 1 (9-12),   1922. 2 (1,2), 1923.

BOLETIN TRIMESTRAL DE INFORMACION, CONFEDERACION DE TRABAJADORES DE MEXICO.   see BOLETIN MENSUAL DE INFORMACION, . . .

CEMLA BOLETIN MENSUAL. Centro de Estudios Monetarios Latinoamericanos. Mexico, D.F.

    EssexU   12, 1966–
    IBank   12 (10), 1966–

*CIENCIAS POLITICAS Y SOCIALES. Escuela Nacional de Ciencias Politicas y Sociales (Mexico). Mexico, D.F. 1, July/Sep 1955–
    [Escuela part of: Universidad Nacional Autonoma de Mexico]
    EssexU*

COMERCIO. Camara Nacional de Comercio de la Ciudad de Mexico. Mexico, D.F.
    1, Aug 1960–

*COMERCIO EXTERIOR (MEXICO). Banco Nacional de Comercio Exterior (Mexico). Mexico, D.F.   1(1), Jan 1951–
    [M. Title varies: also: Comercio Exterior de Mexico]
    BoLSA 1955–
    BoT**
    EssexU *12, 1962–
    Guildhall (Five year file also monthly)
    HispLBC**
    LivPL   1952–54. 1956–
    OxfIES   3, 1957–
    UCL**

COMERCIO EXTERIOR (MEXICO); (ENGLISH EDITION).   Banco Nacional de Comercio
   Exterior (Mexico).   Mexico, D.F.
   EssexU   12(2), 1966—

COMERCIO EXTERIOR (MEXICO); INTERNATIONAL AIR MAIL EDITION. Banco
   Nacional de Comercio Exterior (Mexico).   Mexico, D.F. 1(1), Feb 1955—
   [M. Title varies; also: Comercio Exterior de Mexico; . . .]

COMERCIO INTERNATIONAL.   Asociacion Nacional de Importadores y Exportadores
   de la Republica Mexicana.   Mexico, D.F.   1, 1962—

COMERCIO MEXICANO.   Confederacion de Camaras Nacionales de Comercio (Mexico).
   Mexico, D.F.   No.1, Aug 1951—64, Ap 1961.//
   [Some early issues lack numbering. From no.13 called (2S)]

COMERCIO MUNDIAL.   Asociacion Nacional de Importadores y Exportadores de la
   Republica Mexicana.   Mexico, D.F.   1(1), Ap 1959—
   EssexU   7 (70-73), 1965.

COMUNICACIONES Y TRANSPORTES.   (Mexico) Secretaria de Comunicaciones y
   Transportes.   Mexico. D.F.   1, July/Aug 1959—
   BM   3, 1961—
   EssexU   2(5), 1960— 6 (3), 1965.

CUADERNO, SECRETARIA DEL TRABAJO Y PREVISION SOCIAL (MEXICO).
   Mexico, D.F. 1, 1954—
   BM   18 — 25, 1959.

*CUADERNOS AMERICANOS.   Mexico, D.F.   1, Jan/Feb 1942—

   BM   8 (44), 1949—
   Bodl
   EssexU
   LdsU   14 (84), 1956—
   LivU   24, 1965—
   SheffU   2, 1943— 24, 1965.

ECONOMISTA MEXICANO.   Colegio de Economistas de Mexico.   Mexico, D.F.
   1, Nov/Dec 1961—
   [2M]

ESPEJO.   Coleccion del pensamiento economico moderno. Instituto de
   Investigaciones Sociales y Economicas.   Mexico, D.F.   1, Mar 1960—
ESTADISTICA NACIONAL (MEXICO).   Revista mensual.   (Mexico) Departamento de
   la Estadistica Nacional.   Mexico, D.F.

   BM   53   1927 — 122, 1932.
   StAndU   6, 1930— 7, 1931.

ESTUDIOS, BANCO NACIONAL HIPOTECARIO URBANO Y DE OBRAS PUBLICAS
   (MEXICO).   Mexico, D.F.
   [2M]

EXAMEN DE LA SITUACION ECONOMICA DE MEXICO.   Banco Nacional de Mexico.
   Mexico, D.F.
   BM   35, 1959—
   BoLSA **
   EssexU   40 (461—3, 466, 468—9); 41 (470, 472—3, 475—9).   (1964—6).

GACETA SOCIOLOGICA.   Universidad Nacional Autonoma de Mexico; Instituto de
   Investigaciones Sociales.   Mexico, D.F.   No.1, 1964—
   BM

HOJE DE INFORMACION ECONOMICA. Instituto de Investigaciones Sociales y
   Economicas (Mexico). Mexico, D.F. 1, 1955—
   BoLSA
   LivPL Ap 1956—

INFORMACIONES SOCIALES. (Mexico) Secretaria del Trabajo y Prevision Social.
   Mexico, D.F. 1, 1954—

INFORME ANUAL, BANCO DE MEXICO. Mexico, D.F. 1, 1926—
   BM 1926—
   EssexU 1—31, 1952. 34, 1955— 44, 1965.

INFORME ANUAL, NACIONAL FINANCIERA (MEXICO). Mexico, D.F.
   Bodl 1962—
   BoLSA 1956—
   UCL 1960 (1961)—

INFORME DEL BANCO NACIONAL DE COMERCIO EXTERIOR (MEXICO). Mexico, D.F.
   EssexU 1951—1953. 1955—1956. 1958—1960. 1963—1964.

INFORME, CAMARA NACIONAL DE COMERCIO DE LA CIUDAD DE MEXICO.
   Mexico, D.F.
INTERCAMBIO. British Chamber of Commerce in Mexico. Mexico, D.F.
   BM 253, 1965—
   BoLSA**
   HispLBC**
   LivPL 1953—

*INVESTIGACION ECONOMICA. Revista trimestral. Escuela Nacional de
   Economia (Mexico). Mexico, D.F. 1, 1941—
   EssexU 24, 1964—

INVESTIGACIONES INDUSTRIALES. Banco de Mexico. Mexico, D.F. No.1, 1950—
   GlasU No. 1—3; 6—11; 18—41; 46—

MEMORIA ANUAL, BANCO DE MEXICO. Mexico, D.F.
   BoLSA 1963—
   IBank (Two year file)

MEMORIA ANUAL, COMISION NACIONAL DE VALORES (MEXICO). Mexico, D.F. 1952—
   EssexU 1964.

MEMORIA DE LABORES, DEPARTAMENTO DE ASUNTOS AGRARIOS Y
   COLONIZACION (MEXICO). Mexico, D.F.
   [A]
   BM 1956/57—
   LdsU 1960—1961
   LSE 1955/56—

MEMORIA DE LABORES DE LA SECRETARIA DE RELACIONES EXTERIORES
   (MEXICO). Mexico, D.F.
   BM 1925—1932; 1938—1959; 1964/65—
   Bodl 1925/26—
   GlasU 1925—1928. 1930—1932.
   RIIA 1925/26. 1929/30. 1942/43.

MEMORIA DE LABORES, SECRETARIA DEL TRABAJO Y PREVISION SOCIAL
   (MEXICO). Mexico, D.F.
   BM 1957—
   UCL 1960 (1961)—

MEMORIA, SECRETARIA DE COMUNICACIONES Y OBRAS PUBLICAS (MEXICO).
Mexico, D.F.
BM   1953– 1963.
Bodl   1954/55–

MEMORIA, SECRETARIA DE COMMUNCACIONES Y TRANSPORTES (MEXICO).
Mexico, D.F.   1958/59–
[A. Report year ends 31/Aug. Prev (?part of) : Memoria, Secretaria de
Communicaciones y Obras Publicas (Mex.)]
BM   1959–
EssexU   1958/59–   1959/60.   1962/31.

MEMORIA, SECRETARIA DE LA ECONOMIA NACIONAL (MEXICO).   Mexico, D.F.
BM   1939/40 – 1954
UCL **

MEMORIA DE LA SECRETARIA DE OBRAS PUBLICAS (MEXICO).   Mexico, D.F. ?
?1958/59– [?Prev part of: Memoria, Secretaria de Communicaciones y Obras
Publicas (Mex.)]
BM   1959/60–

MERCADO DE VALORES.   Seminario de Nacional Financiera (Mexico).   Mexico, D.F.
1, 6/Jan 1941–   ["Analisis semanal de sus fluctuaciones"]
BoLSA **
EssexU *20 (2). 1960–

MEXICAN ECONOMIC PANORAMA.   Banco de Comercio (Mexico).   Mexico, D.F.
[M. Engl. ed. of: Panorama Economico]
BoLSA**
LivPL June 1951–

MEXICO.   Facts, figures, trends. Banco Nacional de Comercio Exterior (Mexico).
Mexico, D.F.   1960–
BoT (Current volume)

MEXICO INFORMA.   (Mexico) Direccion General de Informacion.   Mexico, D.F.
1,   1959–

MEXICO MONTHLY BULLETIN.   Banco de la Ciudad de Mexico.   Mexico, D.F.
1, Sep 1965–
BoLSA

MEXLETTER.   Informadora Mexicana de Comercio y Inversione. Mexico, D.F.
1959–
[M]
BoLSA   7, 1965– 9 (16), 1967.

OFICINAS TECNICAS Y ADMINISTRATIVAS DE LA JUNTA DE GOBIERNO, DE LOS
ORGANISMOS Y EMPRESAS DEL ESTADO (MEXICO). Memoria. (Mexico)
Secretaria del Patrimonia Nacional. Mexico, D.F.
Nacional.   Mexico, D.F.
[Part of series: Talleres Graficos de la Nacion]
LSE   1960–

PANORAMA ECONOMICO.   Banco de Comercio (Mexico).   Mexico, D.F.
[Also in Engl. ed. as: Mexican Economic Panorama]
BoLSA **
HispLBC**
LivPL   June 1951–

PRODUCTIVIDAD. Centro Industrial de Productividad (Mexico). Mexico, D.F.

QUARTERLY ECONOMIC REVIEW: MEXICO. Economist Intelligence Unit. London.
No.1, Feb 1962–
BM
LSE*

REVIEW OF THE ECONOMIC SITUATION OF MEXICO. Banco Nacional de Mexico.
Mexico, D.F. 1929–1931; No.71, 1932–
BM 40 (466), 1964–
EssexU *40 (461), 1964–
LivPL 1952–
NottPL 1963–
RIIA no. 319, 1952–
UCL**

REVISTA DE ADMINISTRACION PUBLICA. Instituto de Administracion Publica (Mexico).
Mexico, D.F. 1, Jan/Mar 1956–
BM 3, J1/S 1956–

REVISTA BANCARIA. Asociacion de Banqueros de Mexico. Mexico, D.F.
UCL**

REVISTA DEL BANCO OBRERO. Banco Nacional Obrero de Fomento Industrial (Mexico).
Mexico, D.F. 1, Dec 1937–

*REVISTA DE ECONOMIA. Frente de Economistas Revolucionarios (Mexico). Mexico,
D.F. [1] (1), Jan/Feb 1937–
[Vol. numbering introduced with ?4. To no. 10/12, 1938 issued by :Sindicato
Nacional de Economistas (Mex.)]
EssexU*

REVISTA DE ECONOMIA HISPANO MEXICANA. Camara Espanola de Comercio y Industria
de Mexico. Mexico, D.F.

REVISTA DE ESTADISTICA (MEXICO). (Mexico) Direccion General de Estadistica.
Mexico, D.F. 1, Mar 1938– ; No.1, 1963–
BM 20, 1957–
BodI 1938–1939
BoT**
EssexU 28, 1965–
LdsU 1(2), 1938–2 (12), 1939. [W 1 (4)]
OxfIES Mar 1950–
RIIA No.1, 1963–
UCL No.1, 1963–

REVISTA DE HACIENDA. Mexico, D.F
BodI 1937–1939.
LdsU 2(3), 1948–4 (22), 1949, [W 3(12)]

REVISTA INDUSTRIAL. (Mexico) Secretaria de la Economia Nacional. Mexico.
D.F. 1, 1933–
BM 4–5, 1933.
BodI 1–5, 1935.

REVISTA DEL ITAT. Instituto Tecnico Administrativo del Trabajo (Mexico).
Mexico, D.F.
BM no 14, 1961–
MarshallL no.15.

98

REVISTA MEXICANA DE SEGURIDAD SOCIAL. Instituto Mexicano del Seguridad Social.
Mexico, D.F. 1, Oct 1953—
[Cover title: Seguridad Social]
LSE 1954—

*REVISTA MEXICANA DE SOCIOLOGIA. Universidad Nacional Autonoma de Mexico;
Instituto de Investigaciones Sociales. Mexico, D.F. 1, 1939—

BM *10 (2), 1948—
Bodl
GlasU 26(3), 1963—
LondU 19(2), 1957—

*REVISTA MEXICANA DEL TRABAJO. (1953) (Mexico) Secretaria del Trabajo y
Prevision Social. Mexico, D.F. 1, May 1953— Dec 1953.
[Called '4 epoca' from prev: Revista del Trabajo. Subs again under above
title, from 1, 1954]

REVISTA MEXICANO DEL TRABAJO. (1954) (Mexico) Secretaria del Trabajo y
Prevision Social. Mexico, D.F. 1(1/2), Jan/Feb 1954—
[Called '5 epoca'. Prev also as above, 1, 1953. Earlier as: Revista del
Trabajo]

BM
LdsU 8 (3), 1961—
UCL**

REVISTA DEL TRABAJO. (1937) (Mexico) Secretaria de Trabajo y Prevision
Social. Mexico, D.F. 1(1), Aug 1937— June/Aug 1948.
[From 2 (1), Feb 1938, issues also numbered consecutively, No.1— 160/161,
May/June 1951. Body varies; to 1940 as: (Mexico) Departmento del
Trabajo. Title varies; as above 1937—1940, and 1947—1948. Jan 1941 as:
Revista del Trabajo y Prevision Social. Feb 1941— Dec 1946 as: Trabajo y
Prevision Social. Subs again under above title, numbered from 1, 1948]

BM *1 (3), Oct 1937—
LivU *1—8, 1940.

REVISTA DEL TRABAJO. (1948) (Mexico) Secretaria del Trabajo y Prevision
Social. Mexico, D.F. T.1, Dep 1948— 6, May/June 1951.
[Prev (see); Revista del Trabajo. (1937). Subs: Revista Mexicana del
Trabajo. (1954)]

REVISTA DEL TRABAJO Y PREVISION SOCIAL. Mexico.
see REVISTA DEL TRABAJO. (1937).

REVISTA, TRIBUNAL FISCAL DE LA FEDERACION (MEXICO). Mexico, D.F.

BM 169, 1951—
Bodl 19 (217), 1955—

SALUBRIDAD Y ASISTENCIA. (Mexico) Secretaria de Salubridad y Asistencia.
Mexico, D.F. 1, 1944— 1948.

BM 1946—1947.
BMA *

SALUD PUBLICA DE MEXICO. (Mexico) Secretaria de Salubridad y Asistencia.
Mexico, D.F. 1, July/Sep 1959—
[Called 'Epoca V' in continuation of earlier publs. of the Secretaria, the
latest being: Salubridad y Asistencia.]

BM 1, 1959—
CambU

SEGURIDAD SOCIAL.   Mexico.
see REVISTA MEXICANA DE SEGURIDAD SOCIAL.

SOCIOLOGIA EN MEXICO.   Seminario Mexicano de Sociologia.   Mexico, D.F.
1, Ap   1951—

TECNICAS FINANCIERAS.   Centro de Estudios Monetarios Latinoamericanos.
Mexico, D.F.   1, ?Sep/Oct   1961—
[2M]

HispLBC**

TEMAS CONTEMPORANEOS.   Instituto de Investigaciones Sociales y Economicas
(Mexico).   Mexico, D.F.   1, 1955—

BoLSA

TRABAJO Y PREVISION SOCIAL.   Mexico.   1941—1946.
see REVISTA DEL TRABAJO.   (1937)

*TRIMESTRE ECONOMICO.   Fondo de Cultura Economico (Mexico).   Mexico, D.F.
1, Jan 1934—
[Suspended Jan-Mar 1938).

BM   18, 1951—
BoLSA   1956—
EssexU *
MarshallL   Nos. 102—106, 108—122.
OxfIES   30, 1963—
RIIA
UCL   29, 1962—

NETHERLANDS ANTILLES

BONAIRE;   IN- EN UITVOER STATISTIEK PER GOEDERENSOORT.

   [A]

   BM 1961—
   BoT 1955—

JAARSTATISTIEK VAN DE IN- EN UITVOER PER GOEDERENSOORT VAN DE
NEDERLANDSE ANTILLEN.

   [A]

   BoT 1953—

JAARSTATISTIEK VAN DE IN- EN UITVOER PER LAND DE NEDERLANDSE
ANTILLEN.

   [A]

   BM 1953—1954; 1961.
   BoT 1953—

KWARTAALSTATISTIEK VAN DE IN- EN UITVOER PER LAND VAN CURACAO
EN ARUBA.

   [Q]

   BM no1, 1960—
   BoT 1954—

MAANDSTATISTIEK VAN DE IN- EN UITVOER PER GOEDERENSOORT VAN
CURACAO EN ARUBA

   [M]

   BM 1954—
   BoT 1954—

STATISTIEK JAARBOEK NEDERLANDSE ANTILLEN.

   BM 1961; 1963—
   BoT 1956—

STATISTISCHE MEDEDELINGEN (NETHERLANDS ANTILLES).

   [M. Also titled in Engl.: Statistical Information]

   BM 1 (7), 1954—
   BoT 1954—/W Ja 1956/—

NICARAGUA

ACTIVIDAD PRESUPUESTARIA EN NICARAGUA.   (Nicaragua)   Direccion General de
    Presupuesto. [Managua]   No.1, [1957/58] —
    LSE

ANUARIO ESTADISTICO (NICARAGUA).   (Nicaragua) Direccion General de Estadistica
    y Censos. Managua.

    BoLSA**

BALANCES CONDENSADOS . . . , BANCO NACIONAL DE NICARAGUA.   Managua.
    [Prev: Estado Condensado . . .]
    BM   Je — D, 1960.

BOLETIN, CAMARA NACIONAL DE COMERCIO E INDUSTRIAS DE MANAGUA.
    Managua. [Q]

BOLETIN, DIRECCION GENERAL DEL PRESUPUESTO (NICARAGUA).   Managua.

    BoLSA**

BOLETIN DE ESTADISTICA (NICARAGUA).   (Nicaragua) Direccion General de Estadistica
    y Censos. Managua.
    BM   1957—1964
    BoLSA**
    BoT 1955—
    UCL**

BOLETIN DE LA SUPERINTENDENCIA DE BANCOS Y DE OTRAS INSTITUCIONES
    (NICARAGUA).   Managua.
    [Pub. for the Superintendencia by: Banco Central de Nicaragua]
    UCL   2 (3), 1963—

CIFRAS Y COMENTARIOS, MINISTERIO DE HACIENDA Y CREDITO PUBLICO
    (NICARAGUA).   Managua.

    BoLSA**

INFORME ANUAL, BANCO CENTRAL DE NICARAGUA.   Managua. 1, 1961—

    BM
    BoLSA
    BoT 1961—

MEMORIA DE AGRICULTURA Y GANADERIA (NICARAGUA).   (Nicaragua)
    Ministerio de Agricultura y Ganaderia. Managua.
    BM   1958/59 — 1959/60.
    UCL 1959/60—

MEMORIA, BANCO CENTRAL DE NICARAGUA.   Managua.

    IBank   (Two year file)

MEMORIA, MINISTERIO DE AGRICULTURA Y GANADERIA.
    see MEMORIA DE AGRICULTURA Y GANADERIA (NICARAGUA).

MEMORIA DE LA RECAUDACION GENERAL DE ADUANAS (NICARAGUA).   Managua.
    1951— [Prev: Memoria del Recaudador General de Aduanas y Alta Comision . . .(Nic);
    from 1934 (1935)]
    BM   1916; 1931; 1933; 1935; 1937; 1939; 1952—1953.
    Bodl
    BoLSA   1957—
    BoT

PRESUPUESTO GENERAL DE INGRESOS Y EGRESOS DE LA REPUBLICA
(NICARAGUA).   (Nicaragua) Direccion General del Presupuesto.   [Managua].
   [A]
   LSE   1958/59—

REPORT ON ECONOMIC CONDITIONS IN NICARAGUA.   (Great Britain) Board of
   Trade; Commercial Relations & Exports Dept.   London.   1927 — 1934;
   1951 -- 1954.

   BM
   BoT

REVISTA TRIMESTRAL DEL BANCO CENTRAL DE NICARAGUA.   Managua.   Ano 1,
   1961—
   BM
   BoLSA **

REVISTA, BANCO CENTRAL DE NICARAGUA.   Managua.

   BoLSA **
   BoT 1953 —

PANAMA

ALLGEMEINE STATISTIK DES AUSLANDES; LANDERBERICHTE; PANAMA.
Wiesbaden.   1966–
BM
LSE

ANUARIO DE COMERCIO EXTERIOR (PANAMA).   (Panama) Contraloria General de la
Republica.   Panama.
BM   1953–1957;   1963.
BoT   1952–1959
UCL**

BALANZA DE PAGOS (PANAMA).
see ESTADISTICA PANAMENA;   SERIE D.

COMERCIO EXTERIOR (PANAMA).
see ESTADISTICA PANAMENA; SERIE K.

ESTADISTICA PANAMENA; SERIE A: DEOMGRAFIA.   Poblacion, migracion, asistencia
social y educacion.   (Panama) Direccion de Estadistica y Censo.   Panama.
BM   1947;   1951;   1959–
BoT   1957–
LSE   1957/58–

ESTADISTICA PANAMENA;   SERIE B;   ESTADISTICAS VITALES.   (Panama) Direccion
de Estadistica y Censo.   Panama.
BM   1958–
LSE   1957–

ESTADISTICA PANAMENA; SERIE C: INGRESO NACIONAL.   (Panama) Direccion de
Estadistica y Censo.   Panama.
BM   1950/58–
BoT   1960–
LSE   1950/58–
UCL **

ESTADISTICA PANAMENA; SERIE D: BALANZA DE PAGOS.   (Panama) Direccion de
Estadistica y Censo.   Panama.
BM   1946/54 – 1955/56.
BoT**
LSE   1954/58–

ESTADISTICA PANAMENA; SERIE E: HACIENDA PUBLICA Y FINANZAS.   (Panama)
Direccion de Estadistica y Censo.   Panama.
BM   ano 18, 1958 – 23, 1963.
LSE   1958   (4 trimestre) –
UCL**

ESTADISTICA PANAMENA; SERIE F: INDUSTRIAS.   (Panama) Direccion de Estadistica
y Censo.   Panama.
BM   18, 1958–
BoT   1958–
LSE   1958–
UCL*

ESTADISTICA PANAMENA; SERIE F1: INDUSTRIAS; ENCUESTA.   (Panama) Direccion
de Estadistica y Censo.   Panama.
BM   1957 – 1960
BoT   1952 – 1960
LSE   1957 (1958) –

ESTADISTICA PANAMENA; SERIE G: PRECIOS Y COSTO DE LA VIDA. (Panama)
Direccion de Estadistica y Censo.   Panama

BM   1957—
BoT   1959—
LSE   1957/58—
UCL   21(3),   1962—

ESTADISTICA PANAMENA; SERIE H: INFORMACION AGROPECUARIA. (Panama)
Direccion de Estadistica y Censo.   Panama.
[A]
BM   1958—
BoT   1955—
LSE   1958—

ESTADISTICA PANAMENA; SERIE H1: INFORMACION AGROPECUARIA.   (Panama)
Direccion de Estadistica y Censo.   Panama.
[M]
BM   19, 1960—
UCL   21(9), 1962—

ESTADISTICA PANAMENA; SERIE I: TRANSPORTES Y COMUNICACIONES. (Panama)
Direccion de Estadistica y Censo.   Panama.

BM   1960—
BoT   1958—
LSE   1958—

ESTADISTICA PANAMENA; SERIE K: COMERCIO EXTERIOR.   (Panama) Direccion de
Estadistica y Censo.   Panama.

BM   1946—
BoT**
LSE   1958 (3° trimestre)—
UCL**

ESTADISTICA PANAMENA; SERIE K1: ANUARIO ESTADISTICO.   (Panama) Direccion
de Estadistica y Censo.   Panama.

BM   1958—
UCL**

ESTADISTICAS VITALES (PANAMA).
see ESTADISTICA PANAMENA; SERIE B.

HACIENDA PUBLICA Y FINANZAS (PANAMA).
see ESTADISTICA PANAMENA; SERIE E.

INFORMACION AGROPECUARIA (PANAMA).
see ESTADISTICA PANAMENA; SERIE H (&) H1.

INFORME ANUAL DE LAS ACTIVIDADES, OFICINA DE REGULACION DE PRECIOS
(PANAMA).   Panama.
[Prev. Resumen de las Labores, . . .]
BM   1960
LSE   1952/3; 1955/6—

INFORME DE CONTROLAR GENERAL DE LA REPUBLICA (PANAMA).   Panama.

BM   1954—1961.
UCL   1961—

INGRESO NACIONAL (PANAMA).
see ESTADISTICA PANAMENA; SERIE C.

MEMORIA, BANCO NACIONAL DE PANAMA.   Panama.

    BM   1965—
    IBank   (Two year file)

MEMORIA DEL MINISTERIO DE AGRICULTURA, COMERCIO E INDUSTRIAS . . .
    (PANAMA).   [Panama]

    BM   1951/1952.
    LSE   1952/3 — 1955/6; 1959/60—

MEMORIA, MINISTERIO DE HACIENDA Y TESORO (PANAMA).   Panama.
    [Actual title: Memoria que el Ministerio . . . presenta a la Honorable
    Asamblea Nacional]

    BM   1959
    UCL   1961— [and Suppl., 1961]

PRECIOS Y COSTO DE LA VIDA (PANAMA)
    see ESTADISTICA PANAMENA; SERIE G.

REPORT ON ECONOMIC CONDITIONS IN PANAMA. (Great Britain) Board of Trade;
    Commercial Relations & Exports Dept. London. 1921— 1937; 1950— 1955.

    BM
    BoT

RESUMEN DE LAS LABORES, OFICINA DE REGULACION DE PRECIOS (PANAMA).
    Panama.   [Subs: Informe Anual de las Actividades, . . .]

PARAGUAY

ANUARIO ESTADISTICO DE LA REPUBLICA DEL PARAGUAY.   (Paraguay) Direccion
General de Estadistica y Censos.   Asuncion.

   BM   1886–1887, 1914–1917, 1954–1959.
   RIIA   1946/47.
   UCL**

BOLETIN ESTADISTICO, BANCO CENTRAL DEL PARAGUAY.   Asuncion.
   [2A]

   BoT**

BOLETIN ESTADISTICO MENSUAL, BANCO CENTRAL DEL PARAGUAY.   Asuncion.
   No.1, 1948–

   BM   1958–
   BOLSA   1958–
   BoT
   RIIA   1956– 1963.
   TropProdI   1963–

BOLETIN ESTADISTICO DEL PARAGUAY.   (Paraguay) Direccion General de Estadistico
y Censos.   Asuncion.   1, 1957–

   BM
   BoLSA
   BoT
   UCL   6(16), 1962–

ENCUESTA INDUSTRIAL (PARAGUAY).   (Paraguay)   Ministerio de
Industria y Comercio; Departamento de Estadistica y Censos.   Asuncion.
   [A]

   BoT
   LSE

MEMORIA, BANCO DEL PARAGUAY.   Asuncion.   1944–

   BoLSA   1956–BM 1963–

PARAGUAY INDUSTRIAL Y COMERCIAL.   Organo oficial del Ministerio de Industria
y Comercio.
   [M]

   BM   1952– 1953, 1966–
   BoLSA   1958–

REPORT ON ECONOMIC CONDITIONS IN PARAGUAY.   (Great Britain) Board of Trade;
Commercial Relations & Exports Dept.   London.   1921 – 1936; 1952

   BM

REVISTA DEL INSTITUTO DE PREVISION SOCIAL.   Asuncion.   NO.1, F 1956–
   [Publicada por el Departamento de Divulgacion y Relaciones Internacionales
   del Instituto . . ."]

   BM   1956– 1959

PERU

ACTIVIDADES PRODUCTIVAS DEL PERU. Analisis y perspectivas. Banco
Central de Reserva del Peru. Lima. 1961—
LSE

ACTUALIDAD ECONOMICA. Bolsa de Comercio de Lima. Lima.
BoLSA**
OxfIES   Mr 1956— Dec 1957.

ALGODON.
BoLSA **
OxfIES Mr 1950— Dec 1956

ALLGEMEINE STATISTIK DES AUSLANDES; LANDERBERICHTE; PERU. Wiesbaden.
1966—
LSE

ANDEAN AIRMAIL & PERUVIAN TIMES.
see PERUVIAN TIMES.

ANUARIO DEL COMERCIO EXTERIOR (PERU).
OxfIES   1930— 1943.

ANUARIO ESTADISTICO DEL PERU. (Peru) Direccion Nacional de Estadistica y Censos.
Lima.   1919—
Guildhall   (Current issue)
RIIA   1953— 1956/57.
UCL**

ANUARIO DE LA INDUSTRIA MINERA DEL PERU.
UCL **   BoT**

BALANCES DE LAS EMPRESAS BANCARIAS Y COMPANIAS DE SEGUROS (PERU)
BoLSA   1953—

BOLETIN DEL BANCO CENTRAL DE RESERVA DEL PERU.   Lima.
BoLSA   1956—
BoT **
EssexU   *27, 1957—
HispLBC**
OxfIES   1937—
RIIA   (Current year)
UCL**

BOLETIN COMERCIAL PERUANO-BRITANICO.
Guildhall   July 1964—
HispLBC**
OxfIES   4(26)   1966—

BOLETIN DEMOGRAFICO MUNICIPAL DE LA CIUDAD DE LIMA.
RSocEdin   *8, 1933— 29, 1939.

BOLETIN DE ESTADISTICA PERUANA. (Peru) Direccion Nacional de Estadistica y
Censos. Lima.   1, 1958—
BhmU   1(2), 1958— 4(5), 1961
BoT**
UCL   RIIA 2(3), 1959; 7(3), 1964.

108

BOLETIN MENSUAL, BANCO CENTRAL DE RESERVA DEL PERU.   Lima.   1, 1931–

BOLETIN DEL MINISTERIO DE TRABAJO Y ASUNTOS INDIGENAS (PERU).   Lima.
   BM   3(7), 1958–

ECONOMIA Y AGRICULTURA.   Asociacion Peruana de Economistas Agricolas.   Lima.
   1(1), Sep/Nov   1963–
   [Q]

ESTADISTICA AGRARIA (PERU).   (Peru) Ministerio de Agricultura.   (&)
   Universidad Agraria,   Lima.   Lima.
   HispLBC**
   UCL   1963 (1964)   –

ESTADISTICA DEL COMERCIO EXTERIOR (PERU).   (Peru) Superintendencia General
   de Aduanas.   Lima.   1904–
   [A]
   BoLSA   1955–
   BoT**
   RIIA   1955.

ESTADISTICA PETROLERA DEL PERU.   (Peru) Direccion de Petroleo.   Lima.
   BoT**
   LSE   4, 1952–

INDUSTRIA PERUANA.   Sociedad Nacional de Industrias (Peru).   Lima.
   1, July 1931–
   BoLSA **
   HispLBC**

INFORMACIONES COMERCIALES (PERU).   (Peru) Direccion General de Comercio.
   Lima.   1, Jan 1950–
   [Jan-July 1950 issued by body under earlier name: (Peru) Direccion de
   Asuntos Comerciales]

MEMORIA Y BALANCE, BANCO DEL CREDITO DEL PERU.   Lima.
   BM   1956–

MEMORIA DEL BANCO CENTRAL DE RESERVA DEL PERU.   [Lima]
   BoLSA   1936–
   BoT**
   EssexU   1954–1955; 1964–
   IBank   (Two year file)
   LivPL   1950–
   OxfIES   1934–
   RIIA   1947–
   UCL   1961–

MEMORIA, BANCO DE FOMENTO AGROPECUARIO DEL PERU.   Lima.
   BoLSA**

MEMORIA Y ESTADISTICA, SUPERINTENDENCIA DE BANCOS (PERU).   Lima.
   BoLSA   1934–

MEMORIA, MINISTERIO DE HACIENDA Y COMERCIO (PERU).   Limd.
   BodI   1949–

109

MERCURIO PERUANO. Revista (mensual) de ciencias sociales y letras.
Lima. 1, July 1918—
[Suspended Sep 1931 — July 1939]

NATIONAL ECONOMIC SITUATION (PERU). Banco de Credito del Peru; Departamento
de Estudios Economicos. Lima. (to July 1961).
[Subs: Peruvian Economic Situation]

NEWSLETTER, BANCO CONTINENTAL (PERU). Lima.
BoLSA**

PERU. Monthly business report.
BoLSA**

PERU. Sintesis economica y financiera. Oficina de Estudios para la
Colaboracion Economica Internacional. Buenos Aires.

PERU IN BRIEF. Banco Popular del Peru. Lima.
BoLSA 1958—

PERUVIAN ECONOMIC SITUATION. Banco de Credito del Peru; Departamento de
Estudios Economicos. Lima.
[Prev: National Economic Situation (Peru); to July 1961]
BoLSA

PERUVIAN TIMES. Lima. 1940—
[W. Cover title: Andean Airmail & Peruvian Times]
BoLSA**

PESCA.

PRECIOS Y INDICES DE PRECIOS PARA EL CONSUMIDOR MEDIO (PERU)
BoLSA**
BoT 1962—

RENTA NACIONAL DEL PERU, Banco Central de Reserva del Peru.
Lima.
[A]
BoLSA 1942/52; 1954—
BoT 1952—1959.
OxfIES 1942/47— 1960.
RIIA 1942/60.

REPORT ON ECONOMIC CONDITIONS IN PERU. (Great Britain) Board of Trade;
Commercial Relations & Exports Dept. London. 1919 — 1937; 1949— 1955.
BoT

REPORT ON THE ECONOMIC SITUATION IN PERU. Banco Continental (Peru). Lima.
BoLSA**
HispLBC**

RESENA ECONOMICA Y FINANCIERA. Banco Central de Reserva del Peru.
Lima.
BoLSA 1 Feb 1965—
HispLBC**

RESUMEN ESTADISTICO DE LA PRODUCCION AGROPECUARIA. (PERU).

BoT   1953; 1955; 1958 — 1959: 1963.

UCL**

*REVISTA DE LA FACULTAD DE CIENCIAS ECONOMICAS Y COMERCIALES,
UNIVERSIDAD NACIONAL MAYOR DE SAN MARCOS DE LIMA.   Lima.
(No.1, Ap 1929)- [Title (and body names) vary: No.1—7, Sep 1929 as: Revista
Economica y Financiera, Parent body orig. as: Universidad de San Marcos de Lima.
Subord. body orig. as: Facultad de Ciencias Economicas.]

LdsU   No.60, 1959—
StAndU   Nos. 2—3, 1929.
SheffU   No.60, 1959— 61, 1960; No.64, 1962—

REVISTA MENSUAL, CAMARA DE COMERCIO DE LIMA.   Lima.

BoLSA**

SINTESIS SEMANAL, CORPORACION DE COMERCIANTES DEL PERU.

BoLSA**

SITUACION BANCARIA (PERU).   (Peru) Superintendencia de Bancos. Lima.

BoLSA**
UCL   1962—

SITUACION ECONOMICA NACIONAL (PERU). Banco de Credito del Peru; Departamento
de Estudios Economicos. Lima.
[M]

PUERTO RICO

AGRICULTURA AL DIA. (Puerto Rico) Department of Agriculture and
Commerce. San Juan. 1, July 1954—

   BM   no1, 1958—

ANNUAL REPORT, PUERTO RICO INDUSTRIAL DEVELOPMENT COMPANY. San Juan.

   LSE   (18th) 1960—

ANNUAL STATISTICAL REPORT OF EDA MANUFACTURING PLANTS (PUERTO RICO).
Economic Development Administration (Puerto Rico). [San Juan]

   LSE   [4th]   1958/9—

CENSUS OF MANUFACTURING INDUSTRIES OF PUERTO RICO. (Puerto Rico)
Bureau of Labor Statistics. [San Juan]
[Title also in Span.: Censo de Industrias Manufactureras de Puerto
Rico]

   BM   1957—
   BoT   1955—
   Guildhall   (Current issue only)
   LSE   1957—

EMPLOYMENT, HOURS & EARNINGS IN THE MANUFACTURING INDUSTRIES IN
PUERTO RICO. (Puerto Rico) Bureau of Labor Statistics. San Juan.
[Also titled in Span.: Empleo, Horas y Salarios en las Industrias
Manufactureras de Puerto Rico]

   BM   1954—
   BoT   1953/55—

EMPLOYMENT, HOURS & EARNINGS IN NON-MANUFACTURING INDUSTRIES IN
PUERTO RICO. (Puerto Rico) Bureau of Labor Statistics. San Juan.
[Title varies slightly; also in Span.: Empleo, Horas y Salarios en
Industrias No-manufactureras en Puerto Rico]

   BM   1955—
   LSE   1958—

REVISTA DE AGRICULTURA DE PUERTO RICO. San Juan.

   BM   46 (2),   1959—
   MinAg   42—
   Rothamsted   37 (1)—
   SL   17 (2)

VENTAS AL POR MAYOR DE PRODUCTOS DEL PAIS EN LOS CINCO PRINCIPALES
MERCADOS DE PUERTO RICO. (Puerto Rico) Department of Agriculture &
Commerce. Santurce. 1959—60/1960—61—

   LSE

EL SALVADOR

AGRICULTURA EN EL SALVADOR. (Salvador) Ministerio de Agricultura y
Ganaderia. San Salvador. 1, Jan/Feb 1960—

Bm 1961—
UCL Ano 3/4, Aug 1963—

ALLGEMEINE STATISTIK DES AUSLANDES; LANDERBERICHTE; EL SALVADOR.
Wiesbaden. 1965—

BM
LSE 1965—

ANUARIO ESTADISTICO (SALVADOR). (Salvador) Direccion General de Estadistica
y Censos. San Salvador.
BM 1911—1914; 1916—1919; 1934—1936; 1947—
BoLSA 1946—
BoT**
Guildhall (Current issue)
HispLBC**
RIIA 1947/8; 1954/5; 1958—1959; 1961 (Vol.1.)

BOLETIN ESTADISTICO (SALVADOR). (Salvador) Direccion General de Estadistica
y Censos. San Salvador.
BM 1953-1954; 1960—
BoLSA 1957—
BoT 1952—*
HispLBC**
TropProdI 1958—
UCL No.50, 1961—

BOLETIN GRAFICO, CAMARA DE COMERCIO E INDUSTRIA DE EL SALVADOR.
San Salvador. No.1, 1964—

BOLETIN INFORMATIVO, INSTITUTO SALVADORENO DE INVESTIGACIONES
DEL CAFE. Santa Tocla.
[M]
BM 1963—
EMall No.32, 1962. No.35, 1962—
TropProdI *1959—

CARTA INFORMATIVA PARA LOS SOCIOS. Camara de Comercio e Industria de el
Salvador. San Salvador.

BoLSA**

CARTILLA ECONOMICA (SALVADOR). Consejo Nacional de Planificacion y
Coordinacion Economica (Salvador). San Salvador. No.1, Jan 1963—
LSE

COMERCIO EXTERIOR (SALVADOR). (Salvador) Direccion General de Estadistica
y Censos. San Salvador.
[2/A]
BM 1953—1954; 1958.
BoT 1952— *
UCL 1961—

COSTO Y CONDICIONES DE VIDA EN SAN SALVADOR. (Salvador) Direccion General
de Estadistica y Censos. San Salvador.
BM 1954.

ECONOMIA SALVADORENA. Universidad Nacional de el Salvador; Instituto
de Estudios Economicos. San Salvador. 1, 1952—
["Revista de la Facultad de Economia". Name of parent body varies:
Universidad Autonoma . . .]

    BM   13 (29), 1964—
    BodI   5 (3/4), 1956—
    UCL**

INDUSTRIA. Asociacion Salvadorena de Industriales. San Salvador.

    BoLSA**

MEMORIA, BANCO CENTRAL DE RESERVA DE EL SALVADOR. San Salvador.

    BM   1941—
    BoLSA 1938—
    HispLBC**
    IBank (Two year file)
    LivPL 1950—
    RIIA   1948— 1963.

MEMORIA, BANCO HIPOTECARIO DE EL SALVADOR. San Salvador.

    BM   1960—
    BoLSA **

MEMORIA, INSTITUTO DE COLONIZACION RURAL (SAN SALVADOR). San Salvador.
    [A]

    LSE   1961—

MEMORIA (DE LAS) LABORES DESARROLLADAS POR EL RAMO DE TRABAJO Y
PREVISION SOCIAL . . . (SALVADOR). (Salvador) Ministerio de Trabajo y Prevision.
Social. San Salvador.

    BM   1952/3.
    LSE   1958/9—
    UCL**

MEMORIA DE LAS LABORES DESARROLLADAS POR EL INSTITUTO SALVADORENO
DE FOMENTO DE LA PRODUCCION. San Salvador. 1, 1956—

    UCL   1960   (1961)—

PROGRAMA BIENAL DE INVERSIONES PUBLICAS (SALVADOR). Consejo Nacional de
Planificacion y Coordinacion Economica (Salvador). San Salvador.
    1st,   1964/65—

    BoT   (Current volume)

REPORT ON ECONOMIC CONDITIONS IN EL SALVADOR. (Great Britain) Board of
Trade; Commercial Relations & Exports Dept. London.   1929— 1938;
1951— 1953.

    BM
    BoT

REVISTA DE ECONOMIA DE EL SALVADOR.   Universidad Nacional de el Salvador;
Instituto de Estudios Economicos. San Salvador.

    BM   1950; 1955— 1958
    BoLSA **

REVISTA MENSUAL DEL BANCO CENTRAL DE RESERVA DE EL SALVADOR.
San Salvador.
BM   1967—
BoLSA   1957—
BoT   1958— 1959*;   1960—
HispLBC**
RIIA   (Current year)

SALVADOR EN GRAFICAS.
BM   1966—
BoLSA **
BoT 1956—
HispLBC**

SURINAM

BEDRIJFS- EN BEROEPSTELLING (SURINAM). (Surinam) Algemeen Bureau voor de Statistiek. Paramaribo.
[Also titled in Engl.: Census of Industries and Occupations. Also numbered in general series "Suriname in Cijfers"; e.g., 1961 (1962) = No.20 of general series]

    BoT   1961 (1962)—

JAARCIJFERS VOOR SURINAME. (Surinam) Algemeen Bureau voor de Statistiek. Paramaribo. 1956/60—
[Also titled in Engl.: Statistical Year Book of Suriname]

    BoT   1956/60; 1958/62.
    LSE

MAANDSTATISTIEK VAN DE IN- EN UITVOER PER GOEDERENSOORT EN PER LAND (SURINAM)

    BoT   1961—1963

STATISTISCHE BERICHTEN VAN HET ALGEMEEN BUREAU VOOR DE STATISTIEK (SURINAM). Paramaribo.

    BoT   1956—

SURINAME IN CIJFERS. (Surinam) Algemeen Bureau voor de Statistiek. Paramaribo.

    BoT   (occasional copies kept)

VERSLAG, CENTRALE BANK VAN SURINAME. Paramaribo.   [A]

    BoT   1957—

TRINIDAD & TOBAGO

ANNUAL REPORT, AGRICULTURAL CREDIT BANK OF TRINIDAD & TOBAGO.
Port of Spain.

LondICS   1951—

ANNUAL REPORT, TOURIST BOARD (TRINIDAD & TOBAGO). [Port of Spain]
1958—

BM   1953;   1958.
LSE

ANNUAL RETURNS, PETROLEUM ASSOCIATION (TRINIDAD & TOBAGO).

BoT   1958—1962.

ANNUAL STATISTICAL DIGEST (TRINIDAD & TOBAGO). (Trinidad & Tobago) Central
Statistical Office.   Port of Spain.   No.1, 1935—

BM   1960—
Bodl
BoT**
LondICS   1935— 1951; 1954—

BALANCE OF PAYMENTS OF TRINIDAD & TOBAGO. (Trinidad & Tobago) Central
Statistical Office.   Port of Spain.   1951/59—

LSE

CLASSIFIED LIST OF ACCESSIONS, WEST INDIA REFERENCE COLLECTION, CENTRAL
LIBRARY SERVICES (TRINIDAD & TOBAGO).   Port of Spain.   No.1, Sep 1965—

LondICS

ECA NEWS.   Employers Consultative Association of Trinidad & Tobago.
Port of Spain.   [M]

LondICS   No.11, Nov 1965—

ECONOMIC TRENDS (TRINIDAD & TOBAGO).   (Trinidad & Tobago) Central Statistical
Office.   Port of Spain   1(1), Ap 1958—

BM
Bodl
BoT   1958—1963.
LondICS   1(11), Nov, 1958—

ENTERPRISE.   Trinidad Chamber of Commerce.   Port of Spain.
[Q]

LondICS   2(1), Dec. 1963—

GOVERNMENT REPORTS.   A summary of weekly broadcasts. (Trinidad & Tobago)
Office of the Prime Minister.   Port of Spain.
[W]

LondICS   No.7. Jan 1965—

INTERNATIONAL TRAVEL REPORT (TRINIDAD & TOBAGO). (Trinidad & Tobago)
Central Statistical Office.   Port of Spain.

BM   1961/62.
Bodl   1956—
BoT   1957—1962.
LondICS   1964 (6) —

JOURNAL OF THE AGRICULTURAL SOCIETY OF TRINIDAD & TOBAGO. Port of
Spain.
LondICS   63(4), Dec 1963–

LIST OF PUBLICATIONS CATALOGUED, LIBRARY, INDUSTRIAL DEVELOPMENT
CORPORATION (TRINIDAD & TOBAGO).   Port of Spain.

LondICS (Current year only)

NATIONAL INCOME (TRINIDAD & TOBAGO)
BoT   1952–1962.
LondICS   1951/4.

OBSERVER. Organ of Indian opinion.   Port of Spain.
[M]
LondICS   23(1), Jan 1964–

OVERSEAS TRADE (TRINIDAD & TOBAGO); ANNUAL REPORT. (Trinidad & Tobago)
Central Statistical Office.   Port of Spain.
BM   1951–2954; 1960–
Bodl   1951–
BoT**
LondICS   1951–

OVERSEAS TRADE (TRINIDAD & TOBAGO); MONTHLY REPORT. (Trinidad & Tobago)
Central Statistical Office.   Port of Spain.
BM   1(9), 1951–
Bodl   1(4),   1951–
BoT**
LondICS   (issues retained only until annual vol. received)

POPULATION & VITAL STATISTICS (TRINIDAD & TOBAGO).   Annual report. (Trinidad
& Tobago) Central Statistical Office.   Port of Spain.
BM   1888; 1892–1918; 1920; 1923–1931; 1947–1957.
LondICS   1961/2.

QUARTERLY ECONOMIC REPORT (TRINIDAD & TOBAGO).   (Trinidad & Tobago)
Central Statistical Office.   Port of Spain.   No.1, Ap/June 1950–

BM * 1954–
Bodl   *1951–
BoLSA**
BoT**
LondICS   1950–

REPORT ON THE ADMINISTRATION OF THE CUSTOMS & EXCISE DEPARTMENT
(TRINIDAD & TOBAGO).   Port of Spain.
BM
Bodl   1928–
BoT   1954–1959.
LondICS   1947–

REPORT ON THE MANPOWER SITUATION IN TRINIDAD & TOBAGO. (Trinidad &
Tobago)   Ministry of Labour, Co-operative Development & Social Dervices.
[Port of Spain]   No.1, Mar 1959–
BM
LondICS
LSE

REPORT ON THE NATIONAL INCOME OF TRINIDAD & TOBAGO.   (Trinidad & Tobago)
Central Statistical Office.   Port of Spain.
LondICS   1951/4–

RESEARCH PAPERS, CENTRAL STATISTICAL OFFICE (TRINIDAD & TOBAGO). Port of Spain. No.1, Dec 1963–

    LondICS

SPECTATOR. A monthly journal published in Trinidad. [?Port of Spain]

    LondICS   Mar/Ap 1965–

TEXACO CARIBBEAN. Texaco (Trinidad) Inc. Pointe-a-Pierre, Trin. 1961–
[Prev) 1, 1958–2, 1959 as: Texaco Trinidad News. Then   1960–
Aug 1961 as: Texaco-Trinidad Quarterly. Then as above]

    LondICS   9(1), Aug 1966–

TEXACO TRINIDAD NEWS. Texaco (Trinidad) Inc. Pointe-a-Pierre, Trin. 1,1958– 2, 1959 . . .
[Subs: Texaco–Trinidad Quarterly]

TEXACO-TRINIDAD QUARTERLY. Texaco (Trinidad) Inc. Pointe-a-Pierre, Trin. 3, 1960–   Aug 1961 . . .
[Prev: Texaco Trinidad News. Subs: Texaco Caribbean]

TGG REVIEW. T.Geddes Grant Ltd. Port of Spain.

    LondICS   No.583, Jan 1966–

(TRINIDAD & TOBAGO). Report. (Great Britain) Colonial Office / Commonwealth Office. London.

    BM
    HullU   1949 – 1957.
    LondICS   1933– 1938; 1946– 1957.

TRINIDAD & TOBAGO INDEX. Georgetown, Guyana (etc). No.1, Summer 1965–
["An informal review of social history and research". Published by Dr. Ivar Oxaal, No.1 in Davis, Calif. (Univ. of California; Dept. of Anthropology), No.2. in Hull (Univ. of Hull; Dept. of Sociology), and from no.3 in Georgetown (Univ. of Guyana; Dept. of Sociology)]

    LondICS
    LSE

TRINIDAD & TOBAGO TODAY. (Trinidad & Tobago) Central Statistical Office. Port of Spain. No.1, May 1966–
["A graphic presentation of social and economic statistics"]

    LondICS

TRINIDAD & TOBAGO TRADE DIRECTORY.

    HullU   1963– 1964.

TRINIDAD & TOBAGO YEAR BOOK. Port of Spain.   1865–

    BelfU   1959/60–
    BoT
    LondICS   1950– 1956; 1959/60–

VANGUARD. The voice of labour. Oilfields Workers Trade Union (Trinidad & Tobago). San Fernando, Trin. No.1, 30/Ap 1965–
[W]

    LondICS

WE THE PEOPLE.   St. Barataria, Trin.   1(1), 15/June 1965—

LondICS

[Also the following, available at the Board of Trade Library, not in published form: Monthly and quarterly returns of imports and exports by direction; Monthly return of statistics: imports of textiles]

URUGUAY

ALLGEMEINE STATISTIK DES AUSLANDES; LANDERBERICHTE; URUGUAY.
Wiesbaden. 1966—

    BM
    LSE

ANUARIO ESTADISTICO DE LA REPUBLICA ORIENTAL DEL URUGUAY. (Uruguay)
Direccion General de Estadistica y Censos. Montevideo.

    BM   1884; 1902, 1921; 1927; 1929 — 1937; 1939; 1960—
    Bodl   1902—1918.
    BoLSA   1915—1917; 1931—1932.
    RIIA 1944 (Vol.1); 1941—43 (Vol.2).
    StAndU   19(1); 20(1); *21.

BOLETIN DEL BANCO HIPOTECARIO DEL URUGUAY.

    BM   1884 — 1939
    UCL **

BOLETIN INFORMATIVO, MINISTERIO DE GANADERIA Y AGRICULTURA
(URUGUAY),

    UCL **

BOLETIN MENSUAL DEL BANCO DE LA REPUBLICA ORIENTAL DEL URUGUAY.
Montevideo.   1942—
[Issued by the Banco's Depto. de Investigaciones Economicas. Subtitled:
Seleccion de temas economicos]

    BM   247/248   1963—
    Bodl   11(129), 1953—
    BoLSA**
    LivPL   1955—
    UCL**

BOLETIN URUGUAYO DE SOCIOLOGIA.   Montevideo.   1(1),   June 1961—

    BM   5, 10/11 1966—
    LSE   1(2), 1961—

INFORME ANUAL, CAMARA NACIONAL DE COMERCIO (URUGUAY).   Montevideo.
1919 (1920)—

MEMORIA Y BALANZA GENERAL, BANCO DE LA REPUBLICA ORIENTAL DEL
URUGUAY. Montevideo.

    BM   1940—1941; 1950—1961.
    Bodl   1945—
    BoLSA   1936—
    OxfIES   1937; 1938; 1940—1942.
    RIIA.   1961.

MONTHLY BULLETIN, ASSOCIATION FOR THE DEVELOPMENT OF ANGLO-
URUGUAYAN TRADE   Montevideo.   1, 1941—
[Name of body in Spanish: Asociacion de Fomento del
Intercambio Comercial Anglo-Uruguayo]

    Bodl   54, 1955 — 200, 1958. (Also Spanish ed.)
    BoT   1952—*
    LondU   7 (76), 1947—

MONTHLY BULLETIN, BRITISH CHAMBER OF COMMERCE IN URUGUAY. Montevideo.

    BoLSA**
    HispLBC**
    LivPL   1951—

RECOPILACION ESTADISTICA (URUGUAY). (Uruguay) Direccion General de
    Estadistica y Censos. Montevideo.
    ["Extracto del Mensaje del Poder Ejecutivo a la Asamblea General"]

    LSE   T.2. 1958—   BoT**

REPORT ON ECONOMIC & FINANCIAL CONDITIONS IN URUGUAY. (Great Britain)
    Board of Trade; Commercial Relations & Exports Dept. London. 1921—1935;
    1950—1954.

    BM
    BoT

RESUMEN MENSUAL DE IMPORTACION DE LA REPUBLICA ORIENTAL DEL
    URUGUAY.
    BoT 1957.

RESUMEN DE LOS PRINCIPALES ASPECTOS DE LA ACTIVIDAD ECONOMICA DEL
    URUGUAY. Asociacion de Bancarios del Uruguay.Montevideo.

    BM   1962—
    BoLSA   1956—
    UCL   1961   (1962)—

REVISTA DEL BANCO DE LA REPUBLICA ORIENTAL DEL URUGUAY. Montevideo.
    1, 1942—

    BM   73, 1960—89, 1965
    Bodl*
    BoLSA   1957—
    BoT 1954—
    HispLBC*
    LivPL   1951—1957.

REVISTA DE ECONOMIA.   Montevideo.   1(1), Aug/Sep 1947—

    LSE   No.1 — 51/52, June/Dec 1958.

REVISTA DE ECONOMIA, FINANZAS Y ADMINISTRACION. Asociacion Nacional de
    Contadores y Peritos Mercantiles del Uruguay. Montevideo. 1, 1942—
    [Q: sometimes 3/A]

    LSE   1— 17, 1958; 18 (numero especial), 1959.

REVISTA ECONOMICA; SUPLEMENTO ESTADISTICO. Banco de la Republica Oriental
    del Uruguay. Montevideo. Vol.1/2, 1942/44—

    BM   1960—
    BoLSA   1957—
    BoT**
    LivPL   1952—
    UCL**

REVISTA DE LA FACULTAD DE CIENCIAS ECONOMICAS Y ADMINISTRACION . . . ,
UNIVERSIDAD DE LA REPUBLICA (URUGUAY).   Montevideo.
  [Actual title: Rev. Fac. Ciencias Econ. y Admin. de Montevideo]

  BM 9, 1956; 16, 1959 — 22, 1963.
  EssexU   no.20, 1962 — 25, 1965.
  IChartAccScot   no.20, 1962—

VENEZUELA

ACTIVIDADES PETROLERAS (VENEZUELA). (Venezuela) Ministerio de Minas e
Hidrocarburos. Caracas.

BM   1966–
BodI   3(65), 1951– 5 (107), 1953.

ALGUNOS ASPECTOS DE LAS ACTIVIDADES PETROLERAS VENEZOLANAS Y
MUNDIALES. (Venezuela) Ministerio de Minas e Hidrocarburos; Division
de Economia Petrolera. Caracas.
[A]

LSE   1961–

ANUARIO ESTADISTICO AGROPECUARIO (VENEZUELA). (Venezuela) Ministerio de
Agricultura y Cria. Caracas.

LSE   2, 1962–

ANUARIO ESTADISTICO DE VENEZUELA.

BM 1877; 1894, 1908–1912; 1938; 1942; 1944 – 1956; 1964–
BodI 1948
BolSA   1950–
BoT   1953–1963; 1965–
EssexU   1950– 1952.
Guildhall   (Current issue)
HispLBC**
RIIA   1951– 1955/56.

ANUARIO PETROLERO Y MINERO DE VENEZUELA. (Venezuela) Ministerio de Minas e
Hidrocarburos. Caracas.
[As above from 1952 (1957). Prev: Anuario Petrolero de Venezuela. Above
also titled in English: Venezuelan Petroleum & Minerals Yearbook]

BANCOS DE FOMENTO REGIONAL (VENEZUELA). Corporacion Venezolana de
Fomento. Caracas.
[2/A]

LSE   1956 (1957)–

BOLETIN DEL BANCO CENTRAL DE VENEZUELA. Caracas.

BoLSA   1956– 1957.

BOLETIN, CAMARA DE COMERCIO DE CARACAS. Caracas.
[M]

BOLETIN, CAMARA DE COMERCIO DE MARACAIBO. Maracaibo.

BOLETIN DE COMERCIO EXTERIOR (VENEZUELA). (Venezuela) Direccion General de
Estadistica. Caracas. 1, 1959–
[M]

BM   1, 1959–8, 1966
BoLSA
BoT   1959– (1963–1964*)
HispLBC**
LSE
OxfIES   6 (36), 1964–
UCL

124

BOLETIN DE ECONOMIA Y FINANZAS.   Banco de Venezuela. Caracas.
[M]

BOLETIN INDIGENISTA VENEZOLANO. Comision Indigenista (Venezuela). Caracas.
1, Jan/Mar 1953–
BM
Bodl
UCL

BOLETIN INDUSTRIAL.   (Venezuela) Direccion de Industrias.   Caracas
[M]
BoLSA **

BOLETIN INFORMATIVO DE COMISION DE ESTUDIOS FINANCIEROS Y
ADMINISTRATIVOS. (Venezuela) Ministerio de Hacienda. Caracas.
BM no 80, 1947 – 138, 1962.
MancU *No.84, 1947–

BOLETIN INTERNO, BANCO CENTRAL DE VENEZUELA.   Caracas.
                   [Subs: Boletin Mensual, . . .]
BoLSA   Jan 1957 – June 1958.
LivPl   1951–
OxfIES   Jan 1954– Dec 1955.

BOLETIN MENSUAL, BANCO CENTRAL DE VENEZUELA.   Caracas.
                                    [Prev: Boletin Interno, . . .]
BM 1960–
BoLSA   July 1958–

BOLETIN MENSUAL DE ESTADISTICA (VENEZUELA).   (Venezuela) Direccion General
de Estadistica.   Caracas.
BM   1(1), 1941 – 7 (6), 1947; 10 (12) 1950–
BoLSA
BoT   1952–*
HispLBC**
RIIA
TropProdl   1960.
UCL

BOLETIN DEL MINISTERIO DE SANIDAD Y ASISTENCIA SOCIAL (VENEZUELA).
Caracas. 1, Mar 1936– 4, 1939 . . .
[Subs: Revista de Sanidad y Asistencia Social]
RSM

BOLETIN DE PRECIOS DE PRODUCTOS AGROPECUARIOS (VENEZUELA); SERIE 3:
MONOGRAFIA DE PRECIOS. (Venezuela) Direccion de Economia y
Estadistica Agropecuaria. Caracas.
[M]
LSE   No.42, 1962–

BOLETIN DE LA PROPRIEDAD INDUSTRIAL Y COMERCIAL.

BM   1956–1961; 1966–
Bodl   *71, 1937– 138, 1943.
UCL**

BULLETIN ECONOMIQUE, MISSION DU VENEZUELA AUPRES DE LA COMMUNAUTE
ECONOMIQUE EUROPEENNE.   [?Brussels]

LSE   No.2, Sep 1964–
NCL   No.2 as specimen issue.

125

CARTA SEMANAL, MINISTERIO DE MINAS E HIDROCARBUROS (VENEZUELA).
Caracas.
BM 9, 1966–
BoLSA **
BoR 1959–

CARTA DE VENEZUELA. (Venezuela) Oficina Central de Informacion. Caracas.
BM 1966–
BoLSA 1, 25 Jan 1965–

COMERCIO EXTERIOR DE VENEZUELA. (Venezuela) Direccion de Comercio Exterior
y Consulados, Caracas. 1, 1962–
[M]
BM 3(3), 1964–
HispLBC**
LSE 1(2), 1962. 1(6), 1962–
NLS 3(5), 1964–
OxfIES 2, 1963–

CUADERNOS CVF. Corporacion Venezolana de Fomento. Caracas.
1, Nov/Dec 1961–
[Prev: Cuadernos de Informacion Economica. Subs: Cuadernos de la CVF]
BM 3–6, 1962.
BodI*
LivPL 1962.

*CUADERNOS DE LA CVF. Corporacion Venezolana de Fomento. Caracas.
1(1), Ap/June 1964–
[First issue called "Ano 1, Vol. 1, no.1". Prev: Cuadernos CVF]
BM
LivPL

CUADERNOS DE INFORMACION ECONOMICA. Corporacion Venezolana de Fomento.
Caracas. 1, July 1949– 12(1), May 1961.
[Issues for 1949 actually titled: Cuadernos de Informacion Economica
Venezolana. Suspended 1960– Ap 1961. Subs: Cuadernos CVF]
BM 3, 1951 – 11, 1959.
BodI *2, 1950–
LivPL 1955– 1958.
UCL**

CUADERNOS DE LA SOCIEDAD VENEZOLANA DE PLANIFICACION. Caracas.
[M]
LSE 2(1), 1963–

CVF. Boletin de la Corporacion Venezolana de Fomento. Caracas. 1952–
BM 22, 1956–27, 1957; 1, 1958; 5, 1961.
LivPL *1955–
MarshallL No.1.

*ECONOMIA Y CIENCIAS SOCIALES. Revista de la Facultad de Economia de la
Universidad Central de Venezuela. Caracas. 1, Sep 1958–
BM 1(1), 1958; 5(4), 1963; 6(1–4), 1964.
LdsU 5, 1963–
MarshallL 5(4), 1963.
SouU 6, 1964–
126

ESTUDIOS PRELIMINARES SOBRE INDUSTRIAS (VENEZUELA). Corporacion Venezolana
de Fomento.   Caracas.   No.1, 1960–
[Subs in (2S) of above title]
Bodl
GlasU   No.5, 1960–

ESTUDIOS PRELIMINARES SOBRE INDUSTRIAS (VENEZUELA); (2S).   Corporacion
Venezolana de Fomento; Subgerencia de Servicios Tecnicos.   Caracas.
No.1, 1963–
BM

INFORMACIONES DE VENEZUELA. (Venezuela) Oficina Central de Coordinacion y
Planificacion.   Caracas.   No.1, Jan 1961–
BM   no2, 1961.

INFORME ECONOMICO . . . , BANCO CENTRAL DE VENEZUELA.   Caracas.   1962
[1963] – [Actual title: Informe Economico Correspondiente al ano (date). Prev:
Memoria del Banco . . . , ? 1940– 1961]
BoLSA
BM   1941–
HispLBC**

INFORME, SUPERINTENDENCIA DE BANCOS (VENEZUELA).   Caracas.

BM   1958.
BoLSA   1950–

INMIGRACION (VENEZUELA).   (Venezuela) Ministerio de Agricultura y Cria.
Caracas.
[2/A]
LSE   1963–

LETTER FROM VENEZUELA.   Caracas.

BM   1965–
EssexU   4, 1966–

MEMORIA, BANCO CENTRAL DE VENEZUELA.   Caracas.

BM   1941–
BoLSA   1940–
BoT   1952–1954; 1956–1959.
HispLBC**
IBank (Two year file)
RIIA   1949–1962.
UCL   1962 [1963] –

MEMORIA Y CUENTO, CORPORACION VENEZOLANA DE FOMENTO. Caracas.

BM   1873–1878; 1894; 1896; 1898; 1909; 1918; 1921–1923; 1929–1939; 1947/48.
1953/54–
Bodl * 1937–
BoLSA 1956–
GlasU *1948–
RIIA   1948/9; 1949/50; 1953/4– 1958/9; 1963–
UCL**

MEMORIA Y CUENTO, MINISTERIO DE AGRICULTURA Y CRIA (VENEZUELA).
Caracas.
BM   1937–1940; 1944–1948; 1955; 1957–
Bodl 1962–   (Memoria only?)
HispLBC**
UCL   1960 (1961)–

127

MEMORIA Y CUENTO, MINISTERIO DE FOMENTO (VENEZUELA). Caracas.

BM
GlasU   (Memoria: 1955: Cuento: 1954—5)

PETROLEO Y OTROS DATOS ESTADISTICOS.   (Venezuela) Ministerio de Minas e
Hidrocarburos; Division de Economia Petrolera.   Caracas.
[A]
BM   1964
LSE   [4th] , 1962—

QUARTERLY ECONOMIC REVIEW; VENEZUELA.   Economist Intelligence Unit.
London.   No.1, Ap 1960—
[Prev part of: Q. Econ. Rev.; Colombi a, Venezuela]
BM
LSE*

REPORT ON ECONOMIC CONDITIONS IN VENEZUELA. (Great Britain) Board of
Trade; Commercial Relations & Exports Dept. London.   1921— 1935;
1951—1954.
BM
BoT

REVIEW, AMERICAN CHAMBER OF COMMERCE IN VENEZUELA.   Caracas.
[M]

REVISTA DEL BANCO CENTRAL DE VENEZUELA.   Caracas.

BM   1941—
BoLSA   1958—
HispLBC**
OxfIES   25 (239—241), 1965—
RIIA   (Two year file)
UCL**

*REVISTA DE ECONOMIA LATINOAMERICANA.   Banco Central de Venezuela.
Caracas.   1, June 1961—
[Publ. under the auspices of the Banco]
BM
LSE

REVISTA DE FOMENTO.   (Venezuela) Direccion de Gabinete. Caracas.
[Direccion part of Ministerio de Fomento]
BM   1938—1956
BodI   13 (74), 1951—

REVISTA DE HACIENDA.   (Venezuela) Ministerio de Hacienda.   Caracas
BM   12, 1947
HispLBC**
LondU   12(25), 1947—

REVISTA DE SANIDAD Y ASISTENCIA SOCIAL. (Venezuela) Ministerio de Sanidad
y Asistencia Social.   Caracas.   5, 1940— 24, 1959 . . .
[Prev: Boletin del Ministerio . . . , from 1, 1936. Subs: Revista Venezolana
de Sanidad y Asistencia Social]
BM   1944—
BMA *
BrU
LivU
RSM*
128

REVISTA SHELL. Shell Caribbean Petroleum Co. Caracas. 1(1), Jan 1952–
11(45), Dec 1962.//

BM
BodI   3(12), 1954–
HispLBC**

REVISTA DEL TRABAJO. (Venezuela) Ministerio del Trabajo. Caracas.

UCL**

REVISTA VENEZOLANA DE SANIDAD Y ASISTENCIA SOCIAL. (Venezuela) Ministerio
de Sanidad y Asistencia Social. Caracas.   25, Mar 1960–
[Prev: Revista de Sanidad y Asistencia Social]

BM
LivU   *1960–1961.
RSM

REVISTA VENEZOLANA DE SOCIOLOGIA Y ANTROPOLOGIA. Caracas.   1, 1960–

RAnthroI

VENEZUELA UP-TO-DATE. (Venezuela) Embassy: United States. Washington, D.C.
1, Dec 1949–

BoLSA**
HispLBC**
RIIA

VENEZUELAN ECONOMIC REVIEW.

BoLSA 4 (14), 6 Ap. 1959–

VENEZUELAN PETROLEUM & MINERALS YEARBOOK.
see ANUARIO PETROLERO Y MINERO DE VENEZUELA.

WINDWARD ISLANDS

[Dominica; Grenada; St. Lucia; St. Vincent]

ANNUAL OVERSEAS TRADE REPORT . . . (DOMINICA).   (Dominica) Treasury
　　Dept. Roseau. 1952—
　　[Prev: Import and export statistics for the year . . . , to 1951]

　　BM
　　Bodl
　　BoT
　　LondICS

ANNUAL OVERSEAS TRADE REPORT (GRENADA)
　　St.George's Gren.

　　BM   1959—
　　Bodl   1949—
　　BoT**
　　LondICS   1948—
　　TropProdl 1958—

ANNUAL REPORT ON VITAL STATISTICS . . . (DOMINICA).   (Dominica) Registrar
　　General's Dept. (St.Lucia).

　　BM   1936; 1945—1957.
　　BoT**
　　LondICS   1947— 1952; 1954—

ANUAL TRADE REPORT (ST.VINCENT). (St.Vincent) Customs Dept.
　　Kingstown.   1954—
　　[Prev: Imports and exports; to 1953]

　　BM   1959—
　　Bodl
　　BoT
　　LondICS
　　LSE   1960—

BULLETIN, STATISTICAL UNIT (GRENADA).   St.George's, Gren.
　　[Q]

　　Bodl   1960 (1)—
　　LondICS   1963 (1—3); 1965 (1)—
　　TropProdl   1961—

(DOMINICA). Report. (Great Britain) Colonial Office / Commonwealth
　　Office.   London.

　　BM
　　HullU   1949/50—
　　LondICS   1947—1952; 1953/4—

(GRENADA). Report. (Great Britain) Colonial Office / Commonwealth
　　Office. London.

　　BM
　　HullU   1948/9—
　　LondICS   1935— 1938; 1948—

(GRENADA / CARRIACOU).   Report.   (Great Britain) Commonwealth Office.
　　London.

　　LondICS   1961—

130

IMPORTS & EXPORTS (ST. VINCENT). (St.Vincent) Customs Dept. [Kingstown]
                – 1953.
    [Subs: Annual Trade Report]
    BoT**
    LondICS   1947

IMPORT & EXPORT STATISTICS FOR THE YEAR . . . (DOMINICA). (Dominica)
    Treasury Dept. [Roseau]   – 1951
    [Subs: Annual Overseas Trade Report]
    BoT   1951.   BM   1946–
    LondICS   1950–

JOURNAL OF THE DOMINICA CHAMBER OF COMMERCE.   Roseau.
    [Q]
    LondICS   2, Nov   1963–

JOURNAL OF THE ST. VINCENT CHAMBER OF COMMERCE.
    see ST. VINCENT CHAMBER OF COMMERCE JOURNAL.

MONTHLY OVERSEAS TRADE REPORT (DOMINICA).   (Dominica) Treasury Dept.
    Roseau.
    BoT   1958 – Je 1960.

OVERSEAS TRADE REPORT (ST. LUCIA).   (St.Lucia) Statistical Unit.
    Castries.   No.1, Jan 1960–   [Q]
    LSE

OVERSEAS TRADE OF ST. LUCIA.   (St.Lucia) Statistical Unit.   Castries.
    1960–   [A]
    BM   1960
    Bodl
    LondICS
    LSE

OVERSEAS TRADE (ST. LUCIA); MONTHLY REPORT.
    BoT   Ja 1960.

QUARTERLY DIGEST OF STATISTICS (ST.LUCIA.)   (St.Lucia) Statistical Unit.
    Castries.   No.1, Nov 1959–
    Bodl   No.1, 1959– 2, 1960.
    BoT   1959–1960.
    LSE

QUARTERLY DIGEST OF STATISTICS (ST. VINCENT).
    Bodl   1, Nov   1959–
    BoT   1959–
    TropProdl   1961–

QUARTERLY OVERSEAS TRADE REPORT (GRENADA).
    St.George's.
    BM   1957–
    Bodl   Jan 1959–
    BoT**
    LondICS   (Quarterly issues kept only till annual cumulation received)
    TropProdl   1957–

QUARTERLY OVERSEAS TRADE REPORT (ST. VINCENT)
    BM   1965–
    Bodl   Jan 1957–
    BoT   1957–
    TropProdl   1957–

REPORT OF THE ACCOUNTANT GENERAL (ST. VINCENT).   Kingstown.

>BM   1945—
>LondICS   1963 (1965)—

REPORT OF THE CUSTOMS & EXCISE DEPARTMENT . . . (ST. LUCIA).   Castries.

>[Actual title continues: . . . of the Customs, Revue, Imports and Exports,
>Balance of Trade.   A.   Subs: Overseas Trade of St.Lucia]
>BM   1951—
>Bodl   1962—
>BoT   1954—
>LondICS   1951—

REPORT OF THE REGISTRAR OF CO-OPERATIVE SOCIETIES (ST. VINCENT).
[Kingstown]   June 1958/Dec 1959—

>BM   1958—
>LondICS   1962—
>LSE

REPORT OF THE SENIOR AUDITOR ON THE AUDIT OF THE ACCOUNTS (ST.VINCENT)
(St.Vincent) Audit Dept.   Kingstown.

>BM   1963—1964.
>LondICS   1963—

REPORT ON THE WORKING OF THE INLAND REVENUE DEPARTMENT (ST.VINCENT).
Kingstown.   1959—
[A]

>LSE

(ST.LUCIA). Report.   (Great Britain) Colonial Office / Commonwealth Office.
London.

>BM   1946 — 1964.
>HullU   1946/7; 1949/50—
>LondICS   1933— 1938; 1946— 1952; 1953/54—

ST.LUCIA YEARBOOK.   Castries.   1, 1964—

>LondICS

(ST.VINCENT). Report. (Great Britain) Colonial Office / Commonwealth
Office.   London.
BM   1946 — 1963.
HullU   1949—
LondICS   1933— 1938; 1946— 1949; 1950/51—

ST. VINCENT CHAMBER OF COMMERCE JOURNAL.   Kingstown.   1(1), 1964—
[Q]

>LondICS   [W 1(2)]

TRADE ACCOUNT (ST.LUCIA).
[M]

>BM   1953—1955
>BoT   1956—1959

WINBAN NEWS.   Windward Islands Banana Growers Association.   Castries.
1(1), Jan 1965—
[Vol. 1 publ. 2M. Publ. Q from Vol.2]

>LondICS

132

WINDWARD ISLANDS ANNUAL.   Crawley Down.   1955—

    BM   1955—1963; 1965.
    LondICS   9, 1964—

[Also available in BOT Library, not in published form: (Grenada) Monthly
return of statistics: imports of textiles.   (St.Vincent) Monthly return
of statistics: imports of textiles; Sugar statistics]

INDEX OF SPONSORING BODIES

ACADEMIA DE CIENCIAS ECONOMICAS (Buenos Aires).
— Anales de la Academia . . .
— Bibliotheca de la Academia . . .

AGRICULTURAL CREDIT BANK OF TRINIDAD & TOBAGO.
— Annual Report, . . .

AGRICULTURAL DEVELOPMENT CORPORATION (JAMAICA).
— Report . . .

AGRICULTURAL SOCIETY OF TRINIDAD & TOBAGO.
— Journal of the Agricultural Society . . .

ALALC.
    see ASOCIACION LATINOAMERICANA DE LIBRE COMERCIO.

ALLIANCE FOR PROGRESS INFORMATION TEAM.
— Alliance for Progress Weekly Newsletter.
— Provisional Listing of Alliance for Progress Projects.

AMERICAN BRAZILIAN ASSOCIATION.
— Brazil.

AMERICAN CHAMBER OF COMMERCE IN RIO DE JANEIRO.
— Brazilian Business.

AMERICAN CHAMBER OF COMMERCE IN SAO PAULO.
— Brazilian Newsletter.

AMERICAN CHAMBER OF COMMERCE IN VENEZUELA.
— Review, . . .

AMERICAN UNIVERSITIES FIELD STAFF.
— Letters and Reports from Foreign Countries; [various series]

(ANTIGUA) SOCIAL WELFARE DEPARTMENT.
— Social Welfare Report (Antigua).

ANTIGUA TRADES & LABOUR UNION.
— Workers' Voice.

(ARGENTINA) CONTADURA GENERAL DE LA NACION.
— Memoria de la Contadura . . .

(ARGENTINA) DIRECCION GENERAL DE AGRICULTURA Y DEFENSA AGRICOLA.
— Boletin de Produccion y Fomento Agricola.

(ARGENTINA) DIRECCION GENERAL IMPOSITIVA.
— Boletin de la Direccion . . .

(ARGENTINA) DIRECCION GENERAL DE YACIMIENTOS PETROLIFEROS FISCALES.
— Boletin de Informaciones Petroleras.

(ARGENTINA) DIRECCION NACIONAL DE ESTADISTICA Y CENSOS.
— Anuario del Comercio Exterior de la Republica Argentina.
— Anuario Estadistico de la Republica Argentina.
— Boletin de Estadistica (Argentina).
— Boletin Mensual de Estadistica (Argentina).
— Comercio Exterior (Argentina).
— Comercio Minorista, Precios al por Mayor (Argentina).
— Costo de Vida, Precios Minoristas, Salarios Industriales (Argentina).
— Edificacion (Argentina).
— Embarcaciones de Bandera Argentina en Navigacion Comercial.
— Estadistica Industrial (Argentina).
— Informe, . . .
— Intercambio Comercial Argentino con los Paises de la A.L. de L.C.
— Navegacion Comercial Argentina.
— Sintesis Estadistica Mensual de la Republica Argentina.

(ARGENTINA) DIRECCION NACIONAL DE TURISMO.
— Estadistica sobre Transito Turistico (Argentina).

(ARGENTINA) MINISTERIO DE AGRICULTURA; Direccion de Estadistica.
— Informaciones Estadisticas Agropecuarias (Argentina).

(ARGENTINA) MINISTERIO DE AGRICULTURA Y GANADERA DE LA NACION.
— Memoria, . . .

(ARGENTINA) MINISTERIO DE ASUNTOS AGRARIOS.
— Agro.

(ARGENTINA) MINISTERIO DE COMERCIO.
— Revista del Comercio Exterior Argentino.

(ARGENTINA) MINISTERIO DE COMERCIO Y INDUSTRIA.
— Memoria . . .

(ARGENTINA) MINISTERIO DE EDUCACION NACIONAL.
— Boletin de Comunicaciones.

(ARGENTINA) MINISTERIO DE HACIENDA.
— Boletin, . . .
— Memoria, . . .

(ARGENTINA) MINISTERIO DE OBRAS PUBLICAS.
— Memoria, . . .

(ARGENTINA) MINISTERIO DE SALUD PUBLICA DE LA NACION.
— Boletin Administrativo del Ministerio . . .

(ARGENTINA) MINISTERIO DE TRABAJO Y PREVISION DE LA NACION.
— Memoria, . . .

(ARGENTINA) MINISTERIO DE TRABAJO Y SEGURIDAD SOCIAL.
— Boletin del Trabajo.
— Revista del Ministerio . . .

(ARGENTINA) SECRETARIA DE TRABAJO Y PREVISION.
— Revista del Trabajo y Prevision.

ASOCIACION ARGENTINA DE CIENCIA POLITICA.
— Revista Argentina de Ciencia Politica

ASOCIACION DE BANCARIOS DEL URUGUAY.
— Resumen de los Principales Aspectos de la Economia del Uruguay.

ASOCIACION DE BANQUEROS DE MEXICO.
— Anuario Financiero de Mexico.
— Revista Bancaria.

ASOCIACION DEL CONGRESO PANAMERICANO DE FERROCARRILES.
— Boletin de la Comision Permanente, . . .

ASOCIACION DE DIRIGENTES DE VENTAS DE BUENOS AIRES.
— Panorama de la Economia Argentina.

ASOCIACION LATINOAMERICANA DE LIBRE COMERCIO.
— ALALC Boletin.
— ALALC Sintesis Mensual.
— Libre Comercio.
— Informativo ALALC.

ASOCIACION NACIONAL DE CONTADORES Y PERITOS MERCANTILES DEL URUGUAY.
— Revista de Economia, Finanzas y Administracion.

ASOCIACION NACIONAL DE HACENDADOS DE CUBA.
— Cubazucar.

ASOCIACION NACIONAL DE IMPORTADORES Y EXPORTADORES DE LA REPUBLICA MEXICANA.

135

- Comercio Internacional.
- Comercio Mundial.

ASOCIACION NACIONAL DE INDUSTRIA (HONDURAS).
- Industria.

ASOCIACION PERUANA DE ECONOMISTAS AGRICOLAS.
- Economia y Agricultura.

ASOCIACION SALVADORENA DE INDUSTRIALES.
- Industria.

ASOCIACION DE TECNICOS AZUCAREROS DE CUBA.
- Boletin Oficial, . . .

ASSOCIACAO COMERCIAL E FEDERACAO DAS INDUSTRIAS DO ESTADO DE PARANA.
- Parana Economica.

ASSOCIACAO COMERCIAL DO PARANA.
- Folha do Comercio.

ASSOCIACAO COMERCIAL DE SAO PAULO.
- Digesto Economico.

ASSOCIATION FOR THE DEVELOPMENT OF ANGLO-URUGUAYAN TRADE.
- Monthly Bulletin, . . .

BANCO AGRICOLA DE LA REPUBLICA DOMINICANA.
- Boletin Estadistico, . . .

BANCO DO BRASIL.
- Arquivos Economicos.
- Boletin Trimestrial, . . .
- Boletim da Carteira de Exportacao e Importacao (Brazil).
- Comercio Internacional.
- Relatorio, . . .
- Resenha Economica Mensal, . . .

BANCO CENTRAL DE BOLIVIA.
- Boletin (Mensual) del Banco . . .
- Boletin del Banco . . .; Suplemento Estadistico.
- Memoria Anual del Banco . . .

BANCO CENTRAL DO BRASIL.
- Boletim do Banco . . .

BANCO CENTRAL DE CHILE.
- Balanza de Pagos de Chile.
- Boletin Mensual del Banco . . .
- Memoria Anual, . . .

BANCO CENTRAL DEL ECUADOR.
- Boletin del Banco . . .
- Comercio Exterior Ecuatoriano.
- Memoria del Gerente General del Banco . . .

BANCO CENTRAL DE HONDURAS.
- Boletin Mensual del Banco . . .
- Memoria, . . .
- Revista Trimestral del Banco . . .

BANCO CENTRAL DE NICARAGUA.
- Informe Anual, . . .
- Memoria, . . .
- Revista, . . .

136

BANCO CENTRAL DEL PARAGUAY.
— Boletin Estadistico Mensual, . . .

BANCO CENTRAL DE LA REPUBLICA ARGENTINA.
— Boletin Estadistico, . . .
— Memoria Anual, . . .
— Revista del Banco . . .
— Revista Economica, . . .
— Revista Economica, . . .; Suplemento Estadistico.

BANCO CENTRAL DE LA REPUBLICA DOMINICANA.
— Informe Economico, . . .
— Memoria, . . .

BANCO CENTRAL DE RESERVA DEL PERU.
— Actividades Productivas del Peru.
— Boletin del Banco . . .
— Boletin Mensual, . . .
— Memoria del Banco . . .
— Renta Nacional del Peru.
— Resena Economica y Financiera, . . .

BANCO CENTRAL DE RESERVA DE EL SALVADOR.
— Memoria, . . .
— Revista Mensual del Banco . . .

BANCO CENTRAL DE VENEZUELA.
— Boletin del Banco . . .
— Boletin Interno, . . .
— Boletin Mensual, . . .
— Informe Economico, . . .
— Memoria, . . .
— Revista del Banco . . .
— Revista de Economia Latinoamericana .

BANCO CENTROAMERICANO DE INTEGRACION ECONOMICA.
— Memoria de Labores, . . .

BANCO DE LA CIUDAD DE MEXICO.
— Mexico Monthly Bulletin.

BANCO DE COLOMBIA.
— Informe Referente, . . .
— Newsletter, . . .

BANCO DE COMERCIO (MEXICO).
— Mexican Economic Panorama.
— Panorama Economico.

BANCO CONTINENTAL (PERU).
— Newsletter, . . .
— Report on the Economic Situation in Peru.

BANCO DE CREDITO DEL PERU.
— Memoria y Balance, . . .
— National Economic Situation (Peru).
— Peruvian Economic Situation.
— Situacion Economica Nacional (Peru).

BANCO DE FOMENTO AGROPECUARIO DEL PERU.
— Memoria, . . .

BANCO HIPOTECARIO NACIONAL (ARGENTINA).
— Memoria Anual, . . .

BANCO HIPOTECARIO DE EL SALVADOR.
— Memoria, . . .

BANCO HIPOTECARIO DEL URUGUAY.
— Boletin del Banco . . .

BANCO DE MEXICO.
— Bibliografia Economica de Mexico.
— Informe Anual, . . .
— Investigaciones Industriales (Mexico).
— Memoria Anual, . . .

BANCO DE MEXICO; Biblioteca.
— Boletin Bibliografico, Biblioteca, Banco de Mexico.

BANCO MINERO DE BOLIVIA.
— Memorias Anuales, . . .

BANCO DE LA NACION ARGENTINA.
— Memoria y Balance General, . . .
— Revista del Banco . . .

BANCO NACIONAL DE COMERCIO EXTERIOR (MEXICO).
— Comercio Exterior (Mexico).
— Comercio Exterior (Mexico); (English Edition).
— Comercio Exterior (Mexico); International Air Mail Edition.
— Informe del Banco . . .
— Mexico. Facts, Figures, Trends.

BANCO NACIONAL DE CREDITO EJIDAL (MEXICO).
— Boletin de Estudios Especiales, . . .

BANCO NACIONAL DE CUBA.
— Legislacion Bancaria y Economico—Financiera (Cuba).
— Memoria Anual, . . .
— Revista del Banco . . ..

BANCO NACIONAL DO DESENVOLVIMENTO ECONOMICO (BRAZIL).
— Revista do BNDE.

BANCO NACIONAL DE FOMENTO (ECUADOR).
— Informe Anual de Labores, . . .

BANCO NACIONAL DE FOMENTO (HONDURAS).
— Memoria, . . .

BANCO NACIONAL HIPTECARIO URBANO Y DE OBRAS PUBLICAS (MEXICO).
— Estudios, . . .

BANCO NACIONAL DE MEXICO.
— Annual Report, . . .
— Examem de la Situacion Economica de Mexico.
— Review of the Economic Situation of Mexico.

BANCO NACIONAL DE NICARAGUA.
— Balances Condensados, . . .

BANCO NACIONAL OBRERO DE FOMENTO INDUSTRIAL (MEXICO).
— Revista del Banco Obrero.

BANCO NACIONAL DE PANAMA.
— Memoria, . . .

BANCO DEL PARAGUAY.
— Memoria, . . .

BANCO POPULAR DEL PERU.
— Peru in Brief.

BANCO DE LA PROVINCIA DE BUENOS AIRES.
— Boletin Informativo, . . .

BANCO DE LA PROVINCIA DE CORDOBA (ARGENTINA).
— Revista de Economia.

BANCO DE LA REPUBLICA ARGENTINA.
— Boletin Bibliografico, . . .

BANCO DE LA REPUBLICA DE COLOMBIA.
- Annual Report, . . .
- Archivo de la Economia Nacional (Colombia).
- Disposiciones Economicas (Colombia).
- Informe Anual, . . .
- Revista del Banco . . .

BANCO DE LA REPUBLICA ORIENTAL DEL URUGUAY.
- Boletin Mensual del Banco . . .
- Memoria y Balanza General, . . .

BANCO DE VENEZUELA.
- Boletin de Economia y Finanzas.

BANK OF JAMAICA.
- Annual Report, . . .
- Bulletin, . . .
- Report & Statement of Accounts, . . .

BANK OF LONDON & SOUTH AMERICA.
- Bank and Public Holidays in South & Central America.
- BOLSA Review.
- Fortnightly Review, . . .
- Quarterly Review, . . .
- Report of the Directors [and Statement of Accounts] , . . .
- Review by the Chairman, . . .

BANQUE FRANCAISE ET ITALIENNE POUR L'AMERIQUE DU SUD.
- Evolution de l'Economie des Pays Sud—Americains.

BANQUE NATIONALE DE LA REPUBLIQUE D'HAITI.
- Rapport Annuel du Departement Fiscal, . . .

BARBADOS CHAMBER OF COMMERCE.
- Commercial Journal.
- Journal, . . .

(BARBADOS) COMPTROLLER OF CUSTOMS.
- Administration Report of the Comptroller . . .
- Report on Revenue, Trade and Shipping (Barbados).

BARBADOS EMPLOYERS' CONFEDERATION.
- Monthly Newsletter, . . .

BARBADOS LABOUR PARTY.
- Beacon.

(BARBADOS) STATISTICAL SERVICE.
- Abstract of Statistics (Barbados).
- Census of Tourism (Barbados).
- Overseas Trade (Barbados).
- Overseas Trade Quarterly Report (Barbados).
- Quarterly Digest of Statistics (Barbados).

(BOLIVIA) DIRECCION NACIONAL DE ESTADISTICA Y CENSOS.
- Anuario Demografico (Bolivia).
- Anuario Industrial (Bolivia).
- Balanza Comercial de Bolivia; Comercio Exterior
- Comercio Exterior (Bolivia).
- Indice del Costo de Vida en las Ciudades de La Paz, Cochabamba, Oruro.
- Suplemento Estadistico (Bolivia).

(BOLIVIA) SECRETARIA GENERAL DE LA PRESIDENCIA DE LA REPUBLICA.
- Gaceta Oficial de Bolivia.

BOLSA DE COMERCIO DE BUENOS AIRES.
- Boletin de la Bolsa . . .
- Memoria Correspondiente al Ejercicio, . . .

BOLSA DE COMERCIO DE LIMA.
— Actualidad Economica.

BOLSA DE MERCADORES DA BAHIA.
— Exportacao de Produtos do Estado da Bahia.

BOLSA DE VALORES DO RIO DE JANEIRO.
— Bolsa.

(BRAZIL) CONTADORIA GERAL DA REPUBLICA.
— Boletim da Contadoria . . .

(BRAZIL) DEPARTAMENTO ADMINISTRATIVO DO SERVICO PUBLICO.
— Revista do Servico Publico.

(BRAZIL) DEPARTAMENTO NACIONAL DA PRODUCAO MINERAL.
— Publicacao Especial, . . .
(BRAZIL) EMBASSY: GREAT BRITAIN.
— Brazilian News.

(BRAZIL) EMBASSY: UNITED STATES.
— Survey of the Brazilian Economy.

(BRAZIL) MINISTERIO DE AGRICULTURA.
— Boletim do Ministerio . . .

(BRAZIL) MINISTERIO DA FAZENDA.
— Borracha.
— Relatorio, . . .
— Revista de Financas Publicas (Brazil).

(BRAZIL) MINISTERIO DAS RELACOES EXTERIORES.
— Brasil.
— Brazil.

(BRAZIL) MINISTERIO DE SAUDE.
— Boletim de Bioestadistica e Epidemiologia (Brazil).

(BRAZIL) MINISTERIO DO TRABALHO, INDUSTRIA E COMERCIO.
— Boletim do Ministerio . . .
(BRAZIL) MINISTERIO DA VIACAO E OBRAS PUBLICAS.
— Boletim do Informacoes, . . .
— Brasil Constroi.

(BRAZIL) SERVICO DE ESTATISTICA ECONOMICA E FINANCEIRA.
— Comercio Exterior do Brasil.
— Estatistica do Comercio Exterior (Brazil).
— Mensario Estatistico, . . .
— Movimento Bancario do Brasil.

(BRAZIL) SERVICO DE ESTATISTICA DA PRODUCAO.
— Carnes, Derivados e Subprodutos.
— Oleos e Gorduras Vegetais (e Subprodutos).
— Pecuario e Avicultura, Apicultura e Sericicultura.
— Pesca.
— Previsao Agricola.
— Producao Agricola.
— Producao Animal.
— Producao Mineral.

(BRAZIL) SERVICO FEDERAL DE BIOESTATISTICA.
— Boletim Mensal do Servico . . .

(BRAZIL) SERVICO SOCIAL DOS MENORES.
— Boletim do Servico . . .

(BRAZIL) SUPERINTENDENCIA DA MOEDA E DO CREDITO.
— Boletim SUMOC.

(BRAZIL) SUPERINTENDENCIA DOS SERVICOS DO CAFE.
— Boletim da Superintendencia . . .

BRAZILIAN CHAMBER OF COMMERCE & ECONOMIC AFFAIRS IN GREAT BRITAIN.
- Annual Report, . . .
- Brazil Journal.
- Journal of the Brazilian . . .

BRAZILIAN GOVERNMENT TRADE BUREAU IN GREAT BRITAIN.
- Brazil, Land and People.
- Brazilian Bulletin.

BRITISH CHAMBER OF COMMERCE IN THE ARGENTINE REPUBLIC.
- Monthly Journal, . . .
- Weekly Letter, . . .

BRITISH CHAMBER OF COMMERCE IN BRAZIL.
- Comentario Comercial Anglo-Brasileiro.
- Monthly Bulletin, . . .
- Weekly Supplement of the British . . .

BRITISH CHAMBER OF COMMERCE (MEXICO).
- Intercambio.

BRITISH CHAMBER OF COMMERCE OF SAO PAULO & SOUTHERN BRAZIL.
- Sao Paulo Information Circular.

BRITISH CHAMBER OF COMMERCE IN URUGUAY.
- Monthly Bulletin, . . .

(BRITISH GUIANA)
     see also (GUYANA)

(BRITISH GUIANA) CONTROLLER OF CUSTOMS & EXCISE.
- Annual Report of the Controller . . .

(BRITISH GUIANA) DEPARTMENT OF CUSTOMS & EXCISE.
- Annual Account Relating to External Trade (British Guiana).
- Monthly Account relating to External Trade (British Guiana).

(BRITISH HONDURAS) DEPARTMENT OF CUSTOMS.
- Trade Report (British Honduras).

(BRITISH HONDURAS) DEPARTMENT OF INFORMATION.
- Belize Weekly Newsletter.

(BRITISH HONDURAS) MINISTRY OF FINANCE & DEVELOPMENT.
- Annual Abstract of Statistics (British Honduras).
- Supplementary Abstract of Statistics (British Honduras).

(BUENOS AIRES) POLICIA DE LA CAPITAL FEDERAL.
- Boletin de Estadistica (y Jurisprudencia).

CAJA DE CREDITO AGRARIO (COLOMBIA).
- Carta Agraria.

CAJA DE CREDITO AGRARIO INDUSTRIAL (COLOMBIA).
- Informe del Gerente de la Caja . . .

CAJA NACIONAL DE AHORRO POSTAL (ARGENTINA).
- Ahorro y Seguro.

CAJA NACIONAL DE SEGURIDAD SOCIAL (BOLIVIA).
- Seguridad Social.

CAMARA ARGENTINA DE COMERCIO
- Mercurio.

CAMARA ARGENTINA DE SOCIEDADES ANONIMAS.
- Edocamer.

CAMARA DE COMERCIO ARGENTINO-ALEMANA.
— Boletin de la Camara . . .

CAMARA DE COMERCIO DE BARRANQUILLA.
— Boletin Semanal, . . .

CAMARA DE COMERCIO DE CARACAS.
— Boletin, . . .

CAMARA DE COMERCIO E INDUSTRIA DE EL SALVADOR.
— Boletin Grafico, . . .
— Carta Informativa para los Socios.

CAMARA DE COMERCIO DE LIMA.
— Revista Mensual . . .

CAMARA DE COMERCIO DE MARACAIBO.
— Boletin, . . .

CAMARA DE COMERCIO DE LA REPUBLICA DE CUBA.
— Cuba Economic News.
— Cuba Foreign Trade.

CAMARA ESPANOLA DE COMERCIO Y INDUSTRIA DE MEXICO.
— Revista de Economia Hispano Mexicana.

CAMARA DE EXPANSAO ECONOMICA DO PARANA.
— Parana.   Boletim da Camara . . .

CAMARA NACIONAL DE COMERCIO DE LA CIUDAD DE MEXICO.
— Boletin de la Camara . . .
— Boletin Quincenal, . . .
— Comercio.
— Informe, . . .

CAMARA NACIONAL DE COMERCIO E INDUSTRIAS DE MANAGUA.
— Boletin, . . .

CAMARA NACIONAL DE COMERCIO (URUGUAY).
— Informe Anual, . . .

CAMPANHA NACIONAL DE APERFEICOAMENTO DE PESSOAL DE NIVEL
SUPERIOR (BRAZIL).
— Capes
— Serie Estudos e Ensaios, . . .
— Serie Levantamentos e Analises, . . .

CARIBBEAN COMMISSION.
— Caribbean.
— Caribbean Economic Review.
— Caribbean Market Survey.
— Caribbean Statistical Digest.
— Commodity Bulletin. = Bulletin du Commerce.
— Current Caribbean Bibliography.
— Year Book of Caribbean Research.

CARIBBEAN COMMISSION; Committee on Agriculture, Nutrition, Fisheries &
Forestry.
— Crop Enquiry Series.
— Fisheries Series.

CARIBBEAN COMMISSION; Library.
— Selective List of Recent Additions, Library, Caribbean Commission.

CARIBBEAN CONGRESS OF LABOUR.
— Caribbean Labour.
— CCL Newsletter.

CARIBBEAN ORGANIZATION.
— Caribbean
— Caribbean Agriculture.

- Inter-Caribbean Trade Statistics. = Statistiques du Commerce Intercaraibe.
- Caribbean Plan; Annual Report.
- Co-operative Nesletter.
- Selective List of Recent Additions to the Library, . . .

CARIBBEAN ORGANIZATION; Clearing House on Trade & Tourism Information.
- Clearing House on Trade and Tourism Information Monthly Journal.
- Clearing House on Trade and Tourism Information Weekly.

CARIBBEAN REGIONAL LIBRARY.
- Accessions List, . . .
- Selective List of Recent Additions to the Library.

CARIBBEAN SOCIALIST PARTY.
- Caribbean Socialists' Review.

CARIBBEAN WORKERS: MOVEMENT.
- Carib.
- Caribbean Workers' Weekly.

CEMLA
see CENTRO DE ESTUDIOS MONETARIOS LATINOAMERICANOS.
CENTRAL LIBRARY SERVICES (TRINIDAD & TOBAGO);
- Classified List of Accessions, West India Reference Collection.

CENTRALE BANK VAN SURINAME.
- Verslag, . . .

CENTRO DE ESTUDIOS ARGENTINOS.
- Cuadernos, . . .

CENTRO DE ESTUDIOS ECONOMICO SOCIALES (ARGENTINA).
- Dinamica Social.

CENTRO DE ESTUDIOS MONETARIOS LATINAMERICANOS.
- Aspectos Financieros de las Economias Latinoamericanas.
- Aspectos Monetarios de las Economias Latinoamericanas.
- Boletin Quincenal, . . .
- CEMLA Boletin Mensual.
- Tecnicas Financieras.

CENTRO E FEDERACAO DAS INDUSTRIAS DO ESTADO DE SAO PAULO.
- Boletim Informativo do Centro . . .

CENTRO INDUSTRIAL DE PRODUCTIVIDAD (MEXICO).
- Productividad.

CENTRO DE INVESTIGACIONES PESQUERAS (CUBA).
- Boletin de Divulgacion Tecnica (Cuba).

CENTRO LATINO-AMERICANO DE PESQUISAS EM CIENCIAS SOCIAIS.
- America Latina.
- Bibliografia, . . .
- Boletim do Centro . . .

CENTRO NACIONAL DE ESTUDOS COOPERATIVOS (BRAZIL).
- Arco Iris.

CENTRO DE PESQUISAS DO CACAU (Itabuna).
- Cacau Atualidades.

CHAMBER OF COMMERCE (BRITISH HONDURAS).
- Chamber of Commerce (British Honduras) Bulletin.

CHAMBER OF COMMERCE OF THE CITY OF GEORGETOWN.
- Commercial Review.   [Varies]

CHAMBER OF COMMERCE FOR LATIN AMERICA (New York).
- Inter-American Foreign Trade.

CHAMBER OF COMMERCE OF THE UNITED STATES OF AMERICA IN THE

ARGENTINE REPUBLIC.
— Comments on Argentine Trade.

CHAMBRE DE COMMERCE ARGENTINE-FRANCE.
— France-Argentine.

CHAMBRE DE COMMERCE FRANCE-AMERIQUE LATINE.
— Bulletin, . . .
— Circulaire, . . .

CHAMBRE DE COMMERCE ET D'INDUSTRIE DE LA MARTINIQUE.
— Bulletin, . . .

CHASE MANHATTAN BANK.
— Latin American Business Highlights.

CHASE NATIONAL BANK.
— Noticias Economicas Interamericanas.

(CHILE) CONTRALORIA GENERAL DE LA REPUBLICA.
— Memoria de la Contraloria . . .

(CHILE) DIRECCION DE ESTADISTICA Y CENSOS.
— Sintesis Estadistica (Chile).

(CHILE) DIRECCION GENERAL DE ESTADISTICA.
— Boletin Estadistico (Chile).
— Estadistica Chilena.

(CHILE) DIRECCION GENERAL DE PRODUCCION AGRARIA Y PESQUERA.
— Agricultura y Ganaderia.

(CHILE) SERVICIO DE SEGURO SOCIAL.
— Estadisticas, Servicio . . .

(CHILE) SUPERINTENDENCIA DE BANCOS.
— Estadistica Bancaria (Chile).

CLUBE DE ECONOMISTAS.
— Economica Brasileira.

COCOA INDUSTRY BOARD (JAMAICA).
— Report, . . .

COCOA MARKETING BOARD (JAMAICA).
— Report, . . .

COCONUT INDUSTRY BOARD (JAMAICA).
— Report of the Research Department, . . .

COLEGIO DE ECONOMISTAS DE MEXICO.
— Economista Mexicano.

(COLOMBIA) CONTRALORIA GENERAL DE LA REPUBLICA.
— Economia Colombiana.
— Informe Financiero del Contralor General (Colombia).

(COLOMBIA) DEPARTAMENTO ADMINISTRATIVO NACIONAL DE ESTADISTICA.
— Anuario de Comercio Exterior (Colombia).
— Anuario Estadistico (Colombia).
— Anuario General de Estadistica de Colombia.
— Boletin Mensual de Estadistica (Colombia).
— Economia y Estadistica (Colombia).

(COLOMBIA) MINISTERIO DE AGRICULTURA.
— Memoria de Ministerio . . .

(COLOMBIA) MINISTERIO DE HACIENDA.
— Memoria de Hacienda (Colombia).

(COLOMBIA) MINISTERIO DE MINAS Y PETROLEOS.
— Boletin de Petroleos (Colombia).

144

(COLOMBIA) SUPERINTENDENCIA BANCARIA.
– Boletin, . . .
– Informe, . . .
– Informe Anual, . . .

COMISION INDIGENISTA (VENEZUELA).
– Boletin Indigenista Venezolano.

COMISION INTERAMERICANA DE MUJERES.
see INTER-AMERICAN COMMISSION OF WOMEN.

COMISION NACIONAL BANCARIA (MEXICO).
– Boletin Estadistico, . . .

COMISION NACIONAL DE VALORES (ECUADOR).
– Informe del Gerente, . . .

COMISION NACIONAL DE VALORES (MEXICO).
– Boletin Mensual de la Comision . . .
– Memoria Anual, . . .

COMISSAO DE DESENVOLVIMENTO ECONOMICO DE PERNAMBUCO.
– Boletim Informativo da Codepe.

COMISSAO EXECUTIVA DE DEFESA DA BORRACHA (BRAZIL).
– Anuario de Estatistica e Informacoes, . . .
– Boletim de Estatistica e Informacoes, . . .
– Informacoes Trimestrais, . . .

COMISSAO DE PLANEJAMENTO ECONOMICO DO ESTADO DA BAHIA.
– Boletim de CPE.

COMMITTEE FOR NATIONAL RECONSTRUCTION (GUYANA).
– Simara.

COMPANHIA SIDERURGICA NACIONAL (BRAZIL).
– Lingote.

COMPANIA SALITRERA ANGLO-LAUTARO.
– Desde Chile.

CONFEDERACAO NACIONAL DO COMERCIO (BRAZIL).
– Carta Mensal, Conselho Tecnico Consultivo, . . .
– CNC.

CONFEDERACAO NACIONAL DE INDUSTRIA (BRAZIL).
– Desenvolvimento e Conjuntura.
– Estudos Economicos.

CONFEDERACION DE CAMARAS NACIONALES DE COMERCIO (MEXICO).
– Comercio Mexicana.

CONFEDERACION DE TRABAJADORES DE AMERICA LATINA.
– Notificiero de la CTAL. = CTAL News.

CONFEDERACION DE TRABAJADORES DE MEXICO.
– Boletin Mensual de Informacion, . . .

CONGRESO NACIONAL DE PRODUCTIVIDAD Y BIENESTAR SOCIAL (ARGENTINA).
– Productividad y Bienestar Social.

CONSEJO INTERAMERICANO DE COMERCIO Y PRODUCCION.
– Carta Informativa, Consejo . . .; Serie ALALC.

CONSEJO NACIONAL DE DESAROLLO (ARGENTINA).
– Balance Energetico Argentino.

CONSEJO NACIONAL DE ECONOMIA (CUBA).
– Boletin Informativo, . . .

CONSEJO NACIONAL DE ECONOMIA (HONDURAS).
– Investigacion a la Industria Manufacturera (Honduras).

CONSEJO NACIONAL DE PLANIFICACION Y COORDINACION ECONOMICA

(SALVADOR).
— Programa Bienal de Inversiones Publicas (Salvador).
CONSELHO DE IMIGRACAO E COLONIZACAO (BRAZIL).
— Revista de Imigracao e Colonizacao.
CONSELHO NACIONAL DE ECONOMIA (BRAZIL)
— Revista do Conselho . . .
CONSELHO NACIONAL DE ESTATISTICA (BRAZIL).
— Boletim Estatistico (Brazil).
CONSELHO DE TERRAS DA UNIAO (BRAZIL).
— Revista do Conselho . . .
(CORDOBA, ARGENTINA, PROVINCE) DIRECCION GENERAL DE ESTADISTICA,
CENSOS Y INVESTIGACIONES.
— Revista de la Direccion . . .
CORPORACIONES DE COMERCIANTES DEL PERU.
— Sintesis Semanal, . . .
CORPORACION DE FOMENTO DE LA PRODUCCION (CHILE).
— Memoria, . . .
CORPORACION VENEZOLANA DE FOMENTO.
— Bancos de Fomento Regional (Venezuela).
— Cuadernos CVF.
— Cuadernos de la CVF.
— Cuadernos de Informacion Economica (Venezuela).
— CVF. Boletin de la Corporacion . . .
— Estudios Preliminares sobre Industrias (Venezuela).
— Memoria y Cuento, . . .
(CUBA) DIRECCION GENERAL DE ESTADISTICA.
— Anuario Demografico de Cuba.
— Anuario Estadistico de Cuba.
— Balanza Comercial de Cuba,
— Boletin de Estadisticas (Cuba).
— Exportacion (Cuba).
(CUBA) DIRECCION DE LA OPINION PUBLICA.
— Boletin Oficial, Direccion . . .
(CUBA) DIRECCION DE RELACIONES PUBLICAS.
— Metas.
(CUBA) DIRECTORIO FINANCIERO.
— Trimestre Suplemento del Directorio . . .
(CUBA) EMBASSY: GREAT BRITAIN.
— News from Cuba.
(CUBA) MINISTERIO DE COMERCIO.
— Revista, Ministerio . . .
(CUBA) MINISTERIO DEL COMERCIO EXTERIOR.
— Comercio Exterior (Cuba).
(CUBA) MINISTERIO DE INDUSTRIAS.
— Nuestra Industria (Cuba); Revista Economica.
— Nuestra Industria (Cuba); Revista Tecnologica.
(CUBA) MINISTERIO DE OBRAS PUBLICAS.
— MOP.
(CUBA) MINISTERIO DE TRABAJO.
— Trabajo.
(CUBA) OFICINA DE COORDINACION, DE ESTADISTICAS E INVESTIGACIONES.
— Informe Estadistico Semestral (Cuba).
(CUBA) SECRETARIA DE AGRICULTURA.
— Revista de Agricultura, [Comercio y Trabajo] .

DEVELOPMENT & WELFARE ORGANIZATION IN THE WEST INDIES.
— Development and Welfare in the West Indies; Bulletin.
— Development and Welfare in the West Indies; Report.

DISTRIBUIDORA NACIONAL DE PUBLICACIONES (CUBA).
— Cuba Socialista.

DOMINICA CHAMBER OF COMMERCE.
— Journal of the . . .

(DOMINICA) REGISTRAR GENERAL.
— Annual Report on Vital Statistics (Dominica).

(DOMINICA) TREASURY DEPARTMENT.
— Import and Export Statistics (Dominica).
— Monthly Overseas Trade Report (Dominica).

(DOMINICAN REPUBLIC) DIRECCION GENERAL DE ESTADISTICA.
— Accidentes de Trabajo (Dominican Republic).
— Anuario Estadistico (Dominican Republic).
— Censo Nacional de Industrias y de Comercio (Dominican Republic).
— Censo Nacional de Poblacion (Dominican Republic).
— Comercio Exterior de la Republica Dominica; Resumen del Ano.
— Estadistica Bancaria (Dominican Republic).
— Estadistica Demografia (Dominican Republic).
— Estadistica Industrial de la Republica Dominicana.
— Estadistica de los Negocios de Seguros (Dominican Republic).
— Exportacion de la Republica Dominicana.
— Importacion de la Republica Dominicana.
— Poblacion de la Republica Dominicana.
— Registro Publico (Dominican Republic).
— Sacrificia de Ganada (Dominican Republic).

(DOMINICAN REPUBLIC) SECRETARIA DE ESTADO DE ECONOMIA NACIONAL.
— Revista de la Secretaria . . .

(DOMINICAN REPUBLIC) SECRETARIA DE ESTADO DE JUSTICIA Y TRABAJO.
— Memoria del Ano, . . .

(DOMINICAN REPUBLIC) SECRETARIA DE ESTADO DEL TESORO.
— Memoria, . . .

(DOMINICAN REPUBLIC) SECRETARIA DE ESTADO DE TRABAJO, ECONOMIA Y COMERCIO.
— Revista de la Secretaria.

(DOMINICAN REPUBLIC) SECRETARIA DE ESTADO DE TRABAJO E INDUSTRIA.
— Revista de Trabajo (e Industria).

ECONOMIC & BUSINESS RESEARCH INFORMATION & ADVISORY SERVICE.
— Caribbean Economic Almanac.

ECONOMIC DEVELOPMENT ADMINISTRATION (PUERTO RICO).
— Annual Statistical Report of EDA Manufacturing Plants (Puerto Rico).

ECONOMIC PLANNING UNIT (BARBADOS).
— Series of Economic Surveys (Barbados).

ECONOMIST INTELLIGENCE UNIT.
— Quarterly Economic Review: Argentina.
— Quarterly Economic Review: Brazil.
— Quarterly Economic Review: Colombia.
— Quarterly Economic Review: Mexico.
— Quarterly Economic Review: Venezuela.

(ECUADOR) DIRECCION GENERAL DE ESTADISTICA Y CENSOS.
— Anuario de Estadisticas Vitales (Ecuador).

(ECUADOR) DIRECCION DEL PRESUPUESTO.
— Anuario de Comercio Exterior (Ecuador).
— Comercio Exterior Ecuatoriano.

(ECUADOR) MINISTERIO DEL TESORO.
— Informe a la Nacion, Ministerio . . .

EMPLOYERS CONSULTATIVE ASSOCIATION OF TRINIDAD & TOBAGO.
— ECA News.

EMPRESA NACIONAL DE ELECTRICIDAD (CHILE).
— Produccion y Consumo de Energia en Chile.

ESCOLA DE SERVICO SOCIAL DO PARA.
— Revista Paraense de Estudos Sociais.

ESCUELA BANCARIA Y COMERCIAL (Mexico, D.F.).
— Banca y Comercio.

ESCUELA NACIONAL DE CIENCIAS POLITICAS Y SOCIALES (MEXICO).
— Ciencias Politicas y Sociales.

ESCUELA NACIONAL DE ECONOMIA (MEXICO)
— Investigacion Economica.

FEDERACAO DES ASSOCIACOES COMERCIAIS DE MINAS GERAIS.
— Mensagem Economica.

FEDERACAO DO COMERCIO DO ESTADO DE GOIAS.
— Revista Goiana de Economia.

FEDERACAO DAS INDUSTRIAS DO ESTADO DE MINAS GERAIS.
— Vida Industrial.

FEDERACION LANERA ARGENTINA.
— Exportacion de Cueros Lanaras.

FEDERACION NACIONAL DE CAFETEROS DE COLOMBIA.
— Boletin Estadistica de la Federacion . . .
— Revista Cafetera de Colombia.

FEDERACION NACIONAL DE COMERCIANTES (COLOMBIA).
— Boletin Fenalco.

FEDERACION NACIONAL DE LA PROPRIEDAD (CUBA).
— Revista Nacional de la Propriedad Urbana.

FEDERACION NACIONAL DE TRABAJADORES AZUCAREROS (CUBA).
— Boletin Internacional, . . .

FERROCARRILES NACIONALES (COLOMBIA).
— Ferrocarriles en Cifras (Colombia).

FIRST NATIONAL BANK OF BOSTON.
— Situation in Argentina.

FONDO DE CULTURA ECONOMICO (MEXICO).
— Trimestre Economico.

FRENTE DE ECONOMISTAS REVOLUCIONARIOS (MEXICO).
— Revista de Economia.

FUNDACAO GETULIO VARGAS.
— Revista Brasileira de Economia.

(GREAT BRITAIN) BOARD OF TRADE; COMMERCIAL RELATIONS & EXPORTS DEPT.
— Report on Economic Conditons in Brazil.
— Report on Economic Conditions in Colombia.
— Report on Economic Conditions in Cuba.
— Report on Economic Conditions in Haiti.
— Report on Economic Conditions in Honduras.

- Report on Economic Conditions in Nicaragua.
- Report on Economic Conditions in Panama.
- Report on Economic Conditions in Paraguay.
- Report on Economic Conditions in Peru.
- Report on Economic Conditions in El Salvador.
- Report on Economic Conditions in Venezuela.
- Report on Economic and Financial Conditions in Uruguay.

(GRENADA) STATISTICAL UNIT.
- Bulletin, Statistical Unit (Grenada).

(GUYANA).
see also (BRITISH GUIANA).

GUYANA INFORMATION SERVICES.
- Background to Guyana.
- News from Guyana.

GUYANA INSTITUTE OF INTERNATIONAL AFFAIRS.
- International Affairs (Quarterly).

(GUYANA) MINISTRY OF ECONOMIC DEVELOPMENT; STATISTICAL BUREAU.
- Quarterly Review of Financial Statistics.   (Guyana).

(HAITI) DEPARTEMENT DES AFFAIRES ETRANGERES.
- Bulletin d'Informations, Departement . . .

(HAITI) OFFICE DE CONTROL ET DE DEVELOPPEMENT DES DENREES D'EXPORTATION.
- Rapport Annuel, Office . .

(HONDURAS) DIRECCION GENERAL DE ESTADISTICA Y CENSOS.
- Anuario Estadistico (Honduras).
- Boletin Estadistico (Honduras).
- Comercio Exterior (Honduras).
- Estadisticas Industriales (Honduras).
- Informacion Agropecuaria (Honduras).

(HONDURAS) MINISTERIO DE TRABAJO Y PREVISION SOCIAL.
- Informe de Labores, Ministerio . . .
- Trabajo.

(HONDURAS) SECRETARIA DE HACIENDA, CREDITO PUBLICO Y COMERCIO.
- Informe, Secretaria . . .

INDUSTRIAL DEVELOPMENT BOARD (ANTIGUA).
- Annual Report, . . .

INDUSTRIAL DEVELOPMENT CORPORATION (TRINIDAD & TOBAGO) LIBRARY.
- List of Publications Catalogued, . . .

INFORMADORA MEXICANA DE COMERCIO E INVERSIONE.
- Mexletter.

INSTITUTE OF INTER-AMERICAN STUDIES
- Inter-American Economic Affairs.

INSTITUTO DE ADMINISTRACION PUBLICA (MEXICO).
- Revista de Administracion Publica.

INSTITUTO ANCHIETANO DE PESQUISAS.
- Pesquisas.   [Also in series]

INSTITUTO DE APOSENTADORIA E PENSOES DOS BANCARIOS.
- Revista de Bancarios.

INSTITUTO DE APOSENTADORIA E PENSOES DOS INDUSTRIARIOS.
- Industriarios.

INSTITUTO BAHIANO DO FUMO.
— Boletim Mensal de Informacoes do Instituto . . .

INSTITUTO BRASILEIRO DO CAFE.
— Boletim Estatistico, . . .

INSTITUTO BRASILEIRO DE ECONOMIA, SOCIOLOGIA E POLITICA.
— Cadernos de Nosso Tempo.

INSTITUTO BRASILEIRO DE OPINIAO PUBLICA E ESTATISTICA.
— Boletim das Classes Dirigentes.

INSTITUTO BRASILEIRO DE RELACOES INTERNACIONAIS.
— Revista Brasileira de Politica Internacional.

INSTITUTO DE CACAU DA BAHIA.
— Boletim Informativo do Instituto . . .

INSTITUTO COLOMBIANO DE LA REFORMA AGRARIA.
— Informe de Actividades, . . .

INSTITUTO DE COLONIZACION RURAL (SAN SALVADOR).
— Memoria, . . .

INSTITUTO DE DESARROLLO ECONOMICO Y SOCIAL (ARGENTINA).
— Desarrollo Economico (Argentina).

INSTITUTO DE DIREITO PUBLICO E CIENCIA POLITICA (Rio de Janeiro).
— Revista de Direito Publico e Ciencia Politica.

INSTITUTO DE ECONOMIA "GASTAO VIDIGAL".
— Boletim do Instituto . . .

INSTITUTO DE FOMENTO ALGODONERO (Bogota).
— Algodon y Oleaginosas.
— Informacion Estadistica, Instituto . . .

INSTITUTO INTERAMERICANO DE CIENCIAS AGRICOLAS.
— Extension en las Americas.

INSTITUTO DE INVESTIGACIONES SOCIALES Y ECONOMICAS (MEXICO).
— Espejo.
— Temas Contemporaneos.

INSTITUTO JOAQUIM NABUCO DE PESQUISAS SOCIAIS.
— Boletim do Instituto . . .

INSTITUTO LATINOAMERICANO DEL FIERRO Y EL ACERO.
— ILAFA.   Boletin Informatico.
— Revista Latinoamericano de Siderurgia.

INSTITUTO LATINAMERICANO DE RELACIONES INTERNACIONALES.
— Mundo Nuevo.

INSTITUTO MEXICANO DEL SEGURIDAD SOCIAL.
— Revista Mexicana de Seguridad Social.

INSTITUTO MOVILIZADOR DE INVERSIONES BANCARIAS.
— Memoria, Instituto . . .

INSTITUTO NACIONAL AGRARIO (HONDURAS).
— Reforma Agraria (Honduras).

INSTITUTO NACIONAL DE CAFE (MEXICO)
— Boletin Quincenal, . . .

INSTITUTO NACIONAL DE CONTADORES PUBLICOS (COLOMBIA).
— Contador Publico.

INSTITUTO NACIONAL DO MATE (BRAZIL).
— Boletim Estatistico, . . .

INSTITUTO NACIONAL DE REFORMA AGRARIA (CUBA).
— Boletin de Divulgacion, . . .   [also Suplemento Semanal]

- Cuba. Revista Mensual.
- INRA. Revista Mensual Ilustrada.
- Revista del INRA.

INSTITUTO DE ORGANIZACAO RACIONAL DE TRABALHO.
- IDORT. Revista de Organizacao e Produtividade.

INSTITUTO DE PREVISION SOCIAL (Asuncion).
- Revista del Instituto . . .

INSTITUTO SALVADORENO DE FOMENTO DE LA PRODUCCION.
- Memoria de las Labores Desarroladas.

INSTITUTO SALVADORENO DE INVESTIGACIONES DEL CAFE.
- Boletin Informativo, . . .

INSTITUTO DE SOCIOLOGIA (Buenos Aires).
- Boletin del Instituto de Sociologia.

INSTITUTO TECNICO ADMINISTRATIVO DEL TRABAJO (MEXICO).
- Revista del ITAT.

INSTITUTO TECNOLOGICO DEL SUR.
- Tecnica y Economica. Revista del Instituto . . .
INSTITUTO TORCUATO DI TELLA.
- Revista Latinoamericana de Sociologia.

INTER-AMERICAN COMMERCIAL ARBITRATION COMMISSION.
- Noticias, Comision Interamericana de Arbitraje Comercial.

INTER-AMERICAN COMMISSION OF WOMEN.
- Boletin, Comision Interamericana de Mujeres.
- News Bulletin, . . .
- Noticiero de la Comision Intermaericana de Mujeres.

INTER-AMERICAN ECONOMIC & SOCIAL COUNCIL.
- Servicio Social Interamericano.

INTER-AMERICAN REGIONAL ORGANIZATION OF WORKERS.
- Inter-American Labor Bulletin.

INTER-AMERICAN REGIONAL ORGANIZATION OF WORKERS (CARIBBEAN AREA DIVISION).
- Cadorit Information Bulletin.

INTER-AMERICAN STATISTICAL INSTITUTE.
- America en Cifras.
- Estadistica.

INTERNATIONAL FEDERATION OF COMMERCIAL, CLERICAL & TECHNICAL EMPLOYEES.
- Inter-American Bulletin, . . .

JAMAICA AGRICULTURAL SOCIETY.
- Report, . . .

(JAMAICA) CENTRAL BUREAU OF STATISTICS.
- External Trade of Jamaica.

(JAMAICA) CENTRAL HOUSING AUTHORITY.
- Annual Report, Central Housing Authority (Jamaica).

(JAMAICA), CENTRAL PLANNING UNIT.
- Economic Survey Jamaica.

JAMAICA CHAMBER OF COMMERCE.
- Journal of the . . .

(JAMAICA) DEPARTMENT OF AGRICULTURE.
- Commodity Bulletin (Jamaica).

(JAMAICA) DEPARTMENT OF HOUSING.
— Annual Report, Department of Housing (Jamaica).

(JAMAICA) DEPARTMENT OF STATISTICS.
— Abstract of Statistics (Jamaica).
— Annual Abstract of Statistics. (Jamaica).
— Balance of Payments (Jamaica).
— Digest of Statistics (Jamaica).
— Monetary Statistics (Jamaica).
— Quarterly Abstract of Statistics (Jamaica).
— Quarterly Digest of Statistics (Jamaica).
— Tables on National Income and Expenditure (Jamaica).
— Trade Indices (Jamaica).
— Wage Rates and Hours in Selected Industries (Jamaica).
— Wage Rates in Selected Occupations (Jamaica).

JAMAICA INDUSTRIAL DEVELOPMENT CORPORATION.
— Jamaica Industrial and Commercial Directory.

(JAMAICA) MINISTRY OF EXTERNAL AFFAIRS.
— Handbook of the Ministry . . .

(JAMAICA) MINISTRY OF FINANCE.
— Finance Accounts of Jamaica.

JAMAICA TOURIST BOARD.
— Annual Report, . . .

JUNTA CENTRAL DE PLANIFICACION (CUBA).
— Publicaciones Juceplan (Cuba)

JUNTA NACIONAL DE GRANOS (ARGENTINA).
— Boletin Informativo, . . .

JUNTA NACIONAL PARA COMBATIR LE DESOCUPACION (ARGENTINA).
— Memoria, . . .

JUNTA NACIONAL DE PLANEAMIENTO (BOLIVIA).
— Planeamiento.

JUNTA NACIONAL DE PLANIFICACION Y COORDINACION ECONOMICA (ECUADOR).
— Planificacion.

JUNTA DE PLANIFICACION DE LA PROVINCIA DE BUENOS AIRES.
— Revista de Desarollo Economico.

MAISON DE L'AMERIQUE LATINE (Brussels).
— Belgique—Amerique Latine.

(MARTINIQUE) SERVICE DE LA STATISTIQUE.
— Bulletin de Statistiques (Martinique).

(MEXICO) DEPARTAMENTO DE ASUNTOS, AGRARIOS Y COLONIZACION.
— Memoria de Labores, Departamento . . .

(MEXICO) DEPARTAMENTO DE LA ESTADISTICA NACIONAL.
— Estadistica Nacional (Mexico).

(MEXICO) DIRECCION DE ECONOMIA RURAL.
— Boletin Mensual de la Direccion . . .

(MEXICO) DIRECCION GENERAL DE AGRICULTURA.
— Agricultura Tecnica en Mexico.

(MEXICO) DIRECCION GENERAL DE ESTADISTICA.
— Revista de Estadistica (Mexico).

(MEXICO) DIRECCION GENERAL DE INFORMACION.
— Mexico Informa.

(MEXICO) SECRETARIA DE COMUNICACIONES Y OBRAS PUBLICAS.
— Anales, Secretaria . . .
— Boletin, Secretaria . . .
— Memoria, Secretaria . . .

(MEXICO) SECRETARIA DE COMUNICACIONES Y TRANSPORTES.
— Communicaciones y Transportes (Mexico).
— Memoria, Secretaria . . .

(MEXICO) SECRETARIA DE LA ECONOMIA NACIONAL.
— Memoria, Secretaria . . .
— Revista Industrial (Mexico).

(MEXICO) SECRETARIA DE HACIENDA Y CREDITO PUBLICO.
— Boletin Oficial, Secretaria. . .

(MEXICO) SECRETARIA DE OBRAS PUBLICAS.
— Memoria de la Secretaria. . .

(MEXICO) SECRETARIA DEL PATRIMONIA NACIONAL.
— Oficinas Tecnicas y Administrativas de la Junta de Gobierno, de los
Organismos y Empresas del Estado (Mexico).

(MEXICO) SECRETARIA DE RELACIONES EXTERIORES.
— Memoria de Labores de la Secretaria.

(MEXICO) SECRETARIA DE SALUBRIDAD Y ASISTENCIA.
— Salubridad y Asistencia. (Mexico).
— Salud Publica de Mexico.

(MEXICO) SECRETARIA DEL TRABAJO Y PREVISION SOCIAL.
— Cuaderno, Secretaria . . .
— Informaciones Sociales (Mexico).
— Memoria de Labores, Secretaria . . .
— Revista Mexicana del Trabajo.
— Revista del Trabajo.

(MEXICO) TRIBUNAL FISCAL DE LA FEDERACION.
— Revista, Tribunal . . .

(MINAS GERAIS, BRAZIL) SECRETARIA DA AGRICULTURA, INDUSTRIA,
COMERCIO E TRABALHO.
— Cooperaminas.

NACIONAL FINANCIERA (MEXICO).
— Informe Anual . . .

NATIONAL FOREIGN TRADE COUNCIL (U.S.)
— Noticias.

NEW YORK PUBLIC LIBRARY.
— Index to Latin American Periodicals; Humanities and Social Sciences.
indice General de Publicaciones Periodicas Latinoamericanas; Humanidades y
Ciencias Sociales).

(NICARAGUA) DIRECCION GENERAL DE ESTADISTICA Y CENSOS.
— Anuario Estadistico (Nicaragua).
— Boletin de Estadistica (Nicaragua).

(NICARAGUA) DIRECCION GENERAL DEL PRESUPUESTO.
— Actividad Presupuestaria en Nicaragua.
— Boletin, Direccion . . .
— Presupuesto General de Ingresos y Egresos de la Republica (Nicaragua).

(NICARAGUA) MINISTERIO DE AGRICULTURA Y GANADERIA.
— Memoria de Agricultura y Ganaderia (Nicaragua).

(NICARAGUA) MINISTERIO DE HACIENDA Y CREDITO PUBLICO.
— Cifras y Comentarios, Ministerio . . .

(NICARAGUA) RECAUDACION GENERAL DE ADUANAS.
— Memoria de la Recaudacion . . .

(NICARAGUA) SUPERINTENDENCIA DE BANCOS Y DE OTRAS INSTITUCIONES.
— Boletin de la Superintendencia . . .

OFICINA DE ESTUDIOS PARA LA COLABORACION ECONOMICA INTERNACIONAL.
— Peru.   Sintesis Economica y Financiera.

OILFIELDS WORKERS TRADE UNION (TRINIDAD & TOBAGO).
— Vanguard.

ORDEM DOS ECONOMISTAS DE SAO PAULO.
— Revista de Ciencias Economicas.

ORGANIZATION OF AMERICAN STATES.
— Annuals of the . . .
— OAS Chronicle.

ORGANIZACOES NOVO MUNDO; ASSESSORIA DE ASSUNTOS ECONOMICOS.
— Tendencias Economicas-Financeiras.

PAN AMERICAN . . .
    see (filed as): PANAMERICAN . . .

(PANAMA) CONTRALORIA GENERAL DE LA REPUBLICA.
— Anuario de Comercio Exterior (Panama).
— Informe de Controlar General . . .

(PANAMA) DIRECCION DE ESTADISTICA Y CENSO.
— Estadistica Panamena;   (also in various series).

PANAMA) MINISTERIO DE AGRICULTURA, COMERCIO E INDUSTRIAS.
— Memoria del Ministerio . . .

(PANAMA) MINISTERIO DE HACIENDA Y TESORO.
— Memoria, Ministerio . . .

(PANAMA) OFICINA DE REGULACION DE PRECIOS.
— Informe Anual de las Actividades, Oficina . . .
— Resumen de las Labores, Oficina . . .

PAN-AMERICAN INSTITUTE OF GEOGRAPHY & HISTORY.
— Revista Interamericana de Ciencias Sociales.

PAN AMERICAN UNION.
— Americas.
— Boletin de la Revista Interamericana de Ciencias Sociales.
— Ciencias Sociales.
— Consumer Price (Cost-of-living) Indexes for the American Nations.
    Indices de Precios al Consumidor (Costo de la Vidal) de las
    Naciones Americanas.
— Documentes Oficiales de la Organizacion de los Estados Americanos;
    Indice y Lista General.
— Economia Latinoamericana.
— Informaciones Economicos.
— International Trade of the American States.
— Vivienda y Planeamiento.

PAN AMERICAN UNION; COLUMBUS MEMORIAL LIBRARY.
— List of Books Accessioned and Periodicals Indexed in the Columbus
    Memorial Library.

PAN AMERICAN UNION; OFFICE OF FOREIGN TRADE ADVISERS
— Comercio Interamericano.

(PARAGUAY) DIRECCION GENERAL DE ESTADISTICA Y CENSOS.
— Anuario Estadistico de la Republica del Paraguay.

— Boletin Estadistico del Paraguay.

(PARAGUAY) MINISTERIO DE INDUSTRIA Y COMERCIO.
— Paraguay Industrial y Comercial.

(PARAGUAY) MINISTERIO DE INDUSTRIA Y COMERCIO; Departamento de Estadistico y Censo.
— Encuesta Industrial (Paraguay).

(PARAIBA) DEPARTAMENTO ESTADUAL DE ESTADISTICA.
— Boletin Estatistico (Paraiba).

PARTI COMMUNISTE MARTINIQUAISE.
— Action.

PARTIDO SOCIALISTA (ARGENTINA).
— Anuario Socialista (Argentina).

PATRONATO DE SERVICIO SOCIAL DE CUBA.
— Revista de Servicio Social (Cuba).

PEOPLES NATIONAL CONGRESS (GUYANA).
— New Nation.

PEOPLES PROGRESSIVE PARTY (GUYANA).
— Thunder.

(PERNAMBUCO) DIVISAO DE EPIDEMIOLOGIA E BIOESTATISTICA DO ESTADO.
— Boletim de Bioestatistica (Pernambuco).

(PERU) DIRECCION GENERAL DE COMERCIO.
— Informaciones Comerciales.

(PERU) DIRECCION GENERAL DE ESTADISTICA.
— Anuario Estadistico del Peru.

(PERU) DIRECCION NACIONAL DE ESTADISTICA Y CENSOS.
— Boletin de Estadistica Peruana.

(PERU) DIRECCION DE PETROLEO.
— Estadistica Petrolera del Peru.

(PERU) MINISTERIO DE AGRICULTURA.
— Estadistica Agraria (Peru).

(PERU) MINISTERIO DE HACIENDA Y COMERCIO.
— Memoria, Ministerio . . .

(PERU) MINISTERIO DE TRABAJO Y ASUNTOS INDIGENAS.
— Boletin del Ministerio . . .

(PERU) SUPERINTENDENCIA DE BANCOS
— Memoria y Estadistica, Superintendencia . . .

(PERU) SUPERINTENDENCIA GENERAL DE ADUANAS.
— Estadistica del Comercio Exterior (Peru).

PETROLEUM ASSOCIATION (TRINIDAD & TOBAGO).
— Annual Returns, . . .

(POINTE A PITRE) MUNICIPALITE
— Bulletin Municipal (Pointe a Pitre).

PONTIFICIA UNIVERSIDADE CATOLICA DO RIO DE JANEIRO; INSTITUTO DE ESTUDOS POLITICOS E SOCIAIS.
— Sintese Politica, Economica, Social.

(PUERTO RICO) BUREAU OF LABOR STATISTICS.
— Census of Manufacturing Industries of Puerto Rico.
— Employment, Hours and Earnings in the Manufacturing Industries in Puerto
    Rico. (= Empleo, Horas y Salarios en las Industrias Manufactureras de
    Puerto Rico).
— Employment, Hours and Earnings in Non-Manufacturing Industries in Puerto
    Rico. (= Empleo, Horas y Salarios en Industrias No-Manufactueras en
    Puerto Rico).

(PUERTO RICO) DEPARTMENT OF AGRICULTURE & COMMERCE.
— Agricultura al Dia.
— Ventas al por Mayor de Productos del Pais en los Cinco Principales Mercados
    de Puerto Rico.

PUERTO RICO INDUSTRIAL DEVELOPMENT COMPANY
— Annual Report, . . .

REDE FERROVIARA FEDERAL S.A. (BRAZIL).
— Anuario Estatistico da RFFSA.

(RIO GRANDE DO SUL) DEPARTAMENTO ESTADUAL DE ESTATISTICA.
— Financas Publicas (Rio Grande do Sul).

(RIO GRANDE DO SUL) SECRETARIA DE AGRICULTURA, INDUSTRIA E COMERCIO.
— Sul-Coop.   Boletim Cooperativismo.

ROYAL AGRICULTURAL & COMMERCIAL SOCIETY OF BRITISH GUIANA.
— Timehri.

(ST. CHRISTOPHER-NEVIS) DEPARTMENT OF LABOR.
— Annual Report of the Department   . . .

(ST.LUCIA) CUSTOMS & EXCISE DEPARTMENT.
— Report of the Customs and Excise Department (St. Lucia).

(ST. LUCIA) STATISTICAL UNIT.
— Overseas trade of St. Lucia.
— Quarterly Digest of Statistics (St.Lucia).

(ST. VINCENT) ACCOUNTANT GENERAL.
— . Report of the Accountant General (St.Vincent).

(ST. VINCENT) AUDIT DEPARTMENT.
— Report of the Senior Auditor on the Audit of the Accounts (St.Vincent).

ST. VINCENT CHAMBER OF COMMERCE.
— St. Vincent Chamber of Commerce Journal.

(ST.VINCENT) CUSTOMS DEPARTMENT.
— Annual Trade Report (St.Vincent).
— Imports and Exports (St.Vincent).

(ST.VINCENT) INLAND REVENUE DEPARTMENT.
— Report on the Working of the Inland . . .

(ST.VINCENT) REGISTRAR OF CO-OPERATIVE SOCIETIES.
— Report of the Registrar . . .

(ST. VINCENT) STATISTICAL UNIT.
— Quarterly Overseas Trade Report (St. Vincent)

(SALVADOR) CONSEJO NACIONAL DE PLANIFICACION Y COORDINACION
ECONOMICA. see CONSEJO NACIONAL DE PLANIFICACION Y COORDINACION
ECONOMICA (SALVADOR).

156

(SALVADOR) DIRECCION GENERAL DE ESTADISTICA Y CENSOS.
— Anuario Estadistico (Salvador).
— Boletin Estadistica (Salvador).
— Comercio Exterior (Salvador).
— Costo y Condiciones de Vida en San Salvador.

(SALVADOR) MINISTERIO DE AGRICULTURA Y GANADERA.
— Agricultura en el Salvador.

(SALVADOR) MINISTERIO DE TRABAJO Y PREVISION SOCIAL.
— Memoria (de las) Labores Desarrolladas por el Ramo de Trabajo y Prevision Social (Salvador):

(SAO PAULO, ESTADO) DEPARTAMENTO DE ESTATISTICA.
— Boletim do Departamento ...

(SAO PAULO, ESTADO) DEPARTAMENTO DA PRODUCAO VEGETAL.
— Agricultura em Sao Paulo.

SECRETARIA PERMANENTE DEL TRATADO GENERAL DE INTEGRACION ECONOMICA CENTROAMERICANA (SIECA).
— Compendio Estadistico Centroamericano.

SEMINARIO MEXICANO DE SOCIOLOGIA.
— Sociologia en Mexico

SEMINARIO DE NACIONAL FINANCIERA (MEXICO).
— Mercado de Valores.

(SERGIPE, BRAZIL) SECRETARIA DA FAZENDA, PRODUCAO E OBRAS PUBLICAS; Consultoria Tecnica de Asuntos Economicos e Financeiros.
— Economia e Financas.

SERVICO BANAS (Sao Paulo).
— Banas Informa.

SERVICO DE PESQUISA E DIVULGACAO SOCIO-ECONOMICA LIMITADA (BRAZIL).
— Carta Economica Brasileira.

SHELL CARIBBEAN PETROLEUM CO.
— Revista Shell.

SINDICATO AGRONOMICO DE RIO GRANDE DO SUL.
— Revista Agronomica.

SINDICATO DE OBREROS PANADEROS DE LA PROVINCIA DE LA HABANA.
— Obrero Panadero.

SMALL BUSINESSES LOAN BOARD (JAMAICA).
— Annual Report, ...

SOCIEDADE NACIONAL DE AGRICULTURA (BRAZIL).
— Lavoura.
— Legislacao Agricola do Brasil.

SOCIEDAD NACIONAL DE INDUSTRIAS (PERU).
— Industria Peruana.

SOCIEDAD VENEZOLANA DE PLANIFICACION.
— Cuadernos de la ...

SOCIETE D'ETUDES DEMOGRAPHIQUES ET SOCIALES DE LA MARTINIQUE.
— Cahiers, ...

STANFORD UNIVERSITY; HISPANIC WORK AFFAIRS SEMINAR.
— Hispanic World Report.

STANFORD UNIVERSITY; INSTITUTE OF HISPANIC & LUSO-BRAZILIAN STUDIES.
— Hispanic American Report.

SUMOC.
    see SUPERINTENDENCIA DA MOEDA E DO CREDITO (BRAZIL).

SUPERINTENDENCIA DO DESENVOLVIMENTO DO NORDESTE (BRAZIL).
— Boletim do Estudos de Pesca.

SUPERINTENDENCIA DA MOEDA E DO CREDITO (BRAZIL).
— Relatorio SUMOC.

SUPERINTENDENCIA DO PLANO DE VALORIZACAO ECONOMICA DA AMAZONIA.
— SPVEA. Resenha Informativa.

(SURINAM) ALGEMEEN BUREAU VOOR DE STATISTIEK.
— Bedrijfs- en Bedroepstelling. (Surinam).
— Jaarcijfers voor Suriname. (= Statistical Year Book of Suriname).
— Statistische Berichten van het Algemeen Bureau   . . .
— Suriname en Cijfers.

T.GEDDES GRANT LTD.
— TGG Review.

TEXACO (TRINIDAD) INC.
— Texaco Caribbean.
— Texaco Trinidad News.
— Texaco-Trinidad Quarterly.

TOURIST BOARD (TRINIDAD & TOBAGO).
— Annual Report, . . .

TRADE DEVELOPMENT BOARD (BERMUDA).
— Report of the   . . .

TRINIDAD CHAMBER OF COMMERCE.
— Enterprise.

(TRINIDAD & TOBAGO) CENTRAL STATISTICAL OFFICE.
— Annual Statistical Digest (Trinidad and Tobago).
— Balance of Payments of Trinidad and Tobago.
— Economic Trends (Trinidad and Tobago).
— International Travel Report (Trinidad and Tobago).
— Monthly Overseas Trade Report (Trinidad and Tobago).
— Overseas Trade (Trinidad and Tobago); Annual Report.
— Population and Vital Statistics (Trinidad and Tobago); Annual Report.
— Quarterly Economic Report (Trinidad and Tobago).
— Report on the National Income of Trinidad and Tobago.
— Research Papers, Central . . .
— Trinidad and Tobago Today.

(TRINIDAD & TOBAGO) CUSTOMS & EXCISE DEPARTMENT.
— Report on the Administration of the Customs . . .

(TRINIDAD & TOBAGO) MINISTRY OF LABOUR, CO-OPERATIVE
DEVELOPMENT & SOCIAL SERVICES.
— Report on the Manpower Situation in Trinidad and Tobago.

(TRINIDAD & TOBAGO) OFFICE OF THE PRIME MINISTER.
— Government Reports (Trinidad and Tobago).

UNEMPLOYED WORKERS COUNCIL (JAMAICA).
— National Patriot.

UNION INDUSTRIAL ARGENTINA.
— Revista de la . . .

UNION NACIONAL DE PRODUCTORES DE AZUCAR (MEXICO).
— Boletin Azucarero Mexicano.

UNITED NATIONS.
— Economic Survey of Latin America.

UNITED NATIONS; ECONOMIC COMMISSION FOR LATIN AMERICA.
— Economic Bulletin for Latin America.

- Noticias de la CEPAL.
- Statistical Bulletin for Latin America. [Also: Statistical Supplement]

UNIVERSIDAD DE BAHIA.
- Economista.

UNIVERSIDAD DE BUENOS AIRES.
- Revista de Ciencias Economicas.
- Revista de la Facultad de Ciencias Economicas, . . .
- Revista de la Facultad de Derecho y Ciencias Sociales, . . .

UNIVERSIDAD DE BUENOS AIRES; SEMINARIO DE CIENCIAS JURIDICAS Y SOCIALES.
- Investigaciones del Seminario (. . .),

UNIVERSITY OF CALIFORNIA; CENTER OF LATIN AMERICAN STUDIES.
- Latin America in Periodical Literature.
- Statistical Abstract of Latin America.

UNIVERSIDAD CENTRAL DEL ECUADOR; INSTITUTO DE INVESTIGACIONES ECONOMICAS.
- Boletin de Informacion Economica.
- Boletin Trimestral de Informacion Economica.
- Economia y Adminstracion.

UNIVERSIDAD CENTRAL DE VENEZUELA.
- Economia y Ciencias Sociales. Revista de la Facultad de Economia . . .

UNIVERSIDAD DE CHILE.
- Anales de la Facultad de Ciencias Juridicas y Sociales, . . .
- Economia.

UNIVERSIDAD DE CHILE; INSTITUTO DE ECONOMIA.
- Boletin Informativo, Instituto . . .
- Publicaciones, Instituto . . .

UNIVERSITY OF FLORIDA; SCHOOL OF INTER-AMERICAN STUDIES.
- Journal of Inter-American Studies.

UNIVERSITY OF GUYANA.
- UG Newsletter.

UNIVERSIDAD JAVERIANA.
- Revista Javeriana.

UNIVERSIDAD DE MINAS GERAIS.
- Estudos Economicos, Politicos e Sociais.
- Revista Brasileira de Ciencias Sociais.

UNIVERSIDAD NACIONAL AUTONOMA DE MEXICO; INSTITUTO DE INVESTIGACIONES SOCIALES.
- Gaceta Sociologica.
- Revista Mexicana de Sociologia.

UNIVERSIDAD NACIONAL DE COLOMBIA.
- Revista de la Facultad de Ciencias Economicas, . . .

UNIVERSIDAD NACIONAL DE CORDOBA. (ARGENTINA).
- Boletin de la Facultad de Derecho y Ciencias Sociales, . . .
- Revista de Economia y Estadistica.

UNIVERSIDAD NACIONAL DE LA PLATA.
- Economica.

UNIVERSIDAD NACIONAL DE LA PLATA; ESCUELA SUPERIOR DE CIENCIAS ADMINISTRATIVAS.
- ECA.   Revista de la Escuela . . .

UNIVERSIDAD NACIONAL DE LA PLATA; INSTITUTO DE ESTUDIOS COOPERATIVOS.
- Revista del Instituto . . .

UNIVERSIDAD NACIONAL DE LA PLATA; INSTITUTO DE ESTUDIOS
ECONOMICOS Y FINANCIEROS.
– Boletin del Instituto . . .

UNIVERSIDAD NACIONAL DE LA PLATA; INSTITUTO SUPERIOR DE
CIENCIAS ADMINISTRATIVAS.
– ECA. Revista del Instituto . . .

UNIVERSIDAD NACIONAL DEL LITORAL (ARGENTINA).
– Revista de Ciencias Juridicas y Sociales.
– Revista de la Facultad de Ciencias Economicas, Comerciales y Politicos,
– Trabajos del Seminario, Facultad de Ciencias Economicas, Comerciales y Politicos . . .

UNIVERSIDAD NACIONAL DEL LITORAL (ARGENTINA); INSTITUTO DE
INVESTIGACIONES ECONOMICAS.
– Revista del Instituto . . .

UNIVERSIDAD NACIONAL MAYOR DE SAN MARCOS DE LIMA.
– Revista de la Facultad de Ciencias Economicas y Comerciales, . . .

UNIVERSIDAD NACIONAL DE EL SALVADOR; INSTITUTO DE ESTUDIOS
ECONOMICAS.
– Economia Salvadorena.
– Revista de Economia de el Salvador.

UNIVERSIDAD NACIONAL DEL SUR (ARGENTINA); INSTITUTO DE ECONOMIA.
– Estudios Economicos.

UNIVERSIDAD NACIONAL DE TUCUMAN.
– Revista Agronomica del Noroeste Argentina.

UNIVERSIDAD DO PARA.
– Revista de Ciencias Juridicas, Economicas e Sociais.

UNIVERSITY OF PUERTO RICO; INSTITUTE OF CARIBBEAN STUDIES.
– Caribbean Monthly Bulletin.
– Caribbean Studies.

UNIVERSIDAD DE LA REPUBLICA (URUGUAY)
– Revista de la Facultad de Ciencias Economicas y Administracion de Montevideo.

UNIVERSIDAD TECNICA DE ORURO; CENTRO DE ESTUDIANTES DE
CIENCIAS ECONOMICAS.
– Revista Economica.

UNIVERSITY OF THE WEST INDIES.
– Caribbean Affairs.
– Caribbean Quarterly.
– UWI Quarterly.

UNIVERSITY OF THE WEST INDIES; INSTITUTE OF SOCIAL &
ECONOMIC RESEARCH.
– Progress Report, Institute . . .
– Social and Economic Studies.
– Special Series, Institute . . .

(URUGUAY) DIRECCION GENERAL DE ESTADISTICA Y CENSOS.
– Anuario Estadistico de la Republica Oriental del Uruguay.
– Recopilacion Estadistica (Uruguay).

(URUGUAY) MINISTERIO DE GANADERIA Y AGRICULTURA.
– Boletin Informativo, Ministerio . . .

(VENEZUELA) DIRECCION DE COMERCIO EXTERIOR Y CONSULADOS.
– Comercio Exterior de Venezuela.

(VENEZUELA) DIRECCION DE ECONOMIA Y ESTADISTICA AGROPECUARIA.
– Boletin de Precios de Productos Agropecuarios (Venezuela). [Also: in series]

(VENEZUELA) DIRECCION DE GABINETE.
– Revista de Fomento.

(VENEZUELA) DIRECCION GENERAL DE ESTADISTICA.
— Boletin de Comercio Exterior (Venezuela).
— Boletin Mensual de Estadistica (Venezuela).

(VENEZUELA) DIRECCION DE INDUSTRIAS.
— Boletin Industrial (Venezuela).

(VENEZUELA) EMBASSY: UNITED STATES.
— Venezuela Up-to-date.

(VENEZUELA) MINISTERIO DE AGRICULTURA Y CRIA.
— Anuario Estadistico Agropecuario (Venezuela).
— Inmigracion (Venezuela).
— Memoria y Cuenta, Ministerio . . .

(VENEZUELA) MINISTERIO DE FOMENTO.
— Memoria y Cuenta, Ministerio . . .

(VENEZUELA) MINISTERIO DE HACIENDA.
— Revista de Hacienda (Venezuela.

(VENEZUELA) MINISTERIO DE HACIENDA; COMISION DE ESTUDIOS
FINANCIEROS Y ADMINISTRATIVOS.
— Boletin Informativo de la Comision . . .

(VENEZUELA) MINISTERIO DE MINAS E HIDROCARBUROS.
— Actividades Petroleras (Venezuela).
— Anuario Petrolero y Minero de Venezuela.
— Anuario Petrolero de Venezuela.
— Carta Semanal, Ministerio . . .

(VENEZUELA) MINISTERIO DE MINAS E HIDROCARBUROS; DIVISION DE
ECONOMIA PETROLERA.
— Algunos Aspectos de las Actividades Petroleras Venezolanas y Mundiales.
— Petroleo y otros Datos Estadisticos.

(VENEZUELA) MINISTERIO DE SANIDAD Y ASISTENCIA SOCIAL.
— Boletin del Ministerio . . .
— Revista de Sanidad y Asistencia Social.
— Revista Venezolana de Sanidad y Asistencia Social.

(VENEZUELA) MINISTERIO DEL TRABAJO.
— Revista del Trabajo (Venezuela).

(VENEZUELA) MISSION TO THE EUROPEAN ECONOMIC COMMUNITY.
— Bulletin Economique, Mission du Venezuela aupres de la Communaute Economique
Europeenne.

(VENEZUELA) OFICINA CENTRAL DE COORDINACION Y PLANIFICACION.
— Informaciones de Venezuela.

(VENEZUELA) OFICINA CENTRAL DE INFORMACION.
— Carta de Venezuela.

(VENEZUELA) SUPERINTENDENCIA DE BANCOS.
— Informe, Superintendencia . . .

WEST INDIA COMMITTEE.
— Chronicle of the . . .

(WEST INDIES, FEDERATION) FEDERAL STATISTICAL OFFICE.
— Financial Statistics (West Indies, Federation).
— Monthly Trade Statistics (West Indies, Federation).
— Quarterly Trade Statistics (West Indies, Federation).

(WEST INDIES, FEDERATION) MINISTRY OF NATURAL RESOURCES & AGRICULTURE.
— West Indies Fisheries Bulletin.

(WEST INDIES, Federation) MINISTRY OF TRADE & INDUSTRY.
— Bulletin, Ministry . . .

WEST INDIES NEW HOPE FUND.
— New Hope Chronicle.

WINDWARD ISLANDS BANANA GROWERS ASSOCIATION.
— Winban News.

YACIMIENTOS PETROLIFEROS FISCALES BOLIVIANOS.
— Memoria Anual, . . .

TITLE INDEX

(Letters in right hand margin indicate section in which main entry is found)

Annual Report, Brazilian Chamber of Commerce & Economic Affairs Gt. Br	BRA
Annual Report, Central Housing Authority (Jamaica)	JAM
Annual Report of the Controller of Customs and Excise (British Guiana)	GUY
Annual Report, Department of Housing (Jamaica)	JAM
Annual Report of the Department of Labour (St.Christopher-Nevis) ...	LEE
Annual Report, Industrial Development Board (Antigua)	LEE
Annual Report, Jamaica Tourist Board	JAM
Annual Report, Puerto Rico Industrial Development Company. ...	PUE
Annual Report, Small Businesses Loan Board (Jamaica) ...	JAM
Annual Report, Tourist Board (Trinidad and Tobago).	TRI
Annual Report on Vital Statistics (Dominica).	WIN
Annual Returns, Petroleum Association (Trinidad and Tobago) ...	TRI
Annual Statistical Digest (Trinidad and Tobago)	TRI
Annual Statistical Report of EDA Manufacturing Plants (Puerto Rico).	PUE
Annual Trade Report (Antigua).	LEE
Annual Trade Report (St. Vincent).	WIN
Antigua. (Colonial Office etc. Report).	LEE
Anuario Azucarero de Cuba. (= Cuba Sugar Year Book). ...	CUB
Anuario de Comercio Exterior (Colombia).	COL
Anuario de Comercio Exterior (Ecuador)	ECU
Anuario de Comercio Exterior (Guatemala)	GUA
Anuario de Comercio Exterior (Panama).	PAN
Anuario del Comercio Exterior (Peru).	PER
Anuario del Comercio Exterior de la Republica Argentina. ...	ARG
Anuario Demografico (Bolivia).	BOL
Anuario Demografico de Cuba	CUB
Anuario de Estatistica e Informacoes, Comissao Executiva de Defesa da Bor	BRA
Anuario Estadistico Agropecuario (Venezuela).	VEN
Anuario Estatistico do Brasil	BRA
Anuario Estadistico (Colombia)	COL
Anuario Estadistico de Cuba	CUB
Anuario Estadistico (Honduras)	HON
Anuario Estadistico (Nicaragua)	NIC
Anuario Estadistico (Salvador).	SAL
Anuario de Estadisticas Vitales (Ecuador)	ECU
Anuario Estadistico del Peru.	PER
Anuario Estadistico de la Republica Argentina.	ARG
Anuario Estadistico de la Republica Dominicana ...	DOM
Anuario Estadistico de la Republica Oriental del Uruguay. ...	URU
Anuario Estadistico de la Republica del Paraguay. ...	PAR
Anuario Estatistico da RFFSA.	BRA
Anuario Estadistico de Venezuela	VEN
Anuario Financiero de Mexico	MEX
Anuario General de Estadistica de Colombia.	COL
Anuario Indigenista.	MEX
Anuario de la Industria Minera del Peru.	PER
Anuario Industrial (Bolivia).	BOL
Anuario Petrolero y Minero de Venezuela.	VEN
Anuario Petrolero de Venezuela.	VEN
Anuario Socialista (Argentina)	ARG
APEC	BRA
Apuntes Economicos (Colombia).	COL
Apuntes Economicos (Guatemala)	GUA
Archivo de la Economia Nacional (Guatemala)	GUA
Arco Iris.	BRA
Argentina Austral	ARG
Argentina Financiera	ARG
Argentine Law Bulletin	ARG
Argentine Weekly News Bulletin	ARG
Arquivos Economicos	BRA
Aspectos Financieros de las Economias Latinoamericanas. ...	MEX
Aspectos Monetarios de las Economias Latinoamericanas.	MEX

Boletin de Comercio Exterior (Venezuela). ... ... VEN
Boletin, Comision Interamericana de Mujeres ... ... GEN
Boletin de Comunicaciones. ... ... ARG
Boletin de la Comision Permanente, Asociacion del Congreso Panamericana ARG
Boletim da Contadoria Geral da Republica (Brazil). ... ... BRA
Boletim de CPE. ... ... BRA
Boletin Demografico Municipal de la Ciudad de Lima ... ... PER
Boletim do Departamento de Estatistica do Estado de Sao Paulo ... BRA
Boletin de la Direccion General de Estadistica y Censo (Guatemala) ... GUA
Boletin de la Direccion General Impositiva (Argentina) ... ... ARG
Boletin, Direccion General del Presupuesto (Nicaragua). ... ... NIC
Boletin de Divulgacion, Instituto Nacional de Reforma Agraria (Cuba) CUB
Boletin de Divulgacion, Instit.Nac.de Ref.Ag.(Cuba): Suplemento Semenal.il CUB
Boletin de Divulgacion Tecnica (Cuba) ... ... CUB
Boletin de Economia y Finanzas. ... ... VEN
Boletin Economica de America Latina; Suplemento Estadistico ... GEN
Boletin de Estadistica (Argentina) ... ... ARG
Boletin Estadistico, Asociacion Nacional del Cafe (Guatemala) ... GUA
Boletin de Estadisticas Bancarias (Guatemala) ... ... GUA
Boletin Estadistico, Banco Agricola de la Republica Dominicana ... DOM
Boletin Estadistico, Banco Central de la Republica Argentina ... ARG
Boletin Estadistico del Banco de Guatemala ... ... GUA
Boletin Estadistico (Bolivia) ... ... BOL
Boletin Estadistico (Brazil) ... ... BRA
Boletin Estadistico (Chile) ... ... CHI
Boletin Estadistico, Comision Nacional Bancaria (Mexico) ... ... MEX
Boletin de Estadisticas (Cuba) ... ... CUB
Boletin Estadistica de la Federacion Nacional de Cafeteros de Colombia. COL
Boletin Estadistico (Honduras) ... ... HON
Boletim de Estatistica e Informacoes, Comisao Executiva da Defesa da Borrach BRA
Boletim Estatistico, Instituto Brasileiro do Cafe ... ... BRA
Boletim Estatistico, Instituto Nacional do Mate (Brazil) ... ... BRA
Boletin de Estadistica (y Jurisprudencia) ... ... ARG
Boletin de Estadistica y Jurisprudencia; Anuario ... ... ARG
Boletin Estadistico Mensual, Banco Central del Paraguay ... ... PAR
Boletin Estadistico Mensual (Costa Rica) ... ... COS
Boletin de Estadistica (Nicaragua) ... ... NIC
Boletin Estadistico del Paraguay ... ... PAR
Boletim Estatistico (Paraiba) ... ... BRA
Boletin de Estadistica Peruana ... ... PER
Boletin Estadistico (El Salvador) ... ... SAL
Boletin de Estadisticas de Seguros (Guatemala) ... ... GUA
Boletin de Estudios Especiales, Banco Nacional de Credito Ejidal (Mexico) MEX
Boletim do Estudos de Pesca ... ... BRA
Boletin de la Facultad de Derecho y Ciencias Sociales, Universidad Nacional ARG
Boletin, Federacion Nacional de Comerciantes (Colombia).
            see Boletin Fenalco.
Boletin Fenalco ... ... COL
Boletin Grafico, Camara de Comercio e Industria de el Salvador ... SAL
Boletim de Imposto de Consumo, Imposto de Renda e Tributas en Geral(Br) BRA
Boletin Indigenista ... ... MEX
Boletin Indigenista Venezolano ... ... VEN
Boletin de Industrias ... ... MEX
Boletim de Industria Animal ... ... BRA
Boletin Industrial ... ... VEN
Boletin de Informacion Economica. (Quito)
            see Economia y Administracion.
Boletim do Informacoes, Ministerio da Viacao e Obras Publicas (Brazil) BRA
Boletin de Informaciones Petroleras ... ... ARG
Boletin Informativo, Banco de la Provincia de Buenos Aires ... ARG
Boletin Informativo, Centro e Federacao das Industrias do Estado de S.Paulo BRA
Boletin Informativo da Codepe ... ... BRA

Boletin Informativo de Comision de Estudios Financieros y Administrativos, VEN
    Ministerio de Hacienda (Venezuela)   ...   ...
Boletin Informativo, Consejo Nacional de Economia (Cuba)   ...   CUB
Boletin Informativo, Federacao e Centro das Industrias do Estado deS.Paulo
    see Boletim Informativo, Centro e Federacao   ...
Boletim Informativo (e Estatistico), Instituto Brasileiro do Cafe.   .... BRA
Boletim Informativo, Instituto Salvadoreno de Investigaciones del Cafe. SAL
Boletim Informativo do Instituto de Cacau da Bahia.   ...   ... BRA
Boletim Informativo, Instituto Latinoamericano del Fierro y el Acero.
    see ILAFA.
Boletin Informativo, Junta Nacional de Granos (Argentina).   ... ARG
Boletin Informativo, Ministerio de Ganaderia y Agricultura (Uruguay) URU
Boletim do Instituto de Economia "Gastao Vidigal".   ...   ... BRA
Boletin Informativo, Instituto de Economia, Universidad de Chile. ... CHI
Boletin del Instituto de Estudios Economicos y Finan.Universidad de la Plata ARG
Boletim do Instituto Joaquim Nabuco de Pesquisas Sociais.   ... BRA
Boletin del Instituto de Sociologia (Buenos Aires)   ...   ... ARG
Boletin Internacional de la Federacion Nacional de Trabajadores Azucareros CUB
Boletin Interno, Banco Central de Venezuela. ...   . VEN
Boletin Mensual del Banco Central de Chile   ...   . CHI
Boletin Mensual del Banco Central de Honduras   ...   ... HON
Boletin Mensual, Banco Central de la Republica Dominicana.   ... DOM
Boletin Mensual del Banco de la Republica Oriental del Uruguay   ... URU
Boletin Mensual, Banco Central de Reserva del Peru.   ...   ... PER
Boletin Mensual, Banco Central de Venezuela. ...   . VEN
Boletin Mensual, Centro de Estudios Monetarios Latinoamericanos.
    see CEMLA Boletin Mensual.
Boletin Mensual de la Comision Nacional de Valores (Mexico)   ... MEX
Boletin Mensual de la Direccion de Economia Rural (Mexico).   ... MEX
Boletin Mensual, Direccion General de Estadistica (Guatemala)   ... GUA
Boletin Mensual de Estadistica (Argentina)   ...   . ARG
Boletin Mensual de Estadistica (Colombia)   ...   . COL
Boletin Mensual de Estadistica (Venezuela)   ...   . VEN
Boletin Mensual de Informacion, Confederacion de Trabajadores de Mexico MEX
Boletim Mensal de Informacoes do Instituto Bahiano do Fumo   ... BRA
Boletim Mensal do Servico Federal de Bioestatistica (Brazil)   ... BRA
Boletim do Ministerio de Agricultura (Brazil)   ...   . BRA
Boletin, Ministerio de Hacienda (Argentina)   ...   . ARG
Boletin del Ministerio de Sanidad y Asistencia Social (Venezuela)   ... VEN
Boletin del Ministerio de Trabajos y Asuntos Indigenas (Peru)   ... PER
Boletim do Ministerio do Trabalho, Industria e Comercio (Brazil)   ... BRA
Boletin Oficial de la Asociacion de Tecnicos Azucareros de Cuba   ... CUB
Boletin Oficial, Direccion de la Opinion Publica (Cuba)   ...   ... CUB
Boletin Oficial de la Propiedad Industrial (Cuba)   ...   ... CUB
Boletin Oficial, Secretaria de Hacienda y Credito Publico (Mexico)   ... MEX
Boletin de Petroleos (Colombia)   ...   . COL
Boletin de Precios de Productos Agropecuarios (Venezuela);   ... VEN
Boletin de Produccion y Fomento Agricola (Argentina)   ...   ... ARG
Boletin de la Propiedad Industrial y Comercial (Venezuela)   ... VEN
Boletin Quincenal, Camara Nacional de Comercio de la Ciudad de Mexico MEX
Boletin Quincenal, Central de Estudios Monetarios Latinoamericanos. MEX
Boletin Quincenal, Instituto Nacional del Cafe (Mexico)   ...   ... MEX
Boletin de la Revista Interamericana de Ciencias Sociales ...   ... GEN
Boletin, Secretaria de Comunicaciones y Obras Publicas (Mexico)   ... MEX
Boletin Semanal, Camara de Comercio de Barranquilla   ...   . COL
Boletim do Servico Social dos Menores (Brazil) ...   . BRA
Boletim SUMOC   ...   . BRA
Boletin, Superintendencia Bancaria (Colombia) ...   . COL
Boletin de la Superintendencia de Bancos y de otras Instituciones (Col.) COL
Boletim da Superintendencia dos Servicos do Cafe (Brazil)   ... BRA
Boletin Tecnico, Oficina del Cafe (Costa Rica) ...   . COS
Boletin del Trabajo   ...   . ARG

Boletim Trimestrial, Banco do Brasil ... ... BRA
Boletin Trimestral de Informacion, Confederacion de Trabajadores de Mexico
     see Boletin Mensual de Informacion ...
Boletin Trimestral de Informacion Economica
     see Economia y Administracion.
Boletin Uruguayo de Sociologia ... ... URU
Bolsa ... ... BRA
BOLSA Review ... ... GEN
Booker News ... ... GUY
Borracha ... ... BRA
Brasil ... ... BRA
Brasil Constroi ... ... BRA
Brazil ... ... BRA
Brazil Journal ... ... BRA
Brazil, Land and People ... ... BRA
Brazilian American Survey ... ... BRA
Brazilian Bulletin ... ... BRA
Brazilian Business ... ... BRA
Brazilian Letter ... ... BRA
Brazilian News ... ... BRA
British Guiana. (Colonial Office etc. Report) ... ... GUY
British Honduras   (Colonial Office etc. Report) ... ... BRI
British Virgin Islands (Colonial Office etc. Report) ... ... LEE
Bulletin, Bank of Jamaica. ... ... JAM
Bulletin, British Chamber of Commerce in Sao Paulo ... ... BRA
Bulletin, Chambre de Commerce France-Amerique ... ... GEN
Bulletin, Chambre de Commerce et d'Industrie de la Martinique. ... MAR
Bulletin du Commerce. (Caribbean Commission) ...
     see Commodity Bulletin
Bulletin Economique, Mission du Venezuela aupres de la Communaute
     Economique Europeenne. ... ... VEN
Bulletin d'Informations, Departement des Affaires Etrangeres (Haiti); HAI
Bulletin, Ministry of Trade and Industry (West Indies, Federation) ... CAR
Bulletin Municipal (Pointe a Pitre) ... ... MAR
Bulletin, Statistical Unit (Grenada) ... ... WIN
Bulletin of Statistics (Jamaica); External Trade of Jamaica ... JAM
Bulletin de Statistiques (Martinique) ... ... MAR
Bulletin Trimestriel de Statistique (Haiti) ... ... HAI
Business Conditions in Argentina ... ... ARG

Cacau Atualidades ... ... BRA
Cadernos de Nosso Tempo ... ... BRA
CADORIT Information Bulletin ... ... CAR
Cahiers, Societe d'Etudes Demographiques et Sociales de la Martinique MAR
Capes ... ... BRA
Capital y Hogar ... ... CUB
Carib ... ... CAR
Caribbean. (various publications) ... ... CAR
Caribbean Affairs ... ... CAR
Caribbean Agriculture ... ... CAR
Caribbean Economic Almanac ... ... CAR
Caribbean Economic Review ... ... CAR
Caribbean Labour ... ... CAR
Caribbean Market Survey ... ... CAR
Caribbean Monthly Bulletin ... ... CAR
Caribbean Plan; Annual Report ... ... CAR
Caribbean Quarterly ... ... CAR
Caribbean Socialists Review ... ... CAR
Caribbean Statistical Digest ... ... CAR
Caribbean Studies ... ... CAR

Caribbean Workers Weekly	CAR
Carnes, Derivados e Subprodutos	BRA
Carta Agraria	COL
Carta Economica Brasileira	BRA
Carta Informativa, Consejo Interamericano de Comercio y Produccion; Serie ALALC.	GEN
Carta Informativa para los Socios.	SAL
Carta Mensal, Conselho Tecnico Concultivo, Confed.Nac.do Comercio(Br)	BRA
Carta Semanal de Cafe.	GUA
Carta Semanal, Ministerio de Minas e Hidrocarburos (Venezuela) ...	VEN
Carta de Venezuela	VEN
Cartilla Economica (Salvador)	SAL
Cayman Islands (Colonial Office etc. Report)	CAY
CCL Newsletter	CAR
CEMLA Boletin Mensual	MEX
Censo Nacional de Industrias y de Comercio (Dominican Republic) ...	DOM
Censo Nacional de Poblacion (Dominican Republic)	DOM
Censo de Industrias Manufactureras de Puerto Rico. see Census of Manufacturing Industries of Puerto Rico.	
Census of Manufacturing Industries of Puerto Rico	PUE
Census of Tourism (Barbados)	BAR
Chamber of Commerce (British Honduras) Bulletin	BRI
Chile Industrial	CHI
Chronicle of the West India Committee	CAR
Ciencias Politicas y Sociales	MEX
Ciencias Sociales	GEN
Cifras y Comentarios, Ministerio de Hacienda y Credito Publico (Nicaragua)	NIC
Circulaire, Chambre de Commerce France-Amerique Latine ...	GEN
Circular, West India Committee see West India Committee Circular	
Clarin Economico	ARG
Classified List of Accessions, West India Reference Collection, Central Library Services(Trinidad and Tobago)	TRI
Clearing House on Trade and Tourism Information Monthly Journal	CAR
Clearing House on Trade and Tourism Information Weekly. ...	CAR
CNC.	BRA
Comentario Comercial Anglo-Brasileiro	BRA
Comercio	MEX
Comercio Exterior (Argentina)	ARG
Comercio Exterior (Boliva)	BOL
Comercio Exterior do Brasil	BRA
Comercio Exterior do Brasil por Mercadorias, Segundo os Portos ...	BRA
Comercio Exterior (Chile)	CHI
Comercio Exterior de Costa Rica	COS
Comercio Exterior de Cuba	CUB
Comercio Exterior de Cuba; Importaciones, Exportaciones ...	CUB
Comercio Exterior Ecuatoriano	ECU
Comercio Exterior (Honduras)	HON
Comercio Exterior (Mexico)	MEX
Comercio Exterior (Mexico); (English Edition)	MEX
Comercio Exterior (Mexico); International Air Mail Edition ...	MEX
Comercio Exterior (Panama) see Estadistica Panamena; Serie K.	
Comercio Exterior de la Republica Dominicaca; Resumen del Ano ...	DOM
Comercio Exterior (Salvador)	SAL
Comercio Exterior de Venezuela	VEN
Comercio Interamericano	GEN
Comercio Internacional (Brazil)	BRA
Comercio Internacional (Mexico)	MEX
Comercio Mexicano	MEX
Comercio Minorista, Precios al por Mayor (Argentina)	ARG
Comercio Mundial	MEX

```
Comercio y Produccion (Dominican Republic) ...        ...        ...        DOM
Comments on Argentine Trade         ...        ...        ...        ...        ARG
Commercial Journal         ...        ...        ...        ...        ...        BAR
Commercial Review         ...        ...        ...        ...        ...        GUY
Commodity Bulletin         ...        ...        ...        ...        ...        CAR
Commodity Bulletin (Jamaica)         ...        ...        ...        ...        JAM
Compendio Estadistico Centroamericano         ...        ...        ...        GEN
Comunicaciones y Transportes (Mexico)         ...        ...        ...        MEX
Consumer Price (Cost-of-Living) Indexes for the American Nations  ...        GEN
Contabilidad y Finanzas.         ...        ...        ...        ...        ...        CUB
Contador Publico         ...        ...        ...        ...        ...        COL
Cooperaminas         ...        ...        ...        ...        ...        ...        BRA
Cooperative Newsletter         ...        ...        ...        ...        ...        CAR
Costo y Condiciones de Vida en San Salvador         ...        ...        ...        SAL
Costo de Vida, Precios Minoristas, Salarios Industriales (Argentina)  ...        ARG
"Crash" Estimates of Gross Domestic Product at Factor Cost (Barbados)        BAR
Crop Enquiry Series         ...        ...        ...        ...        ...        CAR
CTAL News
            see Noticiero de la CTAL
Cuadernos Americanos         ...        ...        ...        ...        ...        MEX
Cuadernos, Centro de Estudios Argentinos         ...        ...        ...        ARG
Cuadernos CVF ...         ...        ...        ...        ...        ...        VEN
Cuadernos de la CVF         ...        ...        ...        ...        ...        VEN
Cuadernos de Informacion Economica (Venezuela)         ...        ...        VEN
Cuaderno, Secretaria del Trabajo y Prevision Social (Mexico)         ...        MEX
Cuadernos de la Sociedad Venezolana de Planificacion         ...        ...        VEN
Cuba.        Revista Mensual         ...        ...        ...        ...        CUB
Cuba Economic News         ...        ...        ...        ...        ...        CUB
Cuba Economica y Financiera         ...        ...        ...        ...        CUB
Cuba Foreign Trade         ...        ...        ...        ...        ...        CUB
Cuba Socialista ...         ...        ...        ...        ...        ...        CUB
Cuba Sugar Year Book
            see Anuario Azucarero de Cuba
Cuban Information Service...         ...        ...        ...        ...        CUB
Cubazucar         ...        ...        ...        ...        ...        ...        CUB
Current Caribbean Bibliography         ...        ...        ...        ...        CAR
Customs Administrative Report and Trade Return (Bahamas)         ...        BAH
CVF.         ...        ...        ...        ...        ...        ...        VEN


Derecho Fiscal ...         ...        ...        ...        ...        ...        ARG
Desarrollo Economico (Argentina)         ...        ...        ...        ...        ARG
Desde Chile         ...        ...        ...        ...        ...        ...        CHI
Desenvolvimento e Conjuntura         ...        ...        ...        ...        BRA
Development and Welfare in the West Indies; Bulletin         ...        ...        CAR
Development and Welfare in the West Indies; Report         ...        ...        CAR
Digest of Statistics (Jamaica)         ...        ...        ...        ...        JAM
Digest Economico         ...        ...        ...        ...        ...        BRA
Dinamica Social ...         ...        ...        ...        ...        ...        ARG
Dirigente Industrial         ...        ...        ...        ...        ...        BRA
Disposiciones Economicas (Colombia)         ...        ...        ...        COL
Divulgacion. (Instituto Nacional de Reforma Agraria, Cuba)
            see Boletin de Divulgacion.
Documentos Oficiales de la Organizacion de los Estados Americanos; Indice
Lista General.         ...        ...        ...        GEN
Dominica.        (Colonial Office etc. Report).         WIN


ECA         ...        ...        ...        ...        ...        ...        ARG
ECA News         ...        ...        ...        ...        ...        ...        TRI
Economia         ...        ...        ...        ...        ...        ...        COL
Economia         ...        ...        ...        ...        ...        ...        CHI
Economia y Administracion         ...        ...        ...        ...        ECU
```

170

Industria	...	...	...	...	...	...	GUA
Industria Colombiana	...	...	...	...	...		COL
Industria Peruana		...	...	...	...	...	PER
Industriarios	...	...	...	...	...	...	BRA
Informacion	...	...	...	...	...	...	ARG
Informacion Agropecuaria (Honduras)			...	...	...	HON

Informacion Agropecuaria (Panama)
        see Estadistica Panamena; Serie H.

Informaciones Comerciales (Peru)	...	...	...	...	PER
Informaciones Economicas		...	...	...	...	GEN
Informaciones Estadisticas Agropecuarias (Argentina)		...	...	ARG

Informacion Estadistica, Instituto de Fomento Algodonero	...	COL
Informaciones Sociales (Mexico)	...	...	...	...	MEX
Informacoes Trimestrais, Comissao Executiva de Defesa da Borracha (Brazil)	BRA
Informaciones de Venezuela	...	...	...	...	VEN

Information Bulletin, Caribbean Area Division, Inter-American Regional
        Organization of Workers   ...   .
        see Cadorit Information Bulletin.

Information Circular, British Chamber of Commerce of Sao Paulo and South
        Brazil   see Sao Paulo Information Circular

Information Latine	...	...	...	...	...	GEN
Informativo ALALC	...	...	...	...	GEN
Informe de Actividades, Instituto Colombiano de la Reforma Agraria	COL
Informe Anual de las Actividades, Oficina de Regulacion de Precios	PAN
Informe Anual, Banco Central de Nicaragua	...	...	...	NIC
Informe Anual, Banco de Mexico	...	...	...	MEX
Informe Anual, Banco de la Republica (Colombia)	...	...	COL
Informe Anual, Camara Nacional de Comercio (Uruguay) ...	...	URU
Informe Anual de Labores, Banco Nacional de Fomento (Ecuador) ...	ECU
Informe Anual, Nacional Financiera (Mexico)	...	...	...	MEX
informe Anual, Superintendencia Bancaria (Colombia)	...	COL
Informe del Banco Nacional de Comercio Exterior (Mexico)	...	MEX
Informe, Camara Nacional de Comercio de la Ciudad de Mexico	...	MEX
Informe de Controlar General de la Republica (Panama)	...	PAN

Informe del Departamento de Planes Anuales, Oficine de Planificacion
        (Costa Rica)   ...   .   COS

Informe, Direccion Nacional de Estadistica y Censos (Argentina)	...	ARG
Informe Economico, Banco Central de la Republica Dominicana	...	DOM
Informe Economica, Banco Central de Venezuela	...	...	VEN
Informe Economica, Banco de Guatemala	...	...	GUA
Informe Estadistico Semestral (Cuba)	...	...	CUB
Informe Financiero del Contralor General (Colombia)	...	COL
Informe del Gerente de la Caja de Credito Agrario Industrial (Colombia)	COL
Informe del Gerente, Comision Nacional de Valores (Ecuador)	...	ECU
Informe de Labores, Ministerio de Trabajo y Prevision Social (Honduras)	HON
Informe a la Nacion, Ministerio del Tesoro (Ecuador)	...	...	ECU
Informe de la Oficina del Presupuesto (Costa Rica)	...	...	COS
Informe Referente, Banco de Colombia	...	...	...	COL
Informe, Secretaria de Hacienda, Credito Publico y Comercio (Honduras)	HON
Informe, Superintendencia Bancaria (Colombia)	...	...	COL
Informe, Superintendencia de Bancos (Venezuela)	...	...	VEN

Ingreso Nacional (Panama) ...
        see Estadistica Panamena; Serie C.

Inmigracion (Venezuela)	...	...	...	...	...	VEN
INRA	...	...	...	...	...	...	CUB
Inter-American Bulletin	...	...	...	...	...	GEN
Inter-American Economic Affairs	...	...	...	...	GEN
Inter-American Foreign Trade	...	...	...	...	GEN
Inter-American Labor Bulletin	...	...	...	...	GEN
Intercambio	...	...	...	...	...	...	MEX
Intercambio	...	...	...	...	...	...	BRA

Memoria Anual, Banco Central de la Republica Argentina ...   ...   ARG
Memoria Anual, Banco Hipotecario Nacional (Argentina) ...   ...   ARG
Memoria Anual, Banco de Mexico   ...   .   MEX
Memorias Anuales, Banco Minero de Bolivia   ...   ...   BOL
Memoria Anual, Banco Nacional de Cuba   ...   ...   CUB
Memoria Anual, Comision Nacional de Valores (Mexico) ...   ...   MEX
Memoria Anual, Division de Investigaciones Agropecuarias, Instituto Agropec
    Nacional (Guatemala) ...   .   GUA
Memoria Anual y Estudio Economico, Banco de Guatemala   ...   GUA
Memoria Anual, Instituto de Tierras y Colonizacion (Costa Rica)   ...   COS
Memoria Anual, Ministerio de Economia y Hacienda (Costa Rica)   ...   COS
Memoria Anual, Yacimientos Petroliferos Fiscales Bolivianos   ...   BOL
Memoria v Balance, Banco del Credito del Peru ...   .   PER
Memoria y Balance General, Banco de la Nacion Argentina   ...   ARG
Memoria y Balanza General, Banco de la Republica Oriental del Uruguay   URU
Memoria, Banco Central de Honduras   ...   .   HON
Memoria, Banco Central de Nicaragua   ...   .   NIC
Memoria, Banco Central de la Republica Dominicana   ...   ...   DOM
Memoria del Banco Central de Reserva del Peru.   ...   ...   PER
Memoria, Banco Central de Reserva de el Salvador.   ...   ...   SAL
Memoria, Banco Central de Venezuela   ...   .   VEN
Memoria, Banco de Fomento Agropecuario del Peru   ...   ...   PER
Memoria, Banco Hipotecario de el Salvador.   ...   .   SAL
Memoria, Banco Nacional de Fomento (Honduras)   ...   ...   HON
Memoria, Banco Nacional de Panama.   ...   .   PAN
Memoria, Banco del Paraguay   ...   .   PAR
Memoria de la Contaduria de la Nacion (Argentina)   ...   ...   ARG
Memoria de la Contraloria General (de la Republica) (Chile)   ...   CHI
Memoria, Corporacion de Fomento de la Produccion (Chile)   ...   CHI
Memoria correspondiente al Ejercicio, Bolsa de Comercio (Buenos Aires)   ARG
Memoria y Cuento, Corporacion Venezolana de Fomento ...   ...   VEN
Memoria y Cuento, Ministerio de Agricultura y Cria (Venezuela)   ...   VEN
Memoria y Cuento, Ministerio de Fomento (Venezuela)   ...   ...   VEN
Memoria y Estadistica, Superintendencia de Bancos (Peru)   ...   PER
Memoria del Gerente General del Banco Central del Ecuador   ...   ECU
Memoria de Hacienda (Colombia)   ...   .   COL
Memoria, Instituto de Colonizacion Rural (San Savador) ...   ...   SAL
Memoria, Instituto Movilizador de Inversiones Bancarias (Buenos Aires)   ARG
Memoria, Junta Nacional para Combatir la Desocupacion (Argentina)   ARG
Memoria de Labores, Banco Centroamericano de Integracion Economica   GEN
Memoria de Labores,Dept. De Asuntos Agrarios y Colonizacion(Mexico)   MEX
Memoria de las Labores Desarrolladas por el Instituto Salvadoreno de
    Fomento de la Produccion   ...   ...   SAL
Memoria (de las) Labores Desarrolladas por el Ramo de Trabajo y Previson
    Social (Salvador)   ...   ...   SAL
Memoria de las Labores, Ministerio de Trabajo y Bienestar Social(Guatemala) GUA
Memoria de las Labores Realizadas en los Ministerios de Gobernacion y Policia
    Justicia y Gracia (Costa Rica)   ...   ...   COS
Memoria de Labores de la Secretaria de Relaciones Exteriores (Mexico)   MEX
Memoria de Labores, Secretaria del Trabajo y Prevision Social (Mexico)   MEX
Memoria de Ministerio de Agricultura (Colombia)   ...   ...   COL
Memoria del Ministerio de Agricultura, Comercio e Industrias (Panama).   PAN
Memoria, Ministerio de Agricultura y Ganadera de la Nacion (Argentina)   ARG
Memoria, Ministerio de Agricultura y Ganaderia (Nicaragua)
           see Memoria de Agricultura y Ganaderia (Nicaragua).
Memoria, Ministerio de Comercio y Industria (Argentina).   ...   ARG
Memoria, Ministerio de Hacienda (Argentina)   ...   ...   ARG
Memoria, Ministerio de Hacienda y Comercio (Peru)   ...   ...   PER
Memoria, Ministerio de Hacienda y Tesoro (Panama)   ...   ...   PAN
Memoria, Ministerio de Hacienda y Tesoro (Panama); Suplemento   ...   PAN
Memoria, Ministerio de Obras Publicas (Argentina)   ...   ...   ARG
Memoria, Ministerio de Trabajo y Prevision de la Nacion (Argentina)   ARG

Memoria de la Recaudacion General de Aduanas (Nicaragua) ...	NIC
Memoria, Secretaria de Comunicaciones y Obras Publicas (Mexico) ...	MEX
Memoria, Secretaria de Comunicaciones y Transportes (Mexico) ...	MEX
Memoria, Secretaria de la Economia Nacional (Mexico)	MEX
Memoria, Secretaria de Estado del Tesoro (Dominican Republic)	DOM
Memoria de la Secretaria de Obras Publicas (Mexico)	MEX
Mensagem Economica	BRA
Mensario Estatistico (Brazil)	BRA
Mercado de Valores	MEX
Mercurio	ARG
Mercurio Peruano	PER
Metas	CUB
Mexican Economic Panorama	MEX
Mexico. Facts, Figures, Trends	MEX
Mexico Informa	MEX
Mexico Monthly Bulletin	MEX
Mexletter	MEX
Monetary Statistics (Jamaica)	JAM
Monserrat. (Colonial Office etc. Report)	LEE
Monserrat Mirror	LEE
Monthly Account Relating to External Trade (British Guiana) ...	GUY
Monthly Bulletin, Association for the Development of Anglo-Uruguayan Trade	URU
Monthly Bulletin, British Chamber of Commerce in Brazil ...	BRA
Monthly Bulletin, British Chamber of Commerce in Uruguay ...	URU
Monthly Comment	JAM
Monthly Journal, British Chamber of Commerce in the Argentine Republic	ARG
Monthly Newsletter, Barbados Employers Confederation	BAR
Monthly Overseas Trade Report (Dominica)	WIN
Monthly Return of Statistics (Bahamas); Imports of Textiles ...	BAH
Monthly Trade Statistics (West Indies, Federation)	CAR
MOP. Boletin Oficial, Ministerio de Obras Publicas (Cuba) ...	CUB
Movimento Bancario do Brasil	BRA
Mundo Agrario	ARG
Mundo Industrial	ARG
Mundo Nuevo	GEN

Nacion; Weekly Airmail Edition	ARG
National Accounts, Income and Expenditure (Jamaica)	JAM
National Economic Situation (Peru)	PER
National Income (Trinidad and Tobago)	TRI
National Patriot	JAM
Navegacion Comercial Argentina	ARG
New Hope Chronicle	CAR
New Jamaica	JAM
New Nation	GUY
New World (Fortnightly)	GUY
New World (Quarterly)	JAM
News Bulletin, Inter-American Commission of Women	GEN
News from Cuba	CUB
News from Guyana	GUY
Newsletter, Banco de Colombia	COL
Newsletter, Banco Continental (Peru)	PER
Newsletter, Caribbean Congress of Labour.	
see CCL Newsletter.	
Nieuwe West-Indische Gids	CAR
Noticias. Weekly Digest of Hemispheric Reports.	GEN
Noticias de la CEPAL	GEN
Noticias, Comision Interamericana de Arbitraje Comercial ...	GEN
Noticias Economicas Interamericanas	GEN
Noticiero de la Comision Interamericana de Mujeres	GEN

Noticiero de la CTAL. (=CTAL News) ... ... GEN
Nuestra Industria (Cuba); Revista Economica ... ... CUB

OAS Chronicle ... ... GEN
Obrero Panadero ... ... CUB
Observador Economico e Financeiro ... ... BRA
Observer. Organ of Indian Opinion ... ... TRI
Oficinas Tecnicas y Administrativas de la Junta de Gobierno, de los
          Organismos y Empresas del Estado (Mexico); Memoria. ... MEX
Oleos e Gorduras Vegetais / e Subprodutos. ... ... BRA
Overseas Trade (Barbados) ... ... BAR
Overseas Trade (Trinidad and Tobago); Annual Report ... ... TRI
Overseas Trade (Trinidad and Tobago); Monthly Report ... ... TRI
Overseas Trade Quarterly Report (Barbados) ... ... BAR
Overseas Trade Report (St.Lucia) ... ... WIN
Overseas Trade of St.Lucia ... ... WIN

Panorama de la Economia Argentina ... ... ARG
Panorama Economico ... ... CHI
Panorama Economico ... ... MEX
Panorama Economico Latinamericano ... ... CUB
Paraguay Industrial y Comercial ... ... PAR
Parana. Boletim de Camara de Expansao Economica do Parana ... BRA
Parana Economica ... ... BRA
Pecuaria e Avicultura, Apicultura e Sericicultura (Brasil) ... ... BRA
Peru.   Monthly Business Report ... ... PER
Peru.   Sintesis Economica y Financiera ... ... PER
Peru in Brief ... ... • ... ... PER
Peruvian Economic Situation ... ... PER
Peruvian Times ... ... PER
Pesca ... ... BRA
Pesquisas ... ... BRA
Pesquisas; Communications ... ... BRA
Pesquisas; Historia ... ... BRA
Petroleo y otros Datos Estadisticos (Venezuela) ... ... VEN
Planeamiento ... ... BOL
Planificacion ... ... ECU
Poblacion de la Republica Dominicana ... ... DOM
Politica y Espiritu ... ... CHI
Population and Vital Statistics (Trinidad and Tobago); Annual Report TRI
Precios y Costo de la Vida (Panama) ... ...
                    see Estadistica Panamena; Serie G: ...
Precios y Indices de Precios para el Consumidor Medio (Peru) ... PER
Presupuesto General de Ingresos y Egresos de la Republica (Nicaragua) NIC
Previsao Agricola ... ... BRA
Principal Items of Domestic Exports (Bahamas) ... ... BAH
Principal Items Imported (Bahamas) ... ... BAH
Producao Agricola (Brazil) ... ... BRA
Producao Animal (Brazil) ... ... BRA
Producao Mineral (Brazil) ... ... BRA
Produccion y Consumo de Energia en Chile ... ... CHI
Productividad ... ... MEX
Productividad y Bienestar Social (Argentina) ... ... ARG
Productividade ... . BRA
Program Bienal de Inversiones Publicas (Salvador) ... ... SAL
Progress Report, Institute of Social and Economic Research, University of
                    the West Indies. (varies) ... ... CAR
Provisional Listing of Alliance for Progress Projects ... ... GEN
Public Opinion ... ... JAM

Publicacao Especial, Departamento Nacional da Producao Mineral (Brazil)   BRA
Publicaciones, Instituto de Economia, Universidad de Chile   ... CHI
Publicaciones Juceplan (Cuba)   ... ... CUB

Quarterly Abstract of Statistics (Jamaica)   ... ... JAM
Quarterly Digest of Statistics (Barbados)   ... ... BAR
Quarterly Digest of Statistics (Jamaica)   ... ... JAM
Quarterly Digest of Statistics (St.Lucia)   ... ... WIN
Quarterly Digest of Statistics (St.Vincent)   ... ... WIN
Quarterly Economic Report (Trinidad and Tobago)   ... ... TRI
Quarterly Economic Review; Argentina   ... ... ARG
Quarterly Economic Review; Brazil   ... ... BRA
Quarterly Economic Review; Colombia   ... ... COL
Quarterly Economic Review; Mexico ...   . MEX
Quarterly Economic Review; Venezuela   ... ... VEN
Quarterly Overseas Trade Report (Grenada)   ... ... WIN
Quarterly Overseas Trade Report (St.Vincent) ...   . WIN
Quarterly Review, Bank of London and South America Ltd.   ... GEN
Quarterly Review of Financial Statistics (Guyana)   ... ... GUY
Quarterly Statistical Digest (British Guiana)   ... ... GUY
Quarterly Trade Statistics (West Indies, Federation)   ... ... CAR

Rapport Annuel du Departement Fiscal, Banque Nationale de la Repub d'Haiti HAI
Rapport Annuel, Office de Controle et de Develop. des Denrees d'Export   HAI
Recopilacion Estadistica (Uruguay)   ... ... URU
Reforma Agraria (Honduras)   ... ... HON
Registro Publico (Dominican Republic)   ... ... DOM
Relatorio, Banco do Brasil ...   . BRA
Relatorio, Ministerio de Fazenda (Brazil)   ... ... BRA
Relatorio Sumoc   ... ... BRA
Renta Nacional del Peru   ... ... PER
Report of the Accountant General (St.Vincent)   ... ... WIN
Report, Agricultural Development Corporation (Jamaica) ...   ... JAM
Report, Cocoa Industry Board (Jamaica)   ... ... JAM
Report, Cocoa Marketing Board (Jamaica)   ... ... JAM
Report of the Customs and Excise Department (St.Lucia) ...   ... WIN
Report on the Administration of Customs & Excise Depart.(Trinidad Tobago) TRI
Report of the Directors ..., Bank of London and South America Ltd.   GEN
Report on Economic Conditions in Brazil   ... ... BRA
Report on Economic Conditions in Colombia   ... ... COL
Report on Economic Conditions in Costa Rica ...   . COS
Report on Economic Conditions in Cuba   ... ... CUB
Report on Economic Conditions in Guatemala ...   . GUA
Report on Economic Conditions in Haiti   ... ... HAI
Report on Economic Conditions in Honduras   ... ... HON
Report on Economic Conditions in Nicaragua   ... ... NIC
Report on Economic Conditions in Panama   ... ... PAN
Report on Economic Conditions in Paraguay   ... ... PAR
Report on Economic Conditions in Peru   ... ... PER
Report on Economic Conditions in El Salvador ...   . SAL
Report on Economic Conditions in Venezuela ...   . VEN
Report on Economic and Financial Conditions in Uruguay   ... URU
Report on the Economic Situation in Peru   ... ... PER
Report, Jamaica Agricultural Society ...   . JAM
Report on the Manpower Situation in Trinidad and Tobago   ... TRI
Report on the National Income of Trinidad and Tobago   ... ... TRI
Report of the Registrar of Co-operative Societies (St.Vincent)   ... WIN

Servicio Social Interamericano	GEN
Simara	GUY
Sintesis Estadistica (Chile) ...	CHI
Sintesis Estadistica Mensual de la Republica Argentina	ARG
Sintesis Estadistica Mensual de la Republica Argentina; Suplemento ...	ARG
Sintesis Politica, Economica, Social	BRA
Sintesis Mensual, Asociacion Latinoamericana de Libre Comercio	
see ALALC Sintesis Mensual.	
Sintesis Semanal, Corporacion de Comerciantes del Peru	PER
Situacion Bancaria (Peru) ...	PER
Situacion Economica Nacional (Peru)	PER
Situation in Argentina	ARG
Social and Economic Studies	JAM
Social Welfare Report (Antigua)	LEE
Sociologia	BRA
Sociologia en Mexico	MEX
Special Series, Institute of Social and Economic Research, Univ.of West Ind.	JAM
Spectator	TRI
SPVEA. Resenha Informativa	BRA
Statistical Abstract of Latin America ...	GEN
Statistical Bulletin for Latin America ...	GEN
Statistiques du Commerce Intercaraibe	
see Inter-Caribbean Trade Statistics,	
Statistische Berichten van het algemeen Bureau voor de Statistiek (Surinam)	SUR
Sul-Coop. Boletim Cooperativismo.	BRA
Summary of Imports and Exports of the British Virgin Islands	LEE
Suplemento Estadistico, Banco Central de Bolivia.	
see Boletin del Banco Central de Bolivia; Suplemento Estadistico	
Suplemento Estadistico (Bolivia)	BOL
Supplementary Abstract of Statistics (British Honduras)	BRI
Suriname in Cijfers	SUR
Survey of the Brazilian Economy	BRA
Tables on National Income and Expenditure (Jamaica)	JAM
Tecnica y Economia	BRA
Tecnicas Financieras	MEX
Temas Contemporaneos	MEX
Temas Sociales ...	COS
Tendencias Economicas-Financeiras ...	BRA
Texaco Caribbean	TRI
Texaco Trinidad News	TRI
Texaco-Trinidad Quarterly ...	TRI
TGG Review	TRI
Thunder	GUY
Timehri	GUY
Trabajo	CUB
Tabajo	HON
Trabajo y Prevision Social. (Mexico)	
see Revista del Trabajo	
Trabajos del Seminario, Facultad de Ciencias Economicas, Comerciales y	
Politicas, Universidad Nacional de Litoral (Argentina) ...	ARG
Trabalho e Seguro Social	BRA
Trade Account (St.Lucia)	WIN
Trade and Economic Report (British Guiana)	GUY
Trade Indices (Jamaica)	JAM
Trade Report (British Honduras)	BRI
Trimestre Economico	MEX
Trimestre Estadistico (Guatemala)	GUA
Trimestre Suplemento del Directorio Financiero (Cuba)	CUB
Trinidad and Tobago. (Colonial Office etc. Report)	TRI

HOLDING LIBRARIES

Symbol	Name and address
Aslib	Aslib, 3 Belgrave Square, London SW1
BangUC	University College of North Wales Bangor, North Wales.
BedC	Bedford College, (University of London), Regents Park, London, N.W.1.
BelfPL	Belfast Public Library, Royal Avenue, Belfast 1.
BelfU	Queens University of Belfast, Belfast 7, Northern Ireland.
BhmPL	Birmingham City Libraries, Reference Library, Ratcliffe Place, Birmingham 1.
BhmU	University of Birmingham, Edgbaston, Birmingham 15.
BM	British Museum, Department of Printed Books, London, EC1
BM (NH)	British Museum (Natural History), Cromwell Road, London SW7.
Bodl	Bodleian Library, (University of Oxford), Oxford
BoLSA	Bank of London and South America Ltd., 40 Queen Victoria Street, London EC4
BoT	Board of Trade, 1, Victoria Street, London SW1
BrU	University of Bristol, Queens Road, Bristol 8.
CambU	University of Cambridge, University Library, Cambridge.

ChartInsl	Chartered Insurance Institute, The Hall, 20, Aldermanbury, London EC2
CSA	School of Agriculture, (University of Cambridge), Cambridge.
DurhamU	University of Durham, Palace Green, Durham.
EdinU	University of Edinburgh, George Square, Edinburgh 8.
EMall	East Malling Research Station, East Malling, nr. Maidstone, Kent. [Joint Library with: Commonwealth Bureau of Horticulture and Plantation Crops
EssexU	University of Essex, Wivenhoe Park, Colchester, Essex.
ExU	University of Exeter, Roborough Library, Prince of Wales Road, Exeter,
GlasU	University of Glasgow, Glasgow W2
GrassRI	Grassland Research Institute, Hurley, nr. Maidenhead, Berks.
Guildhall	Guildhall Library, London EC2
Hackney PL	Hackney Central Library, Mare Street, London E8
HispLBC	Hispanic and Luso-Brazilian Councils, Canning House, 2, Belgrave Square, London SW1
HullU	University of Hull, Brynmore Jones Library, Cottingham Road, Hull.
IBank	Institute of Bankers, 10 Lombard Street, London EC3
KensPL	Kensington Public Libraries, Central Library, Phillimore Walk, London W8.

LdsU	University of Leeds, Brotherton Library, Leeds 2.
LeicU	University of Leicester, University Road, Leicester.
LivPL	Liverpool Public Libraries, Central Public Libraries, William Brown Street, Liverpool 3.
LivU	University of Liverpool, Liverpool 3.
LondICS	Institute of Commonwealth Studies, (University of London), 27 Russell Square, London WC1
LondIEd	Institute of Education, (University of London), Malet Street, London WC1
LondU	University of London, Goldsmiths Library, Senate House, London WC1
LSE	London School of Economics and Political Science, British Library of Political and Economic Science, Houghton Street, London WC1
MancPL	Manchester Public Libraries, Central Library St.Peters Square, Manchester 3.
MarshallL	Marshall Library of Economics, Downing Street, Cambridge.
MinAg	Ministry of Agriculture,Fisheries & Food, 3, Whitehall Place, London SW1
NCL	National Central Library, Store Street, London EC1
NIRD	National Institute for Research in Dairying, Shinfield, Reading, Berks.
NLL	National Lending Library for Science and Technology, Boston Spa, Yorks.
NLS	National Library of Scotland, Edinburgh 1.

NottU	University of Nottingham, University Park, Nottingham.
NRL(Holb)	National Refernce Library for Science and Invention (Holborn Division), 25 Southampton Buildings, London WC2.
NuffCOxf	Nuffield College, (University of Oxford), Oxford.
OxfAgEconRI	Agricultural Economics Research Institute, (University of Oxford), Oxford.
OxfDepFor	Department of Forestry, University of Oxford, South Parks Road, Oxford. [Joint library with: Commonwealth Forestry Institute]
OxfICS	Institute of Commonwealth Studies, (University of Oxford), Queen Elizabeth House, 20/21 St. Giles, Oxford.
OxfIES	Institute of Economics and Statistics, (University of Oxford), St. Cross Building, Manor Road, Oxford.
OxfSchGeog	School of Geography, (University of Oxford), Mansfield Road, Oxford.
PrudAssurCo	Prudential Assurance Co. Ltd., Holborn Bars, London EC1.
RadclSL	Radcliffe Science Library, (University of Oxford), Oxford.
RAnthroI	Royal Anthropological Institute, 21 Bedford Square, London WC1
ReadU	University of Reading, Reading, Berks.
RGS	Royal Geographical Society, Kensington Gore, London SW7

RhodesHoOxf	Rhodes House, (University of Oxford), Oxford.
RIIA	Royal Institute of International Affairs, Chatham House, 10 St. James' Square, London SW1
Rothampstead	Rothampstead Experimental Station, Harpenden, Herts.
RSM	Royal Society of Medicine, 1 Wimpole Street, London W1.
RSocEdin	Royal Society of Edinburgh, 22 George Street, Edinburgh 2.
ScottCollComm	Scottish College of Commerce, Pitt Street, Glasgow C2.
ScottPolarRI	Scott Polar Research Institute, (University of Cambridge), Lensfield Road, Cambridge,
SellyOakC	Selly Oak Colleges, Birmingham 29.
SheffU	University of Sheffield, Western Bank, Sheffield 10.
SL	Science Museum Library, South Kensington, London,SW7.
SouU	University of Southampton, University Road, Highfield, Southampton, Hants.
StAndU	University of St.Andrews, St.Andrews, Scotland.
SwUc	University College of Swansea, Singleton Park, Swansea.
TropProdI	Tropical Products Institute, 56-62 Grays Inn Road, London WC1
UCL	University College London, Gower Street, London WC1
UEAnglia	University of East Anglia, Norwich.

WarU	University of Warwick, Coventry, Warwickshire.
WelshPlant	Welsh Plant Breeding Station, (University College of Wales), Plas Gogerddan, Nr. Aberystwyth, Cards.
WimbledonPL	Wimbledon Public Libraries, Hill Road, London.SW19.
YorkU	University of York, Heslington, York.